P...

How...

"A darkly unsettling and unvarnished postmortem of one fractured, complicated American family that will feel deeply, even painfully, familiar to some and shockingly, fascinatingly alien to others, with an emotional power that is universally compelling. This is a masterfully crafted memoir, an elegant tour de force that firmly establishes Mulgrew as a writer of significant literary endowment. The soul mate to Frank McCourt's *Angela's Ashes*, *How to Forget*, despite the promise of its title, cannot be forgotten or ignored."

—Augusten Burroughs, author of *Running with Scissors* and *Toil & Trouble*

"Mulgrew, an actress best known for *Star Trek: Voyager* and *Orange Is the New Black*, plays her best role: as herself. This is no Hollywood tell-all, but a moving personal story about her family, in particular her aging parents, whom she cared for as they faced terminal illnesses."

—*Washington Post*

"This is a passionate book by a passionate writer. Overflowing with the true terrors of family life, with the fight for love and connection and understanding, with an amazing American story of hope and disappointment, sorrow and roots, this memoir will electrify readers and become a part of what we know about who we are."

—Anne Roiphe, journalist, novelist, and
author of the memoir *1185 Park Avenue*

"A rich, eloquent, and emotionally complex portrait of parent-child bonds and a colorful, unforgettable family. . . . [A] candid and moving memoir."

—*Kirkus Reviews*

"Kate Mulgrew is a brilliant actor, which does not conceal her brilliance with the pen. This memoir, *How to Forget*, plunges you into familiar, familial depths of death, disease, and despair, only to pull you up again with a bawdy laugh. Death, disease, and despair are not walls for Mulgrew, but they are steps toward the sunlight of serenity. Read and cry, read and laugh, read and remember *How to Forget*."

—Malachy McCourt, author of *Death Need Not Be Fatal*

"Though both sections of Mulgrew's memoir build to painful good-byes, *How to Forget* is more than just a sad play-by-play of illness and decline. It's a beautiful portrait of a daughter's love for her parents, packed with sharp, amusing recollections, all told with love."

—*New York Times*

"Candid and intimate. . . . A detailed and searing portrait of a family facing the inevitability of death." —*Publishers Weekly*

"[An] engrossing story of a daughter's love, told with brutal honesty."

—*Booklist*

"Mulgrew has written a finely detailed memoir that brings [her parents], ever so briefly and only on its pages, back to life. . . . It's the achingly unique particulars of the relationships between the author, her five brothers and sisters, and their parents that make this book stand out." —*Providence Journal*

How
to
Forget

ALSO BY KATE MULGREW

Born with Teeth

How

to

Forget

A Daughter's Memoir

Kate

Mulgrew

wm

WILLIAM MORROW

An Imprint of HarperCollins*Publishers*

The names and identifying characteristics of some of the individuals featured throughout this book have been changed to protect their privacy.

HarperCollins books may be purchased for educational, business, or sales promotional use. For information, please email the Special Markets Department at SPsales@harpercollins.com.

A hardcover edition of this book was published in 2019 by William Morrow, an imprint of HarperCollins Publishers.

FIRST WILLIAM MORROW PAPERBACK EDITION PUBLISHED 2020.

Designed by Bonni Leon-Berman

The Library of Congress has catalogued a previous edition as follows:

Names: Mulgrew, Kate, 1955– author.
Title: How to forget : a daughter's memoir / Kate Mulgrew.
Description: First edition. | New York, NY : William Morrow, [2018] |
Identifiers: LCCN 2019014753 (print) | LCCN 2019017608 (ebook)
| ISBN 9780062846846 (E-book) | ISBN 9780062846815 (hardcover)
| ISBN 9780062846839 (paperback)
Subjects: LCSH: Mulgrew, Kate, 1955—Family. | Actresses—United States—Biography. | Aging parents—Care—Iowa—Biography. | Parent and adult child.
Classification: LCC PN2287.M785 (ebook) | LCC PN2287.M785 A3 2018 (print)
| DDC 791.4502/8092 [B]—dc23
LC record available at https://lccn.loc.gov/2019014753

ISBN 978-0-06-284683-9 (pbk.)

20 21 22 23 24 LSC 10 9 8 7 6 5 4 3 2 1

In memory of my mother,

Joan Kiernan Mulgrew.

And my father,

Thomas James Mulgrew.

And for my siblings:

Tom, Joe, Laura, Sam, and Jenny

Down, down, down into the
darkness of the
grave

Gently they go, the beautiful,
the tender,
the kind;

Quietly they go, the intelligent,
the witty,
the brave.

I know. But I do not approve.
And I am not
resigned.

EDNA ST. VINCENT MILLAY

PART ONE

My Father

Dedicated to Joan Kiernan,

Who needs and wants a

Husband–lover–father–poet–

Adventurer–philosopher–

Athlete–jester–husband.

I know she'll find him—

In a bottle at Johns Hopkins.

TJM

CHAPTER ONE

He died first, quickly and quietly. It was like my father to outwit my mother, even at the end. Cancer had sprouted in his lung and traveled slowly upward, until it had found an auspicious nesting place on his brain stem. My father, who despised doctors, could probably have bought himself some significant time had it not been for his overweening love of crossword puzzles. He spent his days fastened to a corner of the living room couch, a crossword puzzle laid out before him on the coffee table. To his left, on the dark wood end table, rested his props. A pack of Pall Mall cigarettes, neatly opened, the foil exposing the slim brown and white soldiers stationed within. A heavy gold-plated ashtray with a miniature eagle saddled in such a way as to offer a resting place for the burning cigarette. The requisite silver lighter lay nearby, square and heavy and satisfying to flip open and ignite. A cup of coffee stood innocently by, sipped carefully in the morning, but often left untouched for long periods of time, until the day softened into dusk, at which point it was replaced with a glass of vodka. This beverage, served in a slightly dirty glass with only the suggestion of ice, never stood idly by. It was relished by my father, and his hand left the coolness of the glass only long enough to attend to a challenge on the crossword puzzle before him.

One day, he leaned in to address the problem of a particularly perplexing word and realized he couldn't make out the characters, despite his best efforts. The vision in his left eye would not adjust itself, and the words swam in front of him, causing increasing frustration. My father pulled himself up from his customary place on the couch and made his way slowly to the small bathroom located under the stairwell, where he studied himself in the mirror over the sink. Then he walked back into the living room and peered at the mantel, searching for the small white first aid kit that had rested there, mostly undisturbed, for decades.

Grasping the first aid kit, my father walked into the back of the house, where a long table stood in the middle of the laundry room. He placed the box on the table and quickly withdrew the necessary items: gauze pads and surgical tape. Then he moved into the bathroom off the kitchen and, locking the door behind him, began in earnest to solve the problem of his errant left eye.

This was the sight that greeted my brother Joe when he visited our father later that winter afternoon, and how terrible it must have been for him. All alone, he stood in the middle of the living room and studied his eighty-three-year-old father sitting before him on the couch. The year was 2004, but the old man looked like someone who time had forgotten, peering stoically forward, the left lens of his glasses patched with white gauze and crossed twice over with surgical tape. Joe stared at our father and said, "Jesus, Dad." Joe was no fool and had an intuitive understanding of the game about to be afoot, but neither was he a glutton for punishment, so he tried to slow things down.

"What the hell happened to you?" he asked, sitting across from our father on a black and red floral ottoman, a permanent depression at its center, so that one had no choice but to sink into it. Joe, sunken, looked miserable, as he leaned forward, arms braced on his thighs.

Our father lit a cigarette, inhaled deeply, and said, "Couldn't do the crossword puzzle. Frustrating as hell."

Joe said nothing. His love for his father was complicated, and often ran along parallel lines of anxiety and devotion. When in our father's presence, Joe felt himself helplessly reduced to a kind of childlike insecurity, hesitant to be completely himself with this man, for whom he would do anything. As a result, they often sat together in silence, Dad working on his crossword puzzle and Joe reading the paper. Today, however, Joe found the silence intolerable, and because he could not bear the heaviness that lay over the room, he spoke more boldly than was his custom.

"I think we should visit the ophthalmologist, Dad, and see what's going on. See if we can't get this thing corrected so you can get back to your crossword puzzles."

My father raised an eyebrow and asked, "You think so? Think it's an easy enough fix?"

The two good-looking men, father and son, studied each other. Deceit did not suit their relationship, which was unlike any other in the family. Joe and my father shared a relationship in which each attached a special value to the other, so that in many ways theirs was a secret, unspoken affection, one that defied articulation. Joe's need for his father was primal, the father's need for his son plaintive. This chemistry produced an allegiance at once tenuous and sacred.

After a time, my father looked up from his unfinishable crossword puzzle and fixed his good eye on his son.

"Shit," he said, in acquiescence.

THE PHONE RANG in the bedroom of my apartment in West Palm Beach, where I had retired to take a nap between shows. The tour of *Tea at Five*, a one-woman bio-drama in which I played Katharine Hepburn in both her youth and her dotage, had begun to take its toll. This was precious time for me, since my efforts on the stage were considerable, and when two performances were demanded in one day, it was imperative to lie as still as possible for as long as possible so as to be able to seduce the audience at the evening performance into believing that I was both much younger then I actually was and, fifteen minutes later, much, much older. Therefore, I hesitated before reaching over and then decided, in a moment of curious karmic resolve, to pick up the phone and answer.

"Hello."

"Kate, this is your brother Joe."

The curious formality with which my brother always addressed me had the odd effect of bringing me instantly to attention. My heart skipped a beat, as it did whenever Joe called. This was because Joe was not given to phone calls of a purely social nature. I knew he was not inquiring after my well-being. I intuited, instead, that my brother had something important to tell me and that I had better prepare myself.

"What's up, Bobo? You sound grim," I said.

"Something's up with Dad," Joe replied, shortly.

It was this very curtness of tone that alerted me to the seriousness of the matter at hand. It was not Joe's style to deliver bad news with finesse. He was not one to measure the sound of his remarks, nor was he likely to put himself in the other person's shoes. When darkness was my brother's message, he delivered it with the blunt force of a metal hammer.

"Dad had a problem with his vision and it was fucking with his ability to do his crossword puzzles. This was beginning to drive him nuts, so he taped up the left lens of his glasses in an effort to see more clearly through his right eye. It didn't work, so I convinced him to let me take him to the ophthalmologist."

Joe paused. I swung my legs over the side of the bed and stood up.

"Go on, sweetheart," I urged.

"Looks like there might be—something, some malignancy— somewhere. The ophthalmologist wouldn't tell me much, but he arranged for an appointment with an oncologist at Finley, who immediately ran a number of tests, but I started to get really nervous when he insisted on taking a biopsy. He did, and that's where we are. The doctor wants Dad back at the clinic on Monday."

I sat again, abruptly. An oncologist did not bode well, not in our family. For many years, this clinical title meaning "one who spots death" had been anathema in our house. We disparaged this word, laughed at it, dismissed it, anything to defuse it. It always meant an appointment in a bleak place with a racing pulse, clammy hands, a clock ticking loudly in a dull green corridor. It meant head scarves and autumn leaves, a buckling at the knees, racking sobs on a moonlit night, no more school, a leeching of what was.

"Listen to me, Bo," I said. "Today is Friday. Please make the appointment for next Tuesday, and I'll be there."

"Come on, Kate, you don't have to do that," Joe countered, but I felt him relent, even as he resisted. In that moment, I understood that this had been his intention all along. He knew that of all our siblings, I was in the best position to get our father the care he needed. These circumstances demanded not only compassion but a capable hand and a modicum of fame. I possessed all three.

I didn't for a moment fault my brother for cashing in on my celebrity status. There was even a possibility that he was not conscious of this manipulation, although I found that possibility so remote as to be nonexistent. Joe was grasping for straws in what he anticipated might become a high-stakes game. The medical game. The game of chance, where some are overlooked, some condemned, and some elevated as if by magic to a level of excellent care, thereby increasing their chances to greet another day with the element of promise. Joe was prepared to do anything to ensure my father the greatest number of promising days, where crossword puzzles were dispatched with ease and a vodka on the rocks appeared with happy regularity at the stroke of five. He was prepared to do this because of all the people in the world whom he loved, he loved our father with a singular, unbridled passion.

The tenderness I felt for my brother developed only after years of watching him wreak havoc. I disliked him intensely when he was a young boy and considered him almost pathologically attracted to danger. In a typical summer, he might burn down the barn one day and run away to Chadron, Nebraska, the next.

My father was his own boss and, with his brother, Bob, owned a contracting business called Mulgrew Blacktop. Dressed in khakis and work boots, furious with his son and frustrated by his own impotence, he slammed in and out of the back door over the next two weeks, making for the bottle of J & B when he came in at night and occasionally muttering, "Jesus H. Christ!"

Then, one night the phone rang, and my father picked up the receiver. After listening with intense concentration to whoever was on the other end of the line, he hung up, drained his glass and, looking at his wife and sundry other offspring, burst into laughter and shouted, "The little shit is in Nebraska, for Christ's sake! They picked him up after a bar fight and threw the little creep in jail! He must have really pissed someone off because now he's sitting behind bars with a couple of broken mitts in bleeping Chadron, Nebraska, for Christ's sake! And he somehow managed to rescue a *puppy*, while he was at it! Jesus!"

Early the next morning, I woke to the sound of Dad's car pulling out of the driveway and I knew that he was embarking on the long journey to Chadron, Nebraska, where he would recover his young and completely unmanageable son, whom he would greet with a terrible sternness meant to send shivers down the kid's spine, and the kid would feel those shivers for a while but then somewhere along the highway, the puppy would start to yelp and Dad would mutter invectives about dog shit in his clean car and Joe would smile his shy, crooked smile of phony remorse and hold up his hands, bandaged in gauze, and look at my father with a curious mixture of sweetness and bravado. My father, disarmed, would need to turn away and light up a cigarette.

My younger brother, separated from me by no more than fourteen months, was born with a beautiful face, perfectly formed limbs, a keen intelligence, and a serious penchant for trouble. He was a colicky baby, a hyperactive child, a troubled youth, and an adult male whose beauty captivated and destroyed many women. He and my father looked very much alike, and had either of them acquired in height even so much as two inches more than nature had allotted them, life would have been insupportable. My father stood at five feet six, my brother at five ten, and both men regarded their stature as an affliction. They worked aggressively to dispel the effects of their relative shortness by sharpening their God-given gifts of wit, charm, and sexual allure until it no longer appeared to the naked female eye that they were anything but completely desirable.

One evening in the early summer of 1971, it happened that my father, contrary to custom, joined his family at the dinner table. Tom, the firstborn, favored and openly adored, held the seat of honor, directly to my father's left. Next to him, brimming with resentment at his diminished status, sat Joe. Laura, a soft-spoken and uncertain thirteen-year-old, was placed at our mother's right, and to our mother's left, in a state of perfect contentment, perched Tessie. The two youngest, Sam and Jenny, had eaten earlier in the kitchen under the supervision of Mother's helper, Doris, a painfully shy young woman whose capacity for hard work saved her from making an outright fool of herself with my father, whom she worshipped. My place at the long oval dining table was to my father's right, signifying the importance of my stature as the second-born child and oldest daughter.

There we sat, basking in the sunshine of our father's highly unusual presence. Tales were told, jokes exchanged, candles flickered as we bent to our food, and I thought, How like a normal family we are, after all! Here is our mother, and here is our father! It doesn't matter that he's not eating—he is *here*, and his glass is full, and soon the plates will be cleared and Dad will indicate that he would like me, his eldest daughter, to leave my seat and station myself behind his chair, where I will begin to run my fingers through his hair and where soon the sound of my father's pleasure will escape his lips in low growls, followed by encouragements such as "Ahhh" or "Now you're talking, sugar," when in fact I would not have been talking at all but only rubbing away and now and again twisting his thick, wavy hair into devil's horns and sending my siblings into howls of laughter. Even Mother, from her place at the opposite end of the table, seemed to be enjoying herself. She leaned forward and, putting her elbows on the table, cupped her face in her hands and watched with a kind of vacant amusement as her children chattered and laughed and ate.

Suddenly, the phone rang, startling everyone into silence. The telephone seldom rang in the evening because my father despised the telephone and had put a moratorium on our use of it. He found the empty chatter it inspired to be excessive, irritating, and unduly expensive. Accordingly, we had warned our friends not to call in the evening, when the probability of our father being at home was at its greatest.

The phone rang and continued to ring until finally my father looked up and demanded, "Who the hell is calling at this hour?" It was seven-thirty. I leaned down and, plucking up courage in my role as designated head rubber, whispered, "You better get it, Dad, don't you think?" My father sighed deeply, as if interruptions such as these were unrelenting. He picked up his unused napkin, threw it on the table and, as he marched into the kitchen, exclaimed, "Merde de cheval!"

Minutes passed, as we strained to eavesdrop on the telephone conversation taking place. Occasionally, we heard our father grunt in response, and once he said, "Is that so?" There were long, unbroken moments of silence in the kitchen, and this, we knew instinctively, meant that our father was listening to something that he found particularly interesting. Before he hung up, he deliberately lowered his voice and said, "Okay, pal, we'll see about that."

The door to the dining room opened at last, and our father appeared. He looked directly at Joe, and so severe was his expression that all of us froze in our seats. This expression, specific to our father, signified an immediate end to our revelry, and introduced into the atmosphere an electrifying sensation of tension. No one moved. No one spoke. Our father walked slowly to his place at the end of the table, never once taking his eyes from Joe's face. He stood looking down at his son for some time and then, after a harrowing moment of silence, made a request. Staring at my brother, he said, "Hand me my drink, would you, Dad?"

Startled, my brother looked up. What did our father mean? Was he confused? Was he drunk? Joe slid the glass half full of scotch across the table, offering it to our father. "Thanks, Dad," our father said. We were at once bewildered and intrigued. Only Mother, who until now had said nothing and did not seem particularly alarmed by our father's obvious show of dementia, dared to speak up. "Tom," she demanded, "what on earth are you doing?"

"Well, Jick," our father replied, turning to look at our mother, "it appears our son is about to become a father. That rather distraught fellow on the telephone was the father of a very young mother-to-be, otherwise known as our boy's inamorata, and he informed me that he is slapping you, my fifteen-year-old son, with a paternity suit."

"That's insane!" Joe shouted, jumping to his feet. "She doesn't know it's me—I mean, it *isn't* me—that girl's had everybody in the school! She's easy! She's a slut—"

"*Sit. Down.*" My father's voice, deep and authoritative, was more effective than a blow. Joe abruptly sat. We minor players regarded this interaction with awe, and not a sound could be heard in the room.

Suddenly and without explanation, our father turned his back to the table and stood facing the window. He gazed out over the lawn, utterly silent. Then his shoulders began to move, very slightly, up and down, and this sight more than any other filled each of us with apprehension. Our father never wept. He seldom, if ever, showed any kind of vulnerability. This was completely out of character, and we, as a collective, were stunned. And then we heard what could only be construed as laughter coming from our father's mouth. The laughter grew until it infected each of us and, against our better judgment and despite the bizarreness of the situation, we were soon hysterical. Only Mother rose and left the room, letting the door swing shut behind her.

The corners of Joe's mouth were just about to shape themselves into a smirk of righteous indignation when my father leaned into him and, jabbing a finger in his face, said, "A paternity suit at the age of fifteen. Now, that's a real accomplishment. Something to be proud of. Highly original. And you'll have plenty of time to gloat over it because you are grounded for the next year. No parties. No friends. No sports. No girls. Curfew will begin immediately after school. First, however, you will call the father of this young woman whom you have allegedly impregnated, and you will apologize, and when you are finished apologizing to the father, you will then apologize to his daughter. We'll see whether this paternity suit is an idle threat or a real one, but either way you should know that as far as I'm concerned, you are"—here my father paused, as if thinking twice, before he went on—"in big trouble, pal. *Big* effing trouble."

As my father climbed the staircase, I thought I could make out what sounded like a short chuckle, followed by the words "Well, I'll be damned."

Joe, of course, had interpreted my father correctly. He understood that whereas impregnating a girl of fifteen was hardly laudable, neither was it a criminal offense in Dubuque County in the early seventies, and that soon enough the dramatic allegation would be disproved and his sentence would be commuted, leaving him free to once again enjoy his friends, his sports, his parties, and his girls.

This curious sympathy between my father and my brother developed over the years into something akin to companionship. As soon as alcohol was introduced as a commonality, the relationship was solidified, and the two men, so alike in nature and temperament, could while away whole evenings sipping their respective drinks and speaking only when necessity demanded it. For example, Joe might ask Dad if he could top off his drink and Dad might respond, "Why the hell not." They preferred it that way, didn't care to ruffle the perfect calm of the cocktail hour with superfluous banter, and certainly didn't want to run the risk of welcoming any of the womenfolk, whose voices would shatter the atmosphere like ice picks.

The relationship that grew between my father and my brother was remarkable in that it had been built on a very precarious foundation, one which almost all of us predicted would end in disaster or worse, alienation. Instead, there developed an understanding between them that appeared to the rest of us to be quite effortless, one that was eminently comfortable. Within the confines of this agreement, a love deepened that no one could have predicted, least of all the two leading players, neither of whom could have anticipated such an unexpected intimacy as they leaned into their advancing years.

I looked out at the perpetual sunshine and relentless humidity of West Palm Beach, looked back in my mind at a boy with broken hands, and said, "Don't say another word, Bobo. I'll be there on Tuesday."

CHAPTER TWO

I didn't want to go on the stage that night. I didn't want the ten-minute walk from my apartment to the theater. I didn't want the routine: the application of makeup, the snap of the wig cap over tight pin curls, the shallow breaths that always preceded the first act, the hardest act, the more precipitous slope of this two-sided mountain. In playing Katharine Hepburn, in a production which was staged in two acts, there was no reprieve. In the first act, I played the thirty-year-old Kate, and bounded onstage with youthful energy, equal parts vulnerability and dauntless ego. After intermission, during which I sat zombie-like at my dressing table, I took the audience on a journey through all of the older Hepburn's personal tragedies, each one of which demanded complete focus. If I took my finger off the pulse even for a moment, I ran the risk of losing the thread. This meant that every night, for the two hours I was on the stage, I was in a state of complete immersion.

A challenge such as this is initially very exciting, and I had thrown myself into rehearsals at Hartford Stage with abandon. Every day, from ten until five, we worked in the rehearsal studio. Each night, I walked to the Goodwin Hotel, ordered dinner in the room, and spent the next four hours studying every book I could get my hands on about the life of Katharine Hepburn, watching every movie I could find that starred Katharine Hepburn, and reading my lines aloud so as to perfect every unfamiliar cadence I heard, every affectation. The work was intense and gratifying and, in the beginning, I was not lonely. As the weeks unfolded, however, and the play moved from Hartford to New York, and from New York to a national tour, a pattern developed that was rigid and unalterable. The play became a way of life, one that demanded order and discipline and absolute quiet. My voice, and in particular the tremor I used both physically and vocally in act two, required absolute rest between performances.

This, in itself, was not unusual. What began to take its toll was my inability to justify this lifestyle to my friends and family. I began to sneak out the back door of the theater, avoiding fans, avoiding everyone. Everything outside of the theater threatened the "performance", and, instead of resisting the pull toward asceticism, or at the very least trying to strike a balance, I withdrew into a narrower, much lonelier world. By the time we settled in West Palm Beach for a four-month sit-down, most of the joy I'd known in developing the piece had been replaced by resignation. Loneliness had become routine, the kind of self-imposed exile that is grim and exhausting. My ego was so invested in the performance that I couldn't recognize my own detachment, and this protracted entrenchment in make-believe had the dubious effect of deepening me as an artist while putting the rest of me on ice. When Joe had called and told me about our father, it was as if the little girl in me, a spirit nearly forgotten, suddenly kicked, and swam hard for the surface. Enough, I said to myself.

Thirty years earlier, I had missed the funeral of my sister Tessie, a sister whom I adored, because my father had been adamant that I stay and fulfill my responsibility to the producers, who had, after all, rolled the dice on an unknown actress and given her the lead in a celebrated classic at a well-known theater in Stratford, Connecticut, and who, while confident in her abilities as a performer, might not be so easily inclined to allow this actress to skip four performances so she could go home and attend her younger sister's funeral. My father played this card skillfully, knowing how much I had wanted this part, how badly I had wanted to begin my career as a professional actress, and so I deferred to him, and stayed in Connecticut, where I played the entire weekend to full houses. What my father did not say was that he didn't want me to come to the funeral because I would be a burden to him.

My very presence would exacerbate my father's anxiety and, regardless of the relief it may have provided my mother, he determined that it would be best for all involved if I were to remain back east, and do the honorable thing by staying out of his hair and fulfilling my obligations as a newly minted pro.

In all the years that have passed since Tessie's death, I have never felt anything but intense regret that I missed that last good-bye, that ritual so crucial to those left behind. Tessie, of course, would have been completely indifferent—she lay inside that coffin with her lovely almond-shaped eyes closed tight against the living—but I was left outside, unable to touch her, and made to say good-bye from very far away, on the stage of a summer theater in a small and unfamiliar New England town.

"NO MORE REGRETS," I said, as my dresser fitted the wig snugly onto my head. I had walked to the theater in the moist, dense air of a West Palm Beach evening, and had submitted as I always had to Kara's ministrations. The small clock resting on the vanity table said 7:30 P.M. I felt a familiar tightening in my solar plexus and sighed. Kara smiled at me in her sphinxlike way and whispered, "You do what is right for *you*. They'll get over it."

As, of course, they would. As they always have, and always will. Someone else steps in and before long word on the street is that the replacement is in many ways even better than the original, things happen for a reason, que será, será. This is the getting of wisdom, I thought, something my mother often said before she was afflicted with the getting of dementia. At fifty, I knew what I could not have known at twenty. It had taken thirty years for me to understand that regrets do not dissipate, they do not abate into sadness—they harden until they have formed into a small fist that often rests quietly in the pit of your stomach but that can suddenly, and without warning, land a punch so powerful you are left doubled over in pain, gasping for breath.

"I'll play the weekend and then go home. My father has an appointment with the oncologist on Tuesday. I need to be there for that," I said, summoning the courage to sound confident. Again, Kara smiled softly and turned her attention to my costume, which needed steaming before the evening performance. The room was very quiet, but soon, I knew, the backstage area would fill with the noise of the technical crew, as they moved furniture and adjusted props, checked the lights and ran the sound cues.

There was a knock on the dressing room door, and Christine, the stage manager, looked in and asked, as she always did, "You good? We're at half hour. Can I get you anything?" I didn't immediately respond, so Christine stepped lightly into the room and closed the door behind her. Like Kara, she was sensitive and intuitive, alert to any change in the wind.

She waited until I turned and said, "I have to go home, Christine. We'll need to put the understudy in or cancel the rest of the run. My father's not well. I think it's pretty serious. My brother would not have called me if it weren't serious."

Christine cocked her head to one side, a sign that she was processing this information. The responsibility of delivering the message to the producers would fall to her, and therefore she was careful not to speak until she had formed a clear and honest opinion.

"I'm sorry," she said, at last. "I'm so sorry, Kate. The producers won't like it, but they'll live."

"Whereas my father may not," I said.

"Exactly," Christine agreed, her voice soft.

These two women understood that the central conflict lay not with the producers, but with me. Years of honoring the unspoken laws of the theater had, instead of deepening my self-awareness, done just the opposite. I was confused, and I was scared. Theater etiquette warned me that this sort of thing just wasn't done, not if I wanted to maintain my otherwise unimpeachable reputation. The consummate professional, whose every job had been hard-won, whose every success had meant some sort of sacrifice, whose own children had suffered countless disappointments, warned against the rashness of a decision that might not bode well for the future. What had looked from the outside like fierce independence was, in fact, ferocious ambition.

Now, as I prepared to go onstage, I felt the weariness of someone who has followed orders all her life.

❧

I ROSE FROM my chair and applied the last strokes of lipstick to my mouth, a minor but exacting exercise, which, if not successful, threatened to redefine the entire performance. I then began my journey from the dressing room to stage right, where a small red light would be waiting for me, winking its approval. Too soon, the light would be switched off and, in that moment, everything would be transformed, all the mundane concerns of life forgotten, my sick father and my long-dead sister put summarily and deftly aside, and I would walk onto that stage transfigured, an actress leaping out of the blocks, a shining crusader for Art.

Tonight, as air-conditioning blasted from every conceivable aperture into the soggy atmosphere of the theater, as I listened to the rustling of programs and the putting on of sweaters and the first crunching of candies, I was overcome with loneliness. I could not define myself, I could not defend myself. I felt again, just as I had felt thirty years earlier, that same elemental longing to say good-bye to one I loved, a longing that transcended the hooks of responsibility, and the fear of being permanently unmoored.

I looked up at the cue light, calibrating the switch as I did every night and, as I did every night, offered the performance to Tessie. This night, however, I offered it to Tessie in my father's words. I whispered, "This one's for you, kid," and in the moment of so doing I understood with absolute clarity that I must go home, that I must return to whoever I was before I became this. This creature of unbearable habit.

My father could not have calculated the pain he caused me when he forbade me to attend my sister's funeral. I assumed he had been immersed in his own agony. Likewise, I assumed I had forgiven him.

Just as this long-held assumption felt the first tap of the psychic ice pick, the standby light was switched off, the theater was plunged into darkness and, a mere heartbeat later, the stage was flooded with light.

CHAPTER THREE

You must understand, it was a setup. An arranged marriage masquerading as a romance. There was no love lost between them. My paternal grandfather won her on a bet, having spotted her across the room at the Dubuque Golf & Country Club and, turning to his companion, said, "I'll take that."

"Not in a million years," his friend replied. "She's hands off. Catholic. Teaches at the women's college. Strict family, German."

My grandfather, whose name was Russell, studied the woman who would become my grandmother, and as he watched became increasingly, shall we say, peckish. She was indisputably beautiful, magnificently formed and very graceful, with a pair of the shapeliest legs my grandfather had ever seen. Petite, she may have been called, although I'm more inclined to say she was the ideal size for that time, which would have been around 1918. Standing at five feet, three inches, Genevieve Meysembourg gave the impression of greater height because of her enormous self-regard. Not only was she wonderful to look at but hers were the cadences of an educated woman, as indeed, she was. Genevieve had matriculated at Northwestern University, where she had excelled in speech and drama, in consequence of which she had been offered a teaching position in the speech department at the local women's college in Dubuque, Iowa, which is where this story takes place.

Russell took note and acted. Pulling his wallet from his pocket, he placed a hundred-dollar bill on the table in front of his friend and declared, "A hundred bucks says I get her."

My grandfather's crony, brimming with bonhomie and bourbon, slapped Russell on the back and said, "You're on!"

Six months later, they were married. Genevieve was exquisite in an ivory lace gown with silk-covered buttons running down her spine, disappearing into the fluted train. A veil of similar lace covered her light brown hair, which had been artfully marcelled to frame her heart-shaped face and glittering almond-shaped emerald eyes. My grandfather had her firmly in his grasp, one arm straying around her tiny waist, the hand coming to rest just inches above her hip. Genevieve's eyes remained fixed on the distance, her hands inert within the confines of their ivory kid opera gloves. She knew the jig was up, and that no excuse of faintness or frailness or even monthly indisposition could prevent my grandfather from taking his winnings, that night in the wedding bed.

Genevieve did not immediately become pregnant. She had learned a few worldly tricks, despite her fervid devotion to God, and knew enough to leave the bridal bed immediately after Russell had fallen asleep, and to fill an antiseptic syringe with warm water, and insert it carefully between her lovely legs. We learned this as children at the dinner table when, one evening in early summer, my mother announced she was pregnant once again and my grandmother, from the far end of the table, put down her napkin and, white with anger, said, "Joan, you're not a cow, you know. There is such a thing as a douche."

The douche was rigorously employed until such time as both Genevieve and Russell understood that their marriage was unlikely to produce either passion or camaraderie, so it may as well produce children. The birth of my father in November 1920 undoubtedly gave my grandmother a modicum of satisfaction, if not unalloyed joy, because at last she had a purpose other than pleasing her husband. The baby would engage her, the baby would need her and, most important, the baby would serve as the only acceptable excuse for abandoning the connubial chamber.

My father, Thomas James Mulgrew II, was soon joined by a sister, Jane, and a younger brother, Robert. The children grew up in relative luxury on an estate called Wartburg Place, located on the outskirts of town. Russell had come into a very nice inheritance, and for many years the family money sustained him. My grandfather provided his wife with servants, and the house bustled with activity as the maid did the laundry, the cook prepared the meals, and the nanny, on whom my grandmother soon developed a dependency, looked after the rosy-cheeked, handsome children.

Presently, Genevieve became a sought-after young matron and, while a certain coolness prevented her from becoming inordinately popular, her extraordinary beauty, her innate good taste, and her husband's money raised her to a position of midwestern prominence, which many found enviable. The social demands made on my grandmother were not, in the main, very sophisticated, but they served the important purpose of getting her out of the house and into the company of the local gentry, for whom, adorned in a salmon-pink Worth suit, pearls draped around her swan-like neck, elegant legs sheathed in silk stockings, she could be the undisputed center of attention.

While my grandmother was playing euchre and nibbling on melba crackers at the Dubuque Golf & Country Club, my grandfather was at his favorite speakeasy downtown, getting plastered. Drinking was a habit my grandfather had acquired shortly before marrying my grandmother, and one that did not appear to pose a threat to his equilibrium, particularly since his own father, my great-grandfather, was a confirmed teetotaler. Having had this habit well in check for some time, my grandfather was unsettled to find that it was beginning to get the better of him. One night he stumbled home only to find his alluring wife fast asleep, her bed separated from his by Genevieve's imported Italian prie-dieu, an amenity she had considered, bought, and situated with great care as a reminder to her husband that God alone was her Master. Thus rejected, Russell would descend to the parlor below and begin crashing about in an inebriated search for ice, decanter, and glass. Invariably, this disturbed my grandmother, who slipped out of bed and, covering herself with a robe, crept slowly down the stairs to see if she could prevent her husband from waking the entire household.

Years later, well into his cups, my father told me how, in his bedroom at the top of the stairs, he would awaken to raised voices, the sound of glass shattering, his mother's quiet, insistent pleas. He would lie there for some time, frozen with fear, until the commotion passed. One night, when the noises had subsided, and the house had been restored to order, my father got out of bed and tiptoed into the corridor, where he hid behind a pillar, from which vantage point he had an unobscured view into the parlor downstairs. He could see the figures of his parents quite clearly, and saw that they were standing close to each other, their faces only inches apart, but he was too far away to make out what they were saying. Suddenly, my grandmother turned on her heel and began to run toward the staircase, where she was intercepted by my grandfather, who grabbed her by the arm and, dropping his drink to the floor so that the glass splintered everywhere, slapped her hard across the face.

My father, not yet twelve years old, did not stir from his hiding place behind the pillar. He wanted more than anything to run down to his mother, to defend her, to shout at his father to stop, but he couldn't move, he couldn't breathe, and more disturbing than the fear he felt toward his father was his own inability to go to his mother's side. Even at eleven, my father possessed a strong sense of right and wrong, his character was spoken of as exceptional, and he was often asked to intervene when an argument threatened to erupt in the classroom, or when there were harsh words exchanged on the playing field. It was a well-known fact that his mother had always been his greatest champion, that she admired and worshipped him, that it was she who was the first to say, "Oh, just ask Thos, he'll know what to do." By attaching to her young son the moniker of a much older and worldlier man, she had unwittingly endowed him with a wisdom and sophistication well beyond his years. In the moment of betrayal, however, when he had witnessed his father deliberately break his sacred bond to his mother, when he had ceased to honor and protect her, when in fact he had assaulted her, in this moment the character of my father shrank to the size appropriate to the circumstances at hand, and he was reduced to nothing more than a very young, very frightened boy, who had abruptly lost his place in a world that, until then, had been impregnable. This single slap changed everything, and never again would my father feel, as he had felt during all the years of his childhood, an uncomplicated affection for his parents.

The Russell Mulgrews carried on as usual, the children swam and played tennis at the country club, they learned to ride in the fields abutting Wartburg Place, and my father soon became an accomplished equestrian, winning blue ribbons at county shows, sitting elegantly atop his horse with a ramrod-straight spine and an expression not unlike his mother's, which is to say, inscrutable. It is impossible to know whether that single event in the life of mother and son, the slap, justified their respective retreats behind expressions that no longer conveyed emotion, neither sadness nor joy, or whether they had simply gone to bed that night and made up their minds that Russell would never again know them as he once had. The fact that they did this individually might speak to the strength of the mother-son bond, were it not for the fact that my father removed himself from his mother as well. Gently, and with the utmost courtesy, young Thos disengaged himself from his adoring mother, who could only wonder how it happened that the fond embrace had shifted to a perfunctory kiss on the cheek, and greetings, once affectionate, had transmogrified into formal acknowledgments that now bookended the day: good morning, Mother, good night, Mother.

Russell, dimly aware of the awkward distance between himself and his son, but unwilling and unable to ascertain its genesis, nonetheless attempted a rapprochement by insisting that he buy young Thomas James, whom he pointedly addressed as Tom, his first beer at one of his favorite haunts. Now, whether it was my father's first beer or merely the first beer bought and authorized by my grandfather is not a matter of public record, but I think it is safe to say that the strict enforcement of laws concerning alcohol consumption today in no way resemble the regulations imposed in 1935, and that no objections were raised when my fifteen-year-old father slid onto a barstool in a dingy tavern on the wrong side of town and, accepting the glass of frothy lager, looked steadily at my grandfather and said, "Here's mud in your eye." Russell laughed at his son's precocity, as did the motley crew of inveterate drinkers running the length of the counter, and soon Russell felt that any ill will had been dispelled, and that relations between father and son had been restored to their rightful normalcy.

Meanwhile, back at Wartburg Place, Genevieve nursed a bourbon on the rocks and wondered where her elder son had disappeared to. She didn't have to worry about Janie, who, at thirteen, was short and stocky, square-faced and curious, often referred to by her clique as a "good egg." Robert, taciturn and surly, spent most of his free time in the stables, grooming his horses, whose company he found immeasurably preferable to that of human beings. Genevieve, while continually nurturing a grievance against her husband, whom she considered a bully and a boor and for whom she had developed a visceral abhorrence, at the same time missed the closeness she had once shared with her elder son with an almost palpable sadness. Were it not for an inherent sense of discipline, a trait instilled in her by her father, and a deep, cool pride that she had cultivated because of her celebrated beauty and what she perceived to be her exceptional intelligence, she very likely would have slipped into despondency or what is better known today as depression. Genevieve Meysembourg had been born in tougher times, however, when even the trifecta of beauty, brains, and privilege did not entitle one to undue self-involvement. Instead, my grandmother tapped into the very core of who she was and found there a German hussar of the truest stripe. She transformed her grief into stoicism, and from that time forward it was almost impossible to calculate Genevieve's emotions, hidden as they were beneath a veneer of perfect, imperturbable calm.

Genevieve's detachment, while having no discernible effect on her children, enraged her husband who, after all, had won her fair and square, had courted her assiduously like the hunter he was, bringing gifts of chocolates and, later, gifts of jewelry, had sat on the porch of the Meysembourg house and sipped tea, for Christ's sake, while his future father-in-law bored the bejesus out of him with his talk of progress and industry. Herr Meysembourg, while not possessing any of my grandfather's showmanship, had instead acquired over his lifetime a quiet, dignified reserve from which vantage point he studied others, and as he observed young Russell Mulgrew over the six-month-long courtship of his daughter, he reviewed his options. He had done everything he could to shape his daughter into a creature of uncommon desirability. Nature and superior genetics had endowed her with beauty and health and, although Herr Meysembourg was not a betting man, he had laid down good money on the prospect of a higher education lifting his daughter to a different level of society, and this conviction, combined with Genevieve's discipline, talent, and ambition, had served to produce a young woman any man would covet, and even though it was clear to Herr Meysembourg that Russell's desire for his daughter was essentially superficial, this reality did not in any way alter Herr Meysembourg's opinion of the situation. No other young man of the appropriate class and credentials had come forward, neither during Genevieve's time at Northwestern University nor afterward at home, and he was immovable in his resistance to his daughter's ambition to travel abroad. The girl could do no better, he reasoned, and she was running out of time. No one would want her after she turned twenty-five.

And so it was that Herr Meysembourg delivered his daughter into the hands of Russell Mulgrew, a man he neither knew nor wanted to know. Despite his bluster and a certain coarseness Herr Meysembourg chose to ignore, Russell was a man of means, and that, as far as Herr Meysembourg was concerned, was all that mattered. As it turned out, it was all that mattered to Genevieve, as well. Bloodlines will reveal themselves in choices made, and it was in Genevieve's blood to improve her station in life, whatever the cost.

Certain bloodlines, while undoubtedly advancing superior genes, also foster secrets. In my father's childhood home, and running through his veins, was a coolness that settled like a fine mist over other, more troubling emotions. While alcohol transformed my grandfather into a brutish, mendacious man, unpredictable and often wildly inappropriate, it had the opposite effect on my father. He found that several beers, and perhaps a whiskey or two, steadied him, and quietly flipped a switch that enabled him to lift himself out of his essential aloofness, to abandon his shyness, and enter into a world completely foreign to the one he knew at Wartburg Place.

Everyone in the family drank, but seldom did they drink together. Genevieve, fiercely guarding her reputation, allowed herself two bourbons after six, no more, no less. Robert, a loner, gathered with other loners in bars where there would be no inquiries, and no conversation. He acquired a taste for rum, and this spirit he would imbibe for as long as it took to get good and oiled, so that driving home and then finding his way through the front door and up the stairs to his bedroom was no longer a prospect to be dreaded, but simply a matter of course. Janie sipped cocktails with her friends at the club, but in so doing she was not seeking relief; she was, instead, seeking a permanent way out. In due course, she found it, and left Dubuque to settle in London, where she worked in high-end retail and entertained friends on a modest level in her cozy flat on Dunraven Street. She never married and, whereas this inspired Genevieve's sympathy on one level, on another it thrilled her. There was an extra bedroom in the flat on Dunraven Street, and Genevieve told anyone who would listen that whereas Janie was doing very well in her life abroad, she sorely missed her mother, and that it was therefore her duty to visit her daughter as often as was reasonable.

Russell continued to drink with abandon, and with impunity. The town chose to look the other way as my grandfather indulged his vices, digging his way further and further into debt. He grew fat, and developed a considerable paunch wherein lodged his unfortunate liver which, by this time, showed all the trademarks of the disease that would ultimately be his undoing. His contempt for his wife deepened over the years, and by mutual silent agreement they kept their distance from one another, although this wasn't always convenient.

One summer's night, my grandfather happened to come home early. He wanted to change out of his hunting gear and into his evening clothes and, to ease this transition, he needed a drink. Without removing his jacket and with his rifle still in hand, he walked into the parlor and was surprised to find his wife sitting in an armchair, a book in one hand and a bourbon in the other. Not having encountered each other in this way for some time, my grandparents were caught off guard. My grandfather said something to my grandmother that offended her so deeply she sprang to her feet and, with all the vigor of one who has harbored resentment, rage, and disgust for far too long, hurled her drink across the room and watched as it missed her husband's head by inches and sailed into the foyer, where it landed with a resounding crash on the black-and-white tiled floor.

My grandfather started toward my grandmother when suddenly young Thos appeared in the doorway and, looking directly at his father, very quietly said, "If you lay a hand on her, I'll kill you."

Soon after, my father enlisted in the Army Air Corps. I've often imagined the moment when his train pulled into the East Dubuque station and, turning to the woman who loved him like none other ever would, my father hoisted his standard-issue duffel bag onto his shoulder, then leaned down and, brushing her cool, powdered cheek with his lips said, simply, "Good-bye, Mother."

CHAPTER FOUR

O n the appointed day, I clung to the armrests of my tiny seat in the American Eagle aircraft as it made its descent into the Dubuque Regional Airport, revealing a quilt of fields below, dark and fallow in the bleak winter of 2004. Arriving in my hometown, I marveled, as I always did, that nothing much seemed to have changed, with one glaring exception. No one was there to meet me. This had been agreed on, of course, due to the covert nature of the mission, and the fact that Joe did not want to alarm Dad by notifying him of my visit any sooner than was necessary.

THE ONCOLOGY UNIT at Finley Hospital was long and narrow, modestly appointed and dimly lit. As I approached the nurses' station, a young girl in a pink uniform, which had been tightly fastened across her chest and bore the name SAM on the label affixed to her pocket, looked up and, smiling brightly, asked, "May I help you?"

"You may," I replied, smiling in turn. At that moment, the girl's expression changed, and I knew that she had recognized me. The unspoken plan that Joe and I had hatched appeared to be working, and I was gratified. It could easily have gone another way, I knew, and was grateful that serendipity had placed this girl behind the nurses' desk.

"I'm looking for my father, Tom Mulgrew, and my brother Joe. Do you know if they're here?" I asked, lowering my voice so as not to disturb the climate of perfect calm that pervaded the corridors of the unit.

"Oh, sure! I saw 'em come in about a half hour ago," the young girl said, her face brightening. I looked about the place uncertainly, until Sam registered my confusion and said, "They're just down the way—I can take ya there, if ya want."

"Thanks, that would be great," I replied. "I've never been here before."

Sam chuckled and said, "Why would ya be? Oh look, there's yer dad just down the way!"

She pointed straight ahead, to a room situated at the very end of the corridor. In this room, under a muted overhead light, I made out the figure of a small, old man sitting on a metal stool. A nurse was leaning over this man, doing something to his head. The white head of the old man was slightly bent, as was his back, and I could see that there was no conversation of any kind taking place between the old man and the middle-aged woman attending him. It could have been a scene out of a science fiction movie, so out of place were the woman's ministrations as she applied herself to her task, so detached was the old man, and so bizarre were the surroundings. And yet, curiously, both the man and the woman seemed resigned to their actions, as if sitting on a metal stool under a dim white light in the middle of the day having one's head taped and marked as if in preparation for an elaborate game were ordinary, even perhaps a little dreary, and were it not for Sam's hand on my shoulder, gently pushing me forward, I think I may have stood there indefinitely, trying to work out the puzzle of the small room at the end of the corridor, and the middle-aged woman and old man within it.

"There's yer dad, don't ya see him?" she asked, too loudly.

Startled, I jumped. I did not want Sam's bright voice to disturb the image in front of me, and so I whispered "Thank you" and, moving away from her, found a place against the wall where I could stand, unseen.

Was that my father? Diminutive, slouched, lost, his thinning white hair clipped short, I might not have recognized him were it not for the uniform, familiar to me now for many years. He wore a white T-shirt under a dark blue V-neck sweater, khaki pants, penny loafers, and black rayon socks. He had not deviated from this ensemble in decades, and I had to cast my mind back to my childhood if I wanted to recapture the father who had taken my breath away, a father who had bounded up the stairs two at a time, already pulling off his jacket, calling down to where I stood at the bottom of the staircase, "Kitten, bring me a scotch on the rocks, will you, sugar?" And oh, the privilege of it, and the confident march into the kitchen, where I pulled up a stool so as to retrieve the glass, and leaned over the counter until I could hardly breathe to grasp the bottle of J & B, and carefully poured in the scotch, and then made my way to the refrigerator, where I gathered the ice and watched vigilantly as I released the cubes into the drink, because this required logic and I needed to remember that he liked it cold but not too cold, and when I was satisfied with my labors, the measured, happy walk through the dining room, the glass clasped tightly between my hands, and the deliberate, proud mounting of the stairs, one by one, until I arrived at the top landing, where my father, clad only in blue boxers, stood over the sink in the open bathroom, applying shaving cream to his face and, upon seeing me, shouted, "Atta girl! Now you're talking my lingo!" and how my heart leapt with joy, for I knew I would now be rewarded and would be allowed to sit on the closed toilet seat and watch my handsome young father as he drew the razor over his cheeks, magically making the cream disappear, and splashed his face with warm water and, finally, looking over at me and winking, shook the Old Spice into his hands and patted it, hard and fast, all over his face, and then, as if to punctuate the entire movement, took a big, satisfying sip of his drink and exclaimed, loudly, "Ahhhhh!"

I heard my brother's voice before I saw him and turned just in time to be pulled into a rough embrace.

"Thanks for coming, Kate," Joe said and then, because it interested him to know the inner workings of businesses outside of his own, he

continued. "How the hell did you manage it? Didn't it cost those producers a shitload of money?"

I smiled tightly, dropped my handbag on the floor, crossed my arms,
and replied, "A shitload, as you so elegantly put it. Don't worry, I'll
make up for it, they'll see to that. How are you doing, Bobo?"

My brother assumed a stance that was common to all of us. He
stood with his legs a good two feet apart, his feet firmly planted, arms
crossed tightly over his chest, leaning slightly backward, as if against
a strong but not unpleasant wind. Joe's face, in the unflattering light of
the corridor, looked pale and drawn, his once abundant dark hair had
grown almost white and fell below his shoulders in disheveled curls, his
beard was rough, and his eyes, hooded and heavy, suggested exhaustion. I had always thought of Joe as robust, but observing him now, I
could see clearly that he had lost weight, that he was depleted, and that
whatever it was that was ailing our father, he had internalized.

"What are they doing to him in there?" I whispered, pointing to the
chamber at the end of the corridor, where the nurse, now moving in
slow circles, continued to busy herself with my father's head.

"Jesus, Bo, they're not measuring him for radiation, are they?" I
asked, moving away from the wall so as to command a better view of
the room.

My brother, who had lowered his head, now lifted his eyes to look at
me and said, "You don't understand. It all happened so fast. One minute he was doing his crossword puzzles, telling me his glasses bothered
him, and the next we're here and they're telling me they have to run
more tests, and the sooner the better and, Jesus, what was I supposed
to do, tell them *not* to?"

"I thought we agreed you'd wait for me," I countered.

"They've got their own system, for Christ's sake, Kate, it's a *clinic*,
after all. I couldn't very well tell the attending oncologist to go have
coffee and a donut, my sister's not here yet, she's just coming off a tour,
so could everybody just chill and wait till she shows up!" Joe raked his

fingers anxiously through his hair, looking at me with an expression that betrayed more fear than anger.

This anger of my brother's, so familiar, so easily provoked, would ordinarily have moved me to calm him, would have instantly struck a chord of sympathy, but in this moment, from my vantage point in the corridor that led to the room where my father sat hunched over on a metal stool, it had the opposite effect.

I put my hands on my brother's shoulders and, forcing him to look at me, asked the question that had been germinating since I first glimpsed my father in that strange room at the end of the hall.

"Bo, is Dad even aware of what's going on? Has the doctor talked to him? Has *anyone* talked to him?"

Joe shook his head, then put his face in his hands and rubbed his forehead. I knew that my brother did not feel he had deliberately misled our father, that he had done what had come naturally to him as a son, which was to protect our father from any news that might be unexpected or alarming, in this way allowing him to be carried along by the current so adroitly offered by the medical staff, to be measured and poked, taped and prodded, his gray head drawn on like a child's map. This was more tolerable to my brother than demanding an explanation from the doctor who, my brother knew, would feel compelled to tell the truth. It seemed to Joe that while our father, the doctor, the nurses, and all the medical personnel contrived to play this game, perhaps it wasn't a game at all, and our father was merely undergoing a routine examination, the main purpose of which was to restore his left eye to its normal vision so that he could resume doing his crossword puzzles.

Whereas I could understand my brother's actions, I could not grasp why our father had submitted without question, without protest, to having his head measured and mapped with a Magic Marker. Such behavior was entirely out of keeping with his character. At every point in his life demanding a decision of any importance, my father had exhibited a real dislike of being told what to do, and would respond with contempt, making it clear that no one had authority over him and, if they dared to push it, he could become closed, withdrawn and, finally, intractable.

Something had happened. This wizened creature, bowed over a stool in the back room of a clinic, in no way resembled the man who, all his life, had demanded the truth. In the time that had elapsed since my father's vision had become compromised and his subsequent visit to the ophthalmologist, a seed of terror had been planted, which now prevented him from rising from that absurd metal stool, pushing the nurse aside, and demanding an explanation.

Notwithstanding my natural disinclination to see my father compromised, what rose up inside me was a disgust with the way the entire process had been allowed to unfold, as if this were, indeed, a children's game and my father the designated goose, made to run frantically from one chair to the next until, exhausted, he would simply collapse, and not out of fatigue or despair, but of disgrace.

Joe, standing next to me, his hands thrust deep in his pockets, gazed at our father with an expression of such uncertainty and pain that I instinctively put my arm around him and said, "I get it. You wanted to buy some time, avoid a rush to judgment, but, Bo, this isn't a business decision, or even a family decision, it's *Dad's* decision, and Dad's decision alone. He needs to talk to the doctor and the doctor needs to talk to him—and talk straight. We've got to allow that. Dad will never forgive us if we don't, and you know it."

There was a brief pause, during which I searched my brother's face for signs of resistance and, satisfied there were none, said, "You find the doctor, I'll get Dad."

As I approached the small room at the end of the corridor, the nurse attending my father looked up and, seeing me, put her hand on his shoulder and said, "Mr. Mulgrew, I think your daughter's here."

My father looked at me first in bewilderment and then, with suspicion.

"Kitten, what are you doing here?"

I kissed his cheek and said, "I talked to Joe last week, he told me you had an appointment with Dr. Koenig today, and I wanted to see you," I explained, as my father glared at me. "I wanted to come home."

"Well, in that case, it's nice to see you, kid," he said at last, his expression softening.

"Why don't you come with me, Dad? We're going to have a talk with Dr. Koenig and find out what's going on around here," I said, helping my father to his feet.

Then, turning to the nurse for affirmation, I continued. "That's all right with you, isn't it?"

This nurse, older and wiser than Sam, ran her hand over my father's head as one would a small child's, and replied, "Sure. You do that. I'll see you later, Mr. Mulgrew."

My father, a slave to good manners, turned to the nurse and said, "Thank you, Ruth."

As we left the small room and entered the main artery of the unit, I took my father's arm and asked, "How do you know her name's Ruth?"

"Because it is neatly affixed to her bosom," my father responded.

A door opened in the middle of the corridor, and Joe stepped out.

"Hey, Dad, we're in here," he said.

My father stopped short and stared at my brother.

"We are, are we? And why didn't you tell me your sister was coming?"

Joe, flushing, was at a complete loss.

"I wanted to surprise you, Dad," I prevaricated, then kissed my father again and said, "because I know how much you love surprises."

Dad grunted and looked sideways at his son who, in turn, looked down at his feet. At this moment, the doctor walked in.

Dr. Koenig struck me at once as a man of sympathy. He was tall, well fed, and clean-shaven, and though his was not a striking demeanor, his face not a face to turn heads, because his presence was calming, his expression honest and open, the three of us were immediately put at ease. I thought, when I shook his hand and looked into his clear hazel eyes, that this was a man who understood love.

There was a moment's silence, during which Dr. Koenig placed his file on the exam table and, leaning against it, addressed my father.

"Well, Mr. Mulgrew—" he began, when my father cut him off.

"Tom, call me Tom," he demanded.

Dr. Koenig smiled gently.

"Well, Tom, I understand you'd like to know what's happening to you, is that right?"

My father, referring to neither my brother nor myself, replied affirmatively, "That is correct."

In that single, simple assertion, my father regained a measure of his characteristic composure, and sat tall in his chair.

"Okay, and I have also been led to understand that you want a clear diagnosis and prognosis, with no omissions of fact. Is that right?"

My father, momentarily caught off guard by the seriousness of the doctor's tone, answered, "Roger."

Dr. Koenig shifted his position so that he faced my father directly, the subtlety of which was not lost on either my brother or myself. Joe moved to a corner of the room and made his presence as benign as possible. I, on the other hand, felt a stab of shame at having presumed that the doctor would want me to be a part of the clinical disclosure. Dr. Koenig was interested only in my father, and with expert authority, a deftness learned only after years of practice, relegated my brother and myself to the rank of observers.

"You have cancer, Tom. It probably originated in the lung but has traveled throughout your system and only became apparent when your vision was compromised. That's because a fairly significant tumor has developed on your brain stem, which affects vision, balance, and, in time, many of the brain's functions."

"What do you mean by 'fairly significant'?" my father asked, not moving.

"I'd say it's about the size of a golf ball," Dr. Koenig replied. I inhaled sharply. My father lifted an eyebrow.

"Now, we can treat this, as you have probably guessed, with radiation and chemotherapy. First, we radiate the tumor with the intention of shrinking it, and this will be followed by a program of chemotherapy. Given the size of the tumor and the systemic nature of the malignancy—"

At this point, my father again interrupted the doctor.

"What exactly do you mean by the 'systemic nature of the malignancy'?"

Dr. Koenig was spatially quite close to my father within the confines of the small room, and yet when he adjusted his position so that he was no longer leaning on the examining table but standing away from it, it appeared to my eye that he had situated himself so as to be face-to-face with my father. Neither man acknowledged this, but they continued to look at each other as I imagined soldiers might, which is to say, unflinchingly.

"The cancer has spread from your lung, to your brain, but it is also in your organs—the liver, the kidney—and it is in your spine as well. It is moving quickly and is in an advanced stage. Had we caught it earlier—"

"Advanced stage? How advanced?" my father demanded.

"Stage four, meaning it has moved beyond the lung into other organs and parts of your body," Dr. Koenig explained, quietly, before going on. "But I think we can buy some time if we adhere to the protocols this kind of cancer demands."

My father remained inscrutable. He leaned forward very slightly and, almost smiling, peered into the doctor's face.

"What do you mean by 'buy some time'? What the hell does that mean?"

In the room, it was very quiet. Dr. Koenig, for the first time in his conversation with my father, looked away. Suddenly, I had an image of Dr. Koenig returning to his home at night, after a day's work, after hours of testing and probing, after making onerous decisions that invariably turned into hours of uncertainty, and these hours in turn eclipsed by hopelessness and, finally, despair. How, I wondered, had he learned to battle chronic exhaustion with such forbearance?

"If we follow the radiation with a rigorous course of chemo, I think you will probably have a few weeks more, at the most a couple of months. There will be questionable quality of life because you will be feeling the effects of the toxins from the chemo, but you will have more time."

The silence, intensely felt, remained unbroken. All eyes were on my father, whose own thoughts appeared to have turned inward. He shook his head, ever so slightly, as if to clear it, looked out the window at the gray winter's day, looked down at his feet as if verifying their existence, then slowly raised his eyes to meet the doctor's and said, "Not a lot of laughs in your line of work, are there, pal?"

Dr. Koenig, clearly startled, did not know how to respond. Joe and I chuckled, in a show of solidarity more than anything else, and because responding to our father's humor, however unexpected, was in our DNA.

My father rose to his feet.

"Kitten," he asked, looking at me for the first time since entering this room, "get my coat, will you? Time to go home."

He then extended his hand to the doctor, formally and with intention, and the doctor received it, with equal gravitas. They stood there for a moment, looking at each other, and I silently prayed that Dr. Koenig would say nothing more. He didn't, whereupon my father said, "I want to thank you for all you've done. I have no doubt you are an excellent doctor, but you and I will not be meeting again."

Dr. Koenig ushered us into the corridor and watched as we walked the length of the oncology unit, past the nurses' desk, where Sam waved happily from her station, and through the revolving doors into the bleak afternoon light.

The three of us stood in the parking lot for a moment before making our way slowly to Joe's car. When we reached it, I opened the door for my father, and as he settled into the passenger seat, I leaned into him.

"What do you say to a drink, Dad?" I asked, my hand on the sleeve of his down jacket.

"I'd say, now you're talking my lingo," my father replied, as Joe pulled out of the parking lot, and we started home.

CHAPTER FIVE

The house was quiet, and soon my father and I would be alone. To get there, however, we had first to pass through the stone gates signifying entry into the small estate we called Derby Grange, then through the back door signifying welcome, until finally it was necessary to pass muster with Lucila Ledezma Ruiz, who signified order. Lucy, strong and stoic, beamed when she saw me and said, as she had said for the past twenty-five years upon seeing me after a prolonged absence, "Oh, señora, you here at last." For two decades, she had been my children's nanny, my housekeeper, my cook, and my majordomo. When my children grew up, as inevitably they must, and my parents grew old, Lucy had offered to leave her life in California and transplant herself in Dubuque, Iowa, a place utterly foreign to her, where tall white men sported John Deere caps and spoke sparingly, if at all, and certainly had nothing to say to this diminutive, fierce-looking Mexican woman with her flashing black eyes. She had come to Iowa for me, she had stayed for my mother and, over time and against all odds, she had found herself devoted to my father, so that now, as she divested him of his winter coat, she allowed her hand to rest on his shoulder as she asked, "You hungry, señor? I can fix you a soft-boiled egg and coffee. Or tapioca. You want tapioca?"

My father, unsmiling, said, "No thanks, Lucy. Not hungry. Not yet."

Lucy looked at me, and what passed between us was a shorthand learned over many years, through countless episodes in which it was crucial to protect the vulnerable child, the demoralized sibling, or the confused mother, so that over time a mere lifting of the brow or an almost imperceptible shake of the head was sufficient to convey the message clearly. In this case, it was immediately understood that my father had never been hungry, was not now hungry, and would probably never be hungry again.

A different current, deeper and more intense, delivered the more urgent communication, so that after hanging my father's coat carefully in the closet, Lucy said, "I go check on Beanie, then I go to bed, okay, señora? We talk tomorrow."

"I'll go with you, Luce. Joe, make sure Dad's comfortable, will you?" I asked, already moving toward my mother's room.

Joe, alert to every movement that did not immediately involve him and looking at Lucy with a wariness he reserved for her alone, said, "Yeah, okay, we'll be in the living room, but I can't stay long. The kids will be home soon."

As Lucy and I walked through the dining room, the large ornate mirror over the fireplace reflected the muted light of dusk, and I wondered at the stillness of the table, and at the obedient chairs grouped around it, expecting no one. We passed through the foyer, where I glanced up the stairway that had once seemed so daunting in scale and now appeared unassuming, almost modest, curving just before it reached the top landing and abruptly opening into the single bathroom on the second floor, where, for many years, eight people had been accommodated.

The Good Living Room, just off the foyer, had been converted into a bedroom for my mother, who could no longer climb the stairs. Lucy opened the door quietly, and we entered. The room was in shadow, and I could barely discern the silhouettes of chairs, of the great long mahogany coffee table that sat in the center, of the many lamps and framed photographs that adorned side tables and bookshelves, vivifying the marble counter of the wooden chest that doubled as a bar on festive occasions. Photographs, books, and paintings filled the room. Paintings on every wall, paintings on easels, paintings laid one on top of the other on every available table space. My mother's paintings. My mother's books. Photographs of my mother's children. My mother her-self tucked neatly away in a corner, under a soft quilt, in a well-ordered narrow bed pushed against the wall. As I approached, I saw that her eyes were open, and when I leaned down to kiss her, she looked at me and did not know me.

Even so, I said, "Hello, Mums, it's me, Katy. I'm home."

Still, and even so, she did not respond. Her fingers played with the bedcovers.

"I'm here, darling, and I'll be here when you wake up tomorrow. I love you, Mutti."

Mutti. A sobriquet bestowed on her by a German boyfriend of mine. Mother loved the sound of the word, at once whimsical and unexpected, and so I played along. The nickname that stuck, however, despite my mother's best efforts to abolish it, was Beanie, which attached itself to her one spring day as we passed a small coffee shop on the Upper West Side of Manhattan called the Sensuous Bean. "That's you all over, Mums," I declared. "You're a deadly *sensuous* bean."

"Oh, that's so uninteresting," my mother said, striding off down West Sixty-Ninth Street.

"Nevertheless," I called after her, "you will henceforth be known as Beanie!"

Sitting on the edge of the bed, I was suddenly overcome with fa-tigue and wanted nothing more than to lie down beside my mother and sleep, sleep for hours, sleep without interruption, under the clean white sheets that held my mother secure. I kissed her forehead and looked again into her frightened, vacant eyes, which foraged, still, for some hint of recognition. Our baser impulses are not easily vanquished, nor can they be bent to a stronger will. They rise anew each time we see the face of the one we love, and each time we are pierced by a sliver of hope, that this will be the moment of reclamation, that ours will be the face remembered.

I kissed the soft skin of my mother's sweetly scented face, I stroked her thinning silver hair.

"I like the pink lipstick, Luce." I chuckled.

"She want to be ready for you, señora," Lucy responded, standing at the end of the bed, her arms crossed in what could have been interpreted as a posture of defiance but was, in fact, the way in which Lucy guarded her sense of pride. She had bathed my mother, and washed her hair, she had clipped her nails and moisturized her skin and, at the end of these ablutions, she had applied a hint of rouge to my mother's cheeks and lips. She had done this for my mother, but she had also done this for me.

"I'll get up early tomorrow. You let Mother sleep, and you and I will have breakfast. Alone. Good?" I asked, crossing to where Lucy stood.

"Okay, señora, whatever you say. I go to bed now. You stay up with Señor?"

"Oh, yes. We're going to burn the midnight oil," I replied, kissing the top of her head. "Thank you, Luce. Good night."

"Good night, señora," Lucy responded, closing the door gently behind her as we left my mother's room.

JOE WAS PREPARING to leave and rose as I entered what was pragmatically referred to as the TV Room, thus named because it harbored the only television in the house, and a modest television at that. My father, from his established place at the end of the couch, sat directly across from this television, and we had observed, over the years, that at no point had he shown an inclination to cross the ten-foot distance between the couch and the chest on which rested the TV set, electing, instead, to sit in silence and work on his crossword puzzles. The television set had been purchased and installed for one purpose and one purpose only: to watch Notre Dame football. To that end, we missed television as our cohorts and friends knew it, missed the anticipation of weekly programs, missed the idea of television as a cultural bellwether. We knew it only as a box that facilitated the projection of Notre Dame football games, and for that reason, we feared it. Notre Dame football inspired anxiety, tension, and dread. When the Fighting Irish lost, the entire house was plunged into despair. When they won, the rooms reverberated with euphoria. Tonight, the television looked awkward and out of place, and sat in its customary spot atop the walnut chest like an overweight, unwanted child.

"When was the last time this thing was turned on?" I asked my brother, indicating the television set.

"Who knows," Joe replied curtly, looking at Dad, who was in the process of lighting a cigarette. A relatively thoughtless exercise among the smoking hoi polloi, the lighting of a cigarette could evolve into an elaborate ritual if my father did not wish to participate in the conversation, or if he wished to avoid the conversation altogether, or if he simply wished for silence. With excruciating attention to detail, the cigarette was first selected from the pack of Pall Malls as if chosen for an honorable execution. Turning the pack upside down, he would tap it smartly three times, presumably to bring the soldiers within to attention and to prepare them for evacuation. Then, he would carefully extract the cigarette of his choice with an impressive combination of delicacy and savoir faire, until he held it pinioned between thumb and index finger, where it remained until he brought the flame, ignited only once and with expert precision, to meet the little brown mouth of the cigarette. Satisfied with the effort, my father would settle back on the couch, cross one leg over the other, put his right hand, which held the cigarette, behind his head, and exhale. If he had any surplus energy, or if the hour of the first drink was about to strike, he might shape his lips into a kiss and expel three or four perfect O's of gray smoke from his mouth.

Joe and I did not feel a need to recognize this ritual, which or-dinarily we might have done by gently shouldering each other and shaking our heads, because we understood that all that mattered now was the pleasure our father could extract from it. No one in the fam-ily had ever discussed the dangers of nicotine addiction, not because we feared the repercussions such an opinion might incur, but because we had been taught that debates concerning physical health and well-being were, in the main, insufferable. Even now, Joe and I did not acknowledge the grave price our father's love of nicotine had exacted, because it did not occur to us. We wanted what we had always wanted, our father's pleasure, our father's comfort and, most of all, our father's approval. Joe, cut-glass blue eyes set in a chiseled face, stared at our father. His anxiety was palpable, and nothing could dispel this anxiety except our father's love, the smallest crumb of which would have been sufficient, tossed by a glance, a gesture, a word. Dad looked up and, acknowledging that his son had put on his coat, said, "See you, Joe. Thanks."

I did not walk my brother to his car, knowing that if I did so a hur-ried, whispered conversation would ensue, one in which nothing of any further consequence could be shared. I had in mind an altogether different conversation, one that I could not risk missing.

CHAPTER SIX

The TV Room was hushed. My father, though smoking, was very still. I sat on the faded red and black ottoman opposite him, looking at the fireplace. Someone had swept the floor of the hearth and arranged the logs neatly in a conical fashion, then balled up pages of newspaper and tucked them carefully and strategically under the wood so as to facilitate a good fire.

My father had complicated feelings about fires. He like the idea of a fire but resented the extravagance of all that beautifully cut wood reduced to ash. Tonight, however, I wanted one so badly I decided to circumvent those feelings and approach him from another angle altogether.

"How about a drink, Dad?" I asked, standing.

My father had no such complicated feelings about alcohol but nevertheless glanced at his watch, deliberated for less than a second, and said, "Why not?"

"Good. You've earned it," I said, walking into the adjoining kitchen.

Even now, after a day in which he had been told he had a limited time to live, my father felt compelled to call out the words which had always preceded the offer of a drink. "And easy on the ice."

This ritual was easier in the old days, I mused, when it was scotch on the rocks and no fuss. With his abrupt, unexplained conversion to vodka, the effort was necessarily more involved. I sighed as I pulled the ice tray out of the freezer, dropped the contents into a ceramic bowl, pulled the bottle of Popov from its frozen cot, retrieved my father's favorite, slightly grimy glass from the surface of what was once the dishwasher but had long since been converted into a bar, released three cubes of ice into the glass, poured four fingers of vodka over them, swirled the elixir with my finger, did the same for myself, and returned to the TV Room, where my father welcomed the drink and, lifting it to mine, said, "Thanks, kid."

"Or, as they say in West Palm Beach," I added, "to rose-lipped maidens and fair-haired lads."

My father, squinting, shook his head.

"What the hell are you doing in West Palm Beach?" he asked, although, of course, he knew.

"A by now rather tedious one-woman show based on the life of Katharine Hepburn," I answered, not wanting to pursue this subject but curious to see if my father would. He did not.

"I can't keep track of your goofy life," my father stated, flatly.

"It's goofy all right," I agreed, "I won't argue with that. But I will argue with the temperature in here, Dad. It's freezing. If you won't turn up the heat, could we at least have a fire?"

My father, now drinking as well as smoking, felt he could display a measure of munificence and asked, rhetorically, "Why not?"

These words, the words I had been hoping to hear, were deeply satisfying. It was now clear that my father intended to settle into the evening.

"Tired?"

"Not yet."

"Hungry?"

"Not significantly."

"Not ever, you mean," I parried.

"Not interested," he said.

My father had always disdained food and, observing his face softened by the warmth of the fire, I wondered if he had not developed this curious discipline as a result of having watched his parents indulge their respective neuroses: my grandmother, her extreme vanity and my grandfather, his unapologetic hedonism. Why else would anyone consign himself to a diet that precluded all the reasons to go on living? Those substances he allowed to pass his lips never varied: black coffee, soft-boiled eggs, dry toast, a single hamburger relieved of its bun, a small, well-done filet mignon, and, very occasionally, a dish of tapioca. Only during Lent, when my father took the pledge and practiced abstinence from liquor, did we recognize certain aberrations in his diet. Deprived of alcohol, he experienced a powerful craving for sugar, a craving that, as children, we considered patently cruel. For forty days and forty nights, the freezer was stocked with chocolate bars. Snickers and Milky Ways and Mars bars lined the floor of the otherwise destitute freezer, and to each coveted article my father had taped a warning: PROPERTY OF TJM. DO NOT TOUCH.

Once or twice in the history of this abusive practice, one of us kids, in a paroxysm of lust, would filch a candy bar and, stealing off into a neighboring cornfield, would spend a half hour of inexpressible bliss sucking madly at the slowly melting contents of the bar while mentally repeating the mantra: it's worth it, it's worth it, it's worth it. It never was worth it, because the theft was followed by whole days and nights of suspended terror (we were all guilty by association), and it was only a matter of time before we heard the pop and swish of the freezer door being opened, followed by a profound silence, during which we all sought our respective hiding places, and ending with the freezer door being banged shut, and our father's voice, deep and resonant, shouting in outrage, "Goddammit! Someone in this house is in *big* bleeping trouble!"

"Another?" I asked my father, indicating his drink. "The night is young."

"Why not," he replied, offering the glass to me.

I quickly replenished his drink and replaced it on the rattan coaster, where it had sat for years in its designated spot on the end table. As I approached the fire to give it a nudge with the poker, my father said, "Not necessary."

A small, comfortable silence settled between us, and I was grateful for it. My father's thoughts were well hidden behind eyes that had long ago learned to conceal emotion. He had his mother's wonderful eyes, only his were air force blue, fringed with black lashes, set deep in a face that had once been strikingly handsome. Two flaws served to offset the perfectly symmetrical features, but these imperfections grounded the face, endowing it with character. His mother's genes were immediately in evidence: the mouth full but contained, an elegant nose, broken in a fistfight, rendering it a Celtic masterpiece, and lodged above those slightly slanted eyes were a pair of eyebrows, thick and unruly, which defined his entire face. These were the final, bold strokes of the genetic artist, save for my father's ears, which might be considered the artist's final irony, protruding aggressively, as they did, from the sides of his strong, well-formed head. The ears were spared any undue notoriety mainly because my father's hair was both abundant and wavy, showing the Irish propensity for premature graying, so that from the time he was quite young his black hair was shot through with silver and only now, in his eighty-third year, had his head completed the metamorphosis, and become fully white.

I moved from the ottoman to a matching armchair, put my legs up on the ottoman, and looked at my father. It was only eight o'clock, but on this preternaturally cold, dark January night, it seemed much later. A clock ticked in the distance, and I wondered, dreamily, if the sound could possibly be emanating from my father's wristwatch.

"Well, this has been a hell of a day, hasn't it?" I asked, gently.

My father shifted his body, pursed his lips, and shook his head ever so slightly. I knew that he was irritated. Profoundly irritated. His life had been interrupted, and he resented it. After years of toil and struggle and loss, culminating in the ultimate betrayal when it was made clear that my mother would never again say his name, my father had harbored the small hope that he might live out his days in a quiet, orderly, simple fashion, with coffee in the morning, a drink at night, and crossword puzzles to fill the soft, easy hours in between. That this was not to be hurt him deeply, and he considered it a grave injustice. What harm could a few years of peace do? After the unending years of children being born, the constant noise and turmoil, and then the years of children suffering and dying, when he would not have minded oblivion, after all of that had passed and at last given way to these days of stillness in the house, why should he suddenly be dealt this blow? Just another in a long line of paradoxes that had depleted my father, leeched him of his faith, and now caused him to sit back on the couch and say, "A hell of a day is right. Just wanted to finish the goddam puzzle. Evidently, I should do so without delay."

So, he would choose stoicism and would not be going gentle, after all. This kindled in me a sentimental pride, one I had long nursed regarding my father, and with a stab of terrible sadness I realized that he hadn't been kidding, that this was the real thing. Drunk or sober, he was what he was. Unchanging, and unchangeable, this character trait was potent, captivating, and dangerous. Even now, his power was in evidence. In stillness, he processed the information that had assaulted him earlier. He did not speak, he did not seek comfort, he was in no way agitated. Instead, his usual gravitas assumed an even greater dimension. My father was reckoning with the gods, and I could not leave him alone.

"Dr. Koenig seemed a decent enough guy, don't you think?" I asked.

He turned to look at me, as if pulled rudely from a profound rumination, and answered curtly.

"He was all right, as doctors go. Honest. Direct. Not like some of the clowns I've had to deal with, imposing their half-baked opinions where they're not wanted, or needed."

He was referring to my mother, of course, and the awful nature of her disease. My father didn't believe it, he wouldn't accept it, and so he denied it, and went on denying it until spiders were seen crawling out of the wallpaper, turpentine was set to boil on the stove, the piano rendered mute. The fury fueling his denial was seismic, and it was felt acutely by the kind, brave doctor who made his way out to the house to pay a personal visit to my father. I had organized this visit, of course, but my father had no intention of spending all his well-fermented wrath on me, not when he had what he needed most sitting directly in front of him, the living embodiment of everything my father despised.

My mother's doctor, Mark Fortson, was a thoughtful, levelheaded, compassionate man, who had intentionally forgone greater opportunity to serve a community largely composed of working-class people with little or no regard for the disorders of the nervous system. If you couldn't see it, feel it, treat it with pills, or fix it with an operation, then it was suspect. My father may have received a formal education, but this did not alter the fact that he was a true product of the Midwest, a breed of man unlike any other, men whose curiosity was largely limited to sports and the weather, men who sat in dingy taverns for hours as they downed their beer, men who told jokes about their wives and seldom spoke of their children, who sought their own counsel, men who disdained erudition in its obvious forms but who accepted a man like my father, who wore his work boots and soiled khakis with pride, bought a round only when it was appropriate, and never talked down to anyone. These men feared and distrusted doctors, and while it would be hyperbole to suggest they considered them nothing short of sorcerers, it would be fair to say they avoided them until they were left with no other choice, which typically meant a wife in hard labor, an arm mangled in a thresher, or a dislocated jaw. Despondent spouses, kids with ADHD, a blow to the head from the kick of a cow were dismissed as nuisances and treated with aspirin and indifference.

Six years earlier, on the warm spring afternoon of Dr. Fortson's visit, a few of us had gathered in the TV Room to greet him. As the organizer of this event, I had stood sentinel at the screen door, waiting for the doctor's car to appear in the driveway. In attendance were my brother Joe; my second husband, Tim; and my father, who sat in his customary place on the couch. My sisters, having accepted my mother's diagnosis months earlier, were not present. Joe, exhibiting allegiance to his father, stood rigidly facing the door, arms crossed, seething with anger. He in no way approved of my having scheduled a house call with Dr. Fortson and considered it tantamount to betrayal. My husband loved my mother, had known her long before he ever set eyes on me, and was prepared to serve in this situation as her advocate. Although Tim disliked confrontation, he was not afraid of my father and would, without hesitation, act in the best interests of my mother. My father had agreed to this meeting under duress, and only because I had the necessary authority as my mother's health-care guardian to demand it. He strongly resented having been put in a position of subordination to his own daughter, and this attitude seeped from every pore, from the studied indifference in his posture to the overloud exhalations of his cigarette smoke.

When we heard the approach of Dr. Fortson's car, I noted that no one moved. The powder keg had arrived, and now it was only a matter of the slightest friction before combustion occurred. I went outside to greet the doctor, and when I gave him a cursory description of the atmosphere of the room he was about to enter, the tired, sad smile with which he greeted this information told me he had visited many rooms such as this, and that he was prepared.

Dr. Fortson was met with blatant rudeness when my father refused to rise for the introduction, disdaining a courtesy as natural to him as breathing. He leaned forward grudgingly in his seat and extended his hand halfheartedly to the doctor, who nonetheless accepted it with grace. My father's incivility astounded me, and, despite the circumstances, I was mortified that Dr. Fortson should see him in this light. I indicated a chair for the doctor and, in a gesture of solidarity, sat next to him. A painful silence ensued, during which each person in the room deliberated his next move. My father's defense was impeccable; he said nothing.

After accepting a cup of tea, Dr. Fortson leaned toward my father and said, "So, Tom, I understand you're confused about your wife's condition, and that you'd appreciate some clarification."

My father simply opened his hands and lifted them, in a classic gesture of indifference.

"We have run every test we have at our disposal to determine your wife's diagnosis, and we are almost a hundred percent certain she has Alzheimer's disease."

"That qualification is what interests me. The 'almost.' That's where the whole thing unravels, in my view," my father responded, quickly and incisively. He had prepared himself.

"We say 'almost' because science is still studying this disease, and we have a long way to go before we understand it fully. But I can say with certainty that both the Mini Mental and the MRI show that Joan is in the moderate stages of atypical Alzheimer's disease. Without going into too much detail, the MRI clearly revealed what are commonly known as 'plaques and tangles' in your wife's brain, proteins that cause the degeneration of the cortical region."

In the room, this information settled like a stone in a deep, cool pond.

"Tom," Dr. Fortson continued evenly, "Alzheimer's disease is a progressive, degenerative disease that leads to dementia. As of now, there is no cure and, while there are medications available to slow the progress of the disease, degeneration is inevitable and often extremely difficult for family members to manage. Full-time live-in care is crucial if you wish to keep Joan at home, otherwise I'm afraid you'll have to consider a nursing facility."

At this suggestion, my father blanched. It had not occurred to him that my mother might need to be removed from her home, that this disease was powerful and insidious enough to separate them physically as well as mentally. It was as if Dr. Fortson had gently inserted a needle into my father's lung, causing the air to leak slowly out of him. He lowered his head to his chest. Joe turned away and muttered, "Bullshit."

"It's not bullshit, Joe. Hear the doctor out," Tim said.

Both my father and my brother reacted to this with venomous looks, which were meant to shut Tim up and remind him that he was not a blood member of this family, and that none of this had anything to do with him. Tim kept his eyes fixed on Dr. Fortson's face.

"Have I been clear enough, Tom? Do you have any questions?" Dr. Fortson asked, with great diplomacy.

My father lifted his head and, looking at the doctor, shrugged.

"Sounds like it's all been handled. Everybody seems to have the answers. My daughter has the authority, she's calling the shots, and she says we need to have someone living in the house full-time. Evidently, she's discussed all this with you at length and it's already been resolved, so it seems to me you drove all the way out here for nothing, pal."

When experience meets compassion in the character of a man like Mark Fortson, conflict is ineffective. He had come out to the house to help my father, to edify him, and to comfort him. All these objectives had failed, and yet Dr. Fortson did not abandon my father. He reached out to him with the kind of directness my father most admired, the kind that is fearless.

"Tom, your daughter was made your wife's health-care guardian because your wife wanted it that way. Joan chose Kate to take care of these matters, and Kate agreed. Therefore, we must all defer to Kate in decisions having to do with Joan's welfare and, in this case, strongly advising full-time care in the house for Joan is a sound, practical decision and one I fully support. Your daughter has made it clear that the family has the funds to provide for a caregiver, that the family does not want Joan to leave the house, and that the caregiver is already in place. I know how difficult this must be for you, Tom, but the person whose well-being we need to consider now is Joan. You do want her to stay home, don't you?" Dr. Fortson asked, very calmly.

The tension emanating from my father was not only palpable, but dangerous. I saw him hunched over, held in, the iron doors slamming shut one by one, until he looked as if he had been turned to stone. Not a muscle twitched, the sound of his breathing was barely audible, and he was coiled so tight I thought he might stand and punch Dr. Fortson in the nose, turn and take a whack at Tim, slap me hard. He did none of these things, but in a long life of observing my father I had never seen him in such a state of impotent fury. He was a lame animal who had been kicked to the bottom of a deep pit.

"You bet your ass I want my wife at home," he finally managed to say, looking up at Dr. Fortson through eyes like slits. "I just don't want to be told what to do by every person who comes through that door, do you understand that?"

"I understand completely, Tom. It's hard to learn that someone you love very much has developed a disease like Alzheimer's, especially when it involves someone as vibrant as your wife. We're never prepared for something like this," Mark Fortson said, folding his hands together.

These words, intended to provide solace, instead reverberated like a tired and ill-timed platitude. My father, who loathed platitudes, was eager for this meeting to come to an end and, to my surprise, abruptly stood and extended his hand.

"Thanks for coming out—Fortson, is it?"

"Yes, Tom. Mark Fortson."

"I think I've heard everything I need to hear for one afternoon, Dr. Fortson. We'll handle this." My father lowered his voice and glanced in my direction.

I accompanied the doctor out and, as he opened the car door, I asked him if meetings such as these were predictable, if men such as my father typically responded in this way.

It was a beautiful May afternoon, the sun shone through the maple tree shading Dr. Fortson's car, the bright hood dappled with the shadows of leaves.

"He's lost something, but he's not ready to accept that yet. Maybe he won't ever accept it, but in time he'll learn to live with it. He's a tough character, your father, and he doesn't like being told what to do, does he?" Dr. Fortson asked, a half smile playing at the corners of his mouth.

"That's an understatement," I said, glancing back toward the TV Room, where I knew the men were now gathered in a thick, impenetrable silence.

"You might be surprised," the doctor said, settling into the driver's seat. Then, turning the ignition on, he looked up at me and added, "She was really something, your mother, wasn't she? Someone you don't often encounter in life. And to think, your father has loved her for over fifty years."

The doctor's words, spoken so long ago, resonated in the room where I now sat alone with my father. I wondered if he could possibly have overheard them uttered that afternoon, when Dr. Fortson was preparing to leave and, if so, where they had settled among his tangled emotions.

And to think, your father has loved her for over fifty years.

CHAPTER SEVEN

The vodka had ameliorated my father's mood. He gazed into the fire and, though I knew he was looking inward, I felt he was standing on the precipice of a memory that he both desperately wanted to recover, and at the same time longed to be free of. Torn by the yearning to dip once again into something delicious, he struggled for a moment, and in that moment, without thinking, I pushed him over the edge. I couldn't help myself. Time was running out, and soon everything would be unanswerable.

"Was she the best thing that ever happened to you, Dad?" I asked, watching him carefully.

"Who?" my father asked, rhetorically.

"Who do you think?" I asked, a little too sharply, reverting momentarily to our old jousting ways. "Mother, of course."

"I'd never seen anything like her," my father began, drawing deeply on his cigarette. "Hell, *nobody* had ever seen anything like her. Jesus, she was full of herself! From the East, you know. Slumming in Chicago, working for Kennedy. 'Oh, I wouldn't know where to get a drink on Lake Shore Drive, I'm from the East.' And the Kennedy thing, Christ almighty! You'd think Jack was God and Jean the high priestess, couldn't do anything without first putting it past that bleeping committee."

"Well, Jean was her best friend, they shared an apartment in Chicago, and Mother was working for Jack, so what do you expect?" I interjected.

"Working for Jack was a euphemism for having a helluva good time on the campaign trail. Yeah, yeah, I get it. Hierarchy. But once our romance extended beyond the church steps and I was permitted to see her outside of Mass, we started to have some fun. Not that watching her four pews ahead of me at St. Pat's every Sunday morning wasn't great. She knew I was casing her, and she loved it. But once I actually managed to get her on a date, she dropped the façade and was nothing but pure personality. Jesus, she was fun! Nobody I'd ever met talked like that—you know, the Holyoke routine, but then the *questions*, you wouldn't believe the questions. The strangest, most unbridled curiosity I'd ever experienced. And Christ, she was fast! Do you believe in God or is transubstantiation nothing but indoctrination? Who is God to you? Have you read Kierkegaard, Teilhard de Chardin, Thomas Merton? Do you crave solitude? How did you come to be born in Dubuque, Iowa? Do people in Iowa read?" My father paused to sip his drink, shaking his head with amusement. The memories eclipsed the reality of the silent woman in the adjoining room. He had returned to 1952, and he was young again.

"But when did you know you were in love with her?" I pressed him, modulating my voice. I had learned through the years that whenever I raised my voice, particularly in emotion, my father would respond by beating a fast retreat.

"She was always slipping away, making excuses, and it was always about the East," he mused. "The Kennedys on the Cape, her cronies in Boston, her family in Upper Montclair, New Jersey—men, too, were everywhere, which she made perfectly clear. This was irritating as hell but part of the game and, boy, could that broad play games. I wrote her letters, which she seldom if ever answered, I called her to no avail, it was like hunting a fox, and you know what they say—"

I did know, he had taught me, so I quickly said, "Until one day the fox turns around and shoots the hunter."

"Very good, Kitten." My father smiled approvingly, suggesting that the tale of the fox and the hunter was unsurpassed in his personal lexicon.

"And why, in this case, do you think the fox decided to shoot the hunter?" I asked, wanting to know if tonight my father's slant on the mythic story would be in some way altered.

He sat back on the couch, crossed one leg over the other, put his right arm behind his head, and considered me.

"She had run out of options. None of her beaux in the 'East' had come through. Her two closest pals had outrun her. Jean had married Steve Smith, Effie Shanley had married Bobby Harriss and moved to Mexico, and there she was in her little garret apartment in Boston, painting watercolors of the Common in her sketch pad, single, dateless, and my guess is, getting desperate. So she picked up the phone and called a guy she'd had a few laughs with in Chicago, someone who shared her values, her religion, her *clan*, and she threw her lot in with his. Which was mine. And even then, she didn't make it easy. The hunter had been shot, but he was not quite dead."

An excerpt from a letter I had found among my mother's papers had riveted me. My father had typewritten it to my mother in 1952:

```
The key to the whole thing is you. It's no good
unless you open your eyes and your heart to what
might be. I can't do that for you. And no amount of
"sell" can turn the trick—it has to be natural and
voluntary. We're good for each other, Jick—I know
that. And I also know that I love you and need you
like you'll never be loved or needed again. So get
the hell in gear, sweetie. Give us a chance.
```

He had fought for her, he had wooed her hard and, finally, he had won her—but had he, really? The hunter may have been dead, but the fox, it seemed to me, was bemused. It was a mystery to my mother, this marriage to my father, one that had unfolded with terrific speed, so that there was no time to consider the consequences or look hard at the future that lay before her, no time at all before she had left her be-loved "East" and traveled to Dubuque, Iowa, where, within a year, she had given birth to my brother Tom, followed fourteen months later by myself and then, in rapid succession, Joe, Maggie, Laura, Tess, Sam, and Jenny. After raising these children, and burying two of them, she was left with just a few years to enjoy the beauty of the countryside where she lived, the picnics she shared with Cistercian monks, the wine and the talk, the grown children making her laugh, the studio filled with music, paints, canvases, easels, and rich satisfaction, the books and the trips and the walks down the gravel road. The husband who never joined her for dinner, a man who was cheap and moody and of-ten drunk, was not the husband who had begged her to get the hell in gear. He had changed, he had not kept his promise, and I wondered now, looking at my father as he pulled on his cigarette and quaffed his vodka on what would be one of the last nights of his life, if my mother had simply given up on him.

He had never referred to his love of drink as alcoholism, but my mother had. In the later years of their marriage, when Mother often took trips to visit her friend Jean Smith in New York and immediately upon her return fell victim to a barrage of questions from her oldest daughter, starved for knowledge of what lay beyond the vast cornfields of Iowa, one of these questions invariably led to the next until, in the end, my mother would look out the window and say, resignedly, "I don't talk about your father when I'm away, but if someone persists, I tell them the truth—I tell them my husband is a drunk."

Extraordinary that my mother would say this to a complete stranger at an elegant dinner party in New York. Was it chic to say such a thing? Did laughter follow such a divulgence? Was my mother considered witty, this middle-aged mother of eight from Iowa leaning into some man over cocktails in the Chinese-red drawing room of an Upper East Side townhouse? Or was she considered sad? She had always come back looking, and sounding, depleted, as if the journey home had drained every last scintilla of energy from her body. My father must have picked her up at the Dubuque airport, but I have no recollection of their coming into the house together, no memory of my father carrying her suitcase, following her jauntily up the brick path to the front door. My mother went away for what felt like long periods of time, when in fact it was never more than a week or so, and when she returned the house was restored to life, that much is vivid.

"Things seldom turn out the way we hope they will, especially when it comes to love, right?" This was less a question than a reminder that I was present, and listening, and wanting the night to go on.

My father chortled in that short, derisive way of his, a strange device meant to signal a change of heart. It was seldom, if ever, the unlatching of happiness. Instead, it acted as a warning.

"Ah, hell. Love. I loved your mother. I don't know who she is *now*, I couldn't tell you I know *that* woman, but I love her. We made a contract, and we honored it." My father had to laugh at his own disingenuousness, knowing full well that I was a primary keeper of many of his more salacious secrets, and I, in turn, laughed back.

"I loved your mother, but you see, sugar, I lacked the right kind of ambition, and your mother was attracted to ambition. In the early years, I tried to make a real success of the asphalt business, but I just didn't have the competitive drive, the day-to-day grit. Your mother made me feel as if I could do it—hell, when we started out the sky was the limit. And I had promised her a good life. I mean, I was stealing her from the people and places she knew and loved, and in order to get her to seal the deal, I told her I'd not only give her children and security, but a wonderful life, a life that would satisfy her."

An uncomfortable pause precipitated my putting another log on the fire. My father sat there staring ahead, looking at nothing, recognizing something he had somehow lost along the way and had just this moment recovered in his mind. I did not disturb him, but the intensity of his gaze unsettled me, and I knew he was resolving a conflict that had vexed him for many years.

"I wasn't a loser, but I sure as hell wasn't a winner, either. And your mother wanted a winner. Then Tessie died, and everything fell apart. I didn't handle that well. I became average. And your mother—well, she took trips, didn't she?"

My father glanced at me, knowing this remark was loaded. Wasn't it me, after all, who my mother had taken so many trips to see? Her eldest daughter, a successful actress, always doing a play, or shooting a film on location, or taping a series in New York. It took one phone call and the dates were decided, one more and the tickets booked. I made all the arrangements, of course; my mother merely suggested that it would be sublime if she could get the hell out of Iowa and away from her inebriated husband and live a little. She didn't have to do a thing but sit tight until I'd worked out the details, which I did in a matter of hours. I'd send her pocket money as well, because as soon as my father learned she was taking another trip he'd hit the roof and say, "I'll be damned if I'm paying for it," to which my mother would reply, "Don't worry, Tom, Kitten is taking care of everything." This enraged my father, but he didn't have a leg to stand on. Theirs was not a marriage in which the wife was supplicant to the husband, not when the wife had a daughter who adored her mother's company and was more than willing to pay for it.

"Yes, she took trips. She loved them. It was hardly Mother's fault that you didn't want to go with her, Dad."

"Not my scene."

I suddenly recalled an afternoon many years earlier; I had been sitting on the bed, watching as my mother packed for a trip to New York. As she placed her meager possessions inside the suitcase, I struggled with the anxiety that always attended these preparations. I did not want to be left behind.

"Why doesn't Dad ever go with you?" I'd asked, provocatively.

My mother had considered this question, then said almost sadly, "You know, Kitten, your father is a very shy man."

As I observed my father's tired, ashen face, I allowed the memory to settle. The impression was bruising, and I abruptly let it go, opting, instead, for levity.

"What was she supposed to do, Dad? Sit with you in the front yard, night after night, gazing at the inimitable Iowa moon?"

"Watch it, big shot. The Iowa moon is, in fact, incomparable, as you of all people should know."

For a moment, I thought he might be referring to the nights he and I had sat under the huge oak tree in the wide and generous front yard, bordered on three sides by cornfields, on the fourth by an untended, dappled glen, and on the fifth by a moon that sat in its orb and dazzled the plain fields of Iowa, lit them up like patches of silver, threw out stars as if casting diamonds. In these moments, my father and I were united.

My father was about to say something but changed his mind. He bit down on a fast-moving grin and shook the ice in his glass, indicating that he would not be averse to a top-off. I took his glass, grabbed my own, and headed into the kitchen. The top-off was generous, and my father lifted an eyebrow when I replaced his drink on the rattan coaster. We were both nicely lit, though still short of a snootful.

"You really can't stand the idea of Hollywood, can you?" I challenged him, sitting back in the armchair, the right side of my mouth caught in a fishhook grin.

"Don't understand it. Seems like horseshit. What's in it for you other than the dough?" He was curious, but not receptive. He had long ago made up his mind about Hollywood, and actors, and make-believe. We were a breed apart, an unsavory and unwholesome breed, and my father neither respected nor trusted the way we made a living.

"You can grasp the value of entertainment, can't you? People like to be lifted out of their own lives and taken somewhere else. It's a release, a relief, a pleasure. My God, Dad, there are people out there who absolutely *adore Star Trek* and see Captain Janeway as a heroine. I sure as hell hope I didn't kill myself on that soundstage for seven years for the money alone."

"You've got guts, I'll give you that. I wouldn't last two days in that kind of a cesspool, haven't got the killer instinct—but you do, and it's gotten sharper over the years," my father declared, with conviction. This revelation startled and unsettled me.

"Are you kidding me? You see, this is what comes of never watching me on television. You have no idea what I do, why I do it, or what it means. You think I'm some egomaniac stalking the soundstages of Paramount Studios, ready to jump at the next best offer, happy to walk over anyone who might be in my way. And essentially, only for the profit. Do you honestly think I've done this for thirty-two years because I'm greedy? It's never occurred to you that I've done it because I love it? Come on, Dad, tell me—is that true?"

My father looked at me, pursed his lips, and drew them down, a signal of possible détente. This was because it was growing late, he was buzzed, and because he may have been remembering a hot June day many years earlier, when I was fourteen years old, and he had reluctantly agreed to drive me to Milwaukee, where auditions were being held for the local summer theater. It was highly uncommon for my father to offer me assistance, particularly when it involved the pursuit of my dream. I had always been aware of his distaste for the craft that had so captured my imagination and was shocked when he agreed to drive me the three hours to Milwaukee during the height of his bidding season when, after a brutal winter, most of the roads and bridges in the tristate area were in dire need of repair. It was very unlike him to forgo a chance at winning a good contracting job, and yet he informed me in the early morning that it would be himself, and not my mother, who would be driving me to the audition in Wisconsin.

Incredulous, I climbed into my father's Oldsmobile, and waved good-bye to my mother, who stood at the end of the brick path, her hand raised in a somewhat dubious salute, a gesture which said to me both good luck and good God. She, too, had been amazed at my father's willingness to accommodate me, and couldn't wait to hear about the six hours of agonizing stillness that being in the car with him would mean.

Indeed, an excruciating silence ensued for almost the full three hours of driving time to Milwaukee. Occasionally, my father lit a cigarette and, rolling down the window, turned his head and exhaled great shafts of smoke into the bright summer day. I sat next to him, desperately trying to concentrate on my audition pieces which, of course, I had memorized to the letter, but it was hard not to steal glances at my father's profile, so strong against the sun, his thick black hair moving gently in the breeze, the cigarette caught carelessly, gracefully between index finger and thumb, his eyes fixed on the road ahead.

We stopped only once, to fill up the car with gas, and to allow my father the opportunity to ascertain the correct directions to the summer theater where I was auditioning. I watched him in pantomime through the windshield, leaning casually against the counter, taking the attendant into his confidence, luring him with charm, pointing to something on the map unfolded before him, and suddenly the two men were laughing and I could tell by my father's gestures that he had compressed the story into the tale of a father's duty, albeit toward a daughter who was a little goofy, a little demanding, and more than a little dramatic. Loopy smiles all around, fathers sharing a common burden.

When we pulled into the gravel driveway leading to the theater, I told my father that I didn't know how long it would take, I'd never done this before and wasn't sure exactly what was involved. My father patted the newspaper resting in the center console, pointed to a full carton of Pall Malls, and said, "Give 'em hell, kid."

Inside the barnlike theater, I was met by a forty-something man with sandy hair, who told me to take a seat in the hallway and that I would be called first for the comedy piece and then for the dramatic piece, and that neither should exceed ten minutes, as there were many actors auditioning that day. I sat quietly in a chair somewhat removed from the rest, smoothed back my long brown hair held in place with a light blue ribbon, and prayed to Jesus that I would do well. Jesus was called on in times of crisis but was otherwise left to His druthers. My hands were clammy, and my heart was throbbing in my throat when the sandy-haired man suddenly appeared and summoned me. I followed him onto a wide, dark stage, illuminated by a central light, from which I was able to make out the silhouettes of three people sitting in the fifth row.

The sandy-haired man introduced me to these mysterious figures and then, turning to me, said, "The comedy piece first, Miss Mulgrew. What have you prepared?"

"Kate from *The Taming of the Shrew*," I replied, hoping that such a popular choice would inspire coos of approval from the audition committee. My announcement was met with silence. I knew I had to begin, that time was of the essence, that I was one of many, and yet a sense of dread stole over me, imbuing me with self-consciousness. When I was finished, the judges sat in the darkness, and said nothing. Suddenly, one of them (a short man wearing a tweed jacket, which I found odd on this blisteringly hot day), stood and called out that perhaps it might be best if I did my dramatic piece immediately, rather than having to wait for the other actors to complete their comedy monologues. I agreed, but only because I did not know how to disagree, because it would not have occurred to me to call back to them saying that I would like a few minutes in which to prepare my dramatic piece, that I was sure I'd do better if I could just have a little time to breathe. Immediately, I fell to my knees in the character of Isabella, raised my clasped hands in supplication to the wicked, if invisible, Angelo, and pleaded for my brother's life with all the earnestness of an Eagle Scout. This piece they did regard as brave because I heard the short man in the suit jacket whisper, "*Measure for Measure*—hmm, you don't get that one every day."

When I finished, there was no applause, and I was told to return to my seat in the hallway. The metal chair felt cool and hard under my bony rear end, and I adjusted the folds of my sea-green chiffon dress so that the wrinkles would not show when I was asked to return to the stage for the final judgment. In less than fifteen minutes, the committee had made their decision and I was asked to once again follow the sandy-haired man into the theater. I stood in the center of the stage and faced the fifth row. The short man in the suit jacket did not rise, nor did he speak, but the sole woman among the judges stood up and approached me. When she arrived at the lip of the stage, she beckoned me to come closer to her, and said, "Miss Mulgrew, it is obvious that you have the beginnings of real talent. You have strong potential, but this summer we are doing plays that require adult actors, and you just aren't old enough to pass, so I'm very sorry to have to tell you that it won't work this summer, but that we appreciate the effort and hope you will try again next year."

I mumbled something meant to sound confident and mature, and then walked quickly off the stage and did not stop until I found the bathroom, whereupon I threw myself into a stall and clapped both hands over my mouth to stifle the sobs that overcame me. Not only had I failed, but I had failed on the one day my father had offered to take me to an audition. Now he would know that my passion was, in fact, nothing more than posturing, and that my protestations of devotion to the art of acting were simply the histrionics of an awkward kid who bit her nails, thought she was a cut above, and drove everybody nuts with her demands. There was no way around it—I had to face him, but at that moment, in the humid bathroom of that summer theater where self-important men wore inappropriate jackets and where my impressionable ego had been dealt a severe blow, all I wanted was to disappear.

Looking in the mirror, I combed my hair and splashed cold water on my face, then I tucked my audition pieces into my book bag and headed for the driveway, where my father was waiting for me. I opened the door to the passenger side, slid into the car, and immediately said, "I didn't make it. They think I'm too young. I'm sorry, Dad."

My father looked at me, took a last pull on his cigarette, tossed it out the window, and turned the key in the ignition. He shook his head but said nothing. As we started down the highway, I experienced an overwhelming sense of shame, and knew that there was no way to conceal my anguish from my father, so I made a herculean effort to sit still and contain myself. This way, at least, he could not accuse me of talking too much on the way home.

We drove for miles, down that long, dusty highway, and not two words were spoken between us. After an hour and a half of strained silence, during which the audition played over and over in my mind like a nightmare, my father suddenly signaled that he was turning left and, indeed, he pulled the car off the highway and continued down another road until, after about a mile, he came to a large sign that announced itself as a supper club in bright red neon letters. Once he had pulled the car into the parking lot, he turned to me and said, "Let's get a bite to eat."

Inside, it was cool and hushed and the booths were cushioned with red leather. My father slid into one of them and indicated that I should take the opposite banquette. In the center of the table stood a low glass condiment dish garnished with carrots, breadsticks, black olives, and minced ham. Glasses of ice water were placed in front of us by a plump waitress wearing a red dress with cap sleeves and a white frilly apron who, when she handed my father his menu, said, "Well, T. J., my God, haven't seen you in a donkey's age. How've ya been?"

My father smiled and said, "Not too bad, Betty, how about yourself?"

Betty, it was clear, had known my father long before I entered the picture, and their rapport was immediately warm and lively.

"Oh, ya know, T. J., same old."

"Betty, this is my daughter Kate," my father continued, looking at me to see if the shock of the audition had blunted my manners.

"It's very nice to meet you, ma'am," I said, rising a little in my seat, and Betty nodded not at me but at my father, as if to say she expected nothing less from the daughter of Tom Mulgrew.

Without referring to the menu, my father looked up at Betty and said, "We'll both have the filet mignon, medium, with a baked potato and a shrimp cocktail to start. I'd like a J & B on the rocks, and my daughter will have a Coke."

When the shrimp cocktail arrived, splayed elegantly in a cut-glass cordial dish with a small container of cocktail sauce in its center, I sat taller in my seat and pulled the starched white napkin into my lap. My father, lighting a cigarette, merely said, "Take one and dip it in the sauce, but don't rush it, Kitten. They're all yours."

We didn't rush it, we took our time, and when the shrimp cocktail was replaced with the filet mignon and the baked potato, I beheld the feast before me and thought, My brothers and sisters are going to kill me when they find out, and then, just as quickly, I thought, My brothers and sisters are not going to kill me because they are *never going to find out*. I am never going to tell them. And so it was. I didn't share this story with my youngest sister, Jenny, until I was well into middle age, and when at last, over a good bottle of wine, I did reveal this adventure, her expression first softened, then saddened, and finally fixed itself into a mask of resignation. To her, it was a fairy tale.

My father had driven me to Milwaukee, where I had failed, and where he had seen and acknowledged my failure, and he had then taken me to a supper club by way of reminding me that I was his daughter, his first girl, and that he would not forsake me.

As I studied him now, in the deepening hours of the evening, his ill-repaired glasses removed and set to rest on the side table, his face drawn and gray, I thought again about the miracle of time, its manifest cruelty and its sublime mercy. There he was, an old man close to death, his legs sticklike in his khaki trousers, his beard gray and rough, the fine red lines of abuse woven across his cheeks like a spiderweb, and yet in my mind's eye he was forty-five years old, charismatic and striking, and it struck me with the force of a blow that this would never change, that this was the image of my father I would carry to my grave.

CHAPTER EIGHT

My father sent mixed messages throughout my youth, to keep me on my toes or simply to amuse himself, I'm not sure which, but when it came to sex he was present in a way that was both unsettling and very revealing. Completely uninterested in my scholastic or theatrical accomplishments, my father would occasionally exhibit curiosity about the boys who now appeared in my life and, depending on his mood, could be generous toward them or inexplicably rude. High school football players and lovely, fine-limbed Irish-Catholic boys from town were dismissed out of hand and, because he responded so cavalierly, I followed suit, looking always for the intrigue that would capture my father's imagination.

In a way, my father had rehearsed me well for what lay in store. He could not have known on a conscious level that he was preparing me for the real world of men, and yet for years I was exposed to the lascivious underpinnings of my father's friends, who prowled around our house like drunk, hungry bears. Sometimes, they hit pay dirt, and would stumble across my path in the Good Living Room, where I had paused under the Christmas tree at exactly the moment Ella Fitzgerald's voice rose in provocative scat, standing stock-still as they came forward and, not for a moment releasing the drink clutched in one hand, caught me with the other hand and pulled me into a dance, as naturally as if we were at a church fair.

A country house in the dead of winter is a kind of church, I suppose, littered with bodies of all ages and types, fires banked in every hearth, music soaring through the rooms, but it lacks the escape routes of a proper church and offers the young girl no option but to accept the outstretched hand, and to pretend that she is enjoying the silly, whimsical steps she is taking from side to side with her father's inebriated friend who, as he pulls her closer, keeps mumbling that he should introduce her to his teenage son, but then crushes her foot as he stumbles and uses this moment to bring her to her knees, whereupon his drink is knocked out of his hand, the amber streaks of bourbon staining her pretty Christmas dress, and she is saved by this mishap and rises quickly, leaving him there, looking bewilderedly into his empty glass and wondering what happened to all the fun.

Alternatively, the man could be used as the means to an end, and this behavior was not only allowed, but tacitly condoned. One of my father's friends, a member of a different, more affluent, and slightly younger set, a man I'll call Teddy, came one night and stayed for a week, waiting for the hour when he and my father had consumed enough alcohol to safely risk breaching domestic protocol, at which time he would steal into the Good Living Room, where he knew he would find me reading on the couch, close the door behind him, and settle in next to me. He pleaded for a kiss. He reached for my hand. Would I let him kiss me if he returned tomorrow with enough McDonald's for the whole family? This proposal would be met with a shy, if provocative, smile, and Teddy would remain uncomfortably slumped over on the couch for the duration of the night, until I would awaken him in the morning on my way to school and remind him of his promise to bring McDonald's to the house that night.

In the evening, he would return bearing great greasy bags of hamburgers and fries, my siblings squealing with delight as they ripped the bags open, and my mother—relieved, weary, and grateful—would usher Teddy into the TV Room, where he would wait patiently for my father to come home. Sometimes I waited for Teddy to unlatch the door to the Good Living Room, and sometimes I didn't. I was learning about titillation, and boundaries, and the thrill of scaling those boundaries, and I was also learning that men, whether drunk or sober, had little regard for propriety and would like nothing better than to break all the rules that had been imposed on them from time immemorial. In me, they had found a cool coconspirator, a girl who would never talk because there was, after all, nothing to talk about. My father's mixed messages filled the house with understated chaos, but through it all I was able to grasp the rudimentary mandate: withhold, but as for the rest, who's looking?

Strange, then, that my father should react as he did when Frank O'Connor entered my life. Another friend from the past, this man was also a member of the younger set and was initially warmly welcomed by my father.

I will never forget the first time I saw him, because earlier that evening my life had been threatened by a young man whom I had met at the community theater, someone I had been attracted to because of his extraordinary beauty, but whom I had subsequently slapped lightly on the cheek when he stood me up on our first date and heatedly warned, "No one stands me up—do you get it?" He got it, all right, and begged to be allowed another chance, to which I grudgingly acquiesced, naming the precise time and place for the pickup the following night.

He drove me deep into the country, past familiar signposts, past streetlights, past the road that would take me home. I looked out the window and felt the first hairs rising at the back of my neck. "You missed the turnoff," I said, with an attempt at confidence. The beautiful boy looked straight ahead and said nothing.

He pulled into a field about ten miles outside of the city limits, and we bumped along in the pitch black until we came to a large maple tree. There, he turned off the ignition and told me to get out. I stood by the side of the car as he went around to the trunk and, opening it, took out a rough woolen blanket and a crowbar.

"Sit," he ordered, throwing the blanket on the ground. I did, never taking my eyes from his face.

Lifting the crowbar slightly, he approached until he stood over me.

Then he leaned down and said, "Nobody ever stands you up, huh? Well, nobody ever *slaps* me. Do you get that, you fucking cunt?"

With that, he raised the crowbar over his head and stood there for a moment, looking down at me. Then he lowered his arm, walked quickly to his car, threw the crowbar in the backseat, and drove away.

I waited until I saw his headlights disappear at the end of the long road, and then crawled off the woolen blanket onto the dirt field, which felt much safer. I was shaking from the ordeal and at the same time trying to retain as much of it as I was able, so that I could recount the drama as accurately as possible. Eclipsing the physical shock was the far greater horror of having been called a cunt. No one had ever used that word in my presence, let alone used it to describe me. *Cunt* signified everything that was most abhorrent about women, and to have had it flung at me with apparent ease filled me with apprehension. Could it possibly be true that I was a cunt? And if so, what other demonic traits lay dormant within me, ready to spring forth at the first provocation? Boys do not drive girls into the middle of the countryside and threaten them with a crowbar unless those girls have deeply and profoundly pissed them off. The realization settled over me that I had this ability, and I wondered if it was dangerous and, if so, how dangerous? Standing in the dark field, completely disoriented, I realized I had no other option than to walk home.

Hours passed before I reached the house, where the windows were lit up, and the driveway was snaggled with cars. I knew, of course, that the TV Room would be full of men well on their way to getting baked, and this somehow emboldened me to climb up the side porch steps and open the screen door which led directly into the room. A group of about ten men turned to look at me and, pausing in their revelry, gave me the once-over before my father laughed loudly and said, "The prodigal daughter returns!"

My cheeks burned, and tears stung my eyes, but I was determined to tell my father what had happened, convinced that my tale would send him and his posse on an immediate hunt for the culprit, and that the psychotic pervert who had threatened me with a crowbar would be brought to justice. I stood in the middle of the room and began to recount the nightmare that had befallen me not two hours earlier, when it dawned on me that no one was actually listening to my story; they were instead *pretending* to listen, this was part of the game of adult male inebriation, particularly when it involved a teenage girl known for her histrionics and a father who liked nothing more than cutting her down to size.

I persevered because I knew that it was imperative to get through to them, that they must be made to understand, but when I came to the moment in which the boy had called me a cunt, something happened that I could not possibly have foreseen. The room went dead silent. Shockingly, uncomfortably silent. I had overstepped my bounds, and they, as a collective, would teach me where to draw the line. *Cunt* was against the rules—it wasn't used, it wasn't thought, it was completely out of line. It was debasing, and dark, and belonged in the mouths of people from the other side of the tracks, not in the pretty, pink, privileged mouth of Tom Mulgrew's young daughter.

"That's enough," my father said, standing.

"But it's true, Dad, it's all true," I insisted, desperately trying to control my emotions and maintain a measured tone of voice. But this was a room full of strangers who had lost interest in their subject, for she had somehow disappointed them, and now it was time for her to go.

I walked quickly through the smoke-filled room and, as I approached the door to the hallway, a good-looking man of medium height, with limpid blue eyes and thick, wavy, burnished red-gold hair, suddenly stood up and, extending his hand, said, "I don't think we've met. I'm a friend of your father's, home for a visit. Frank O'Connor."

Because my father had humiliated me, it was hard to look into this stranger's eyes. I paused just long enough to awkwardly shake his hand and mumbled, "Must be nice to visit, and even nicer to leave. Good night."

In the morning, Frank O'Connor was waiting for me. He blanched when I appeared at the top of the staircase in my school uniform, stammering, "I thought you were at least nineteen—I mean, maybe a TA or even a—it's the middle of summer, what are you—I guess I wasn't thinking straight—"

"You're right you weren't thinking straight," I interrupted. "You were completely hammered. I'm going to summer school, so I can get out of this place as soon as humanly possible and start my life as a thinking person. You can give me a ride, if you're going my way."

FRANK O'CONNOR DROVE me to school and was there to pick me up when school ended at 2:00 P.M. He was thirty-one years old and I was sixteen, taking summer classes to graduate early from high school and be on my way to acting conservatory before the year was out. He was on his way back to Southern California, where he was a practicing psychologist, stopping just long enough to visit his mother. Although he came from a big Irish-Catholic family and got along well with his siblings, there was no love lost between him and his father, who made no secret of the fact that while he tolerated his oldest son stopping for a few days to see his mother, he sure as hell wasn't running a hotel. In the brief time he'd be around, O'Connor saw no harm in giving T. J.'s daughter a ride to and from school, a gesture which was met with little resistance from the home guard, who expressed scant interest in the movements of their older children.

As the summer waned, and Frank O'Connor appeared more and more regularly on the front porch in the early evening hours, my father began to prick up his ears and would sometimes throw open the screen door and, looking straight at Frank, say, "Drive in here, pal. Let's have a belt."

It wasn't long before Frank could no longer conceal his motives and went directly to my father to ask his permission to date me. My father was flabbergasted and wanted to know what the hell Frank found so appealing about an outspoken, freckle-faced kid who had just finished her junior year in high school. Frank, to his infinite credit, had the balls to tell my father the truth.

"I'm smitten with her, T. J. What can I say?"

"Not much," my father replied, shortly. "What the hell do you expect *me* to say?"

"Well, I hope you'll say yes. I mean, you know I would never hurt her, and that I'll honor your rules. I'd just like the opportunity to spend some time with her," Frank said, simply.

My father looked at Frank and, after a moment, shrugged.

"I don't think you're playing with a full deck and you're probably full of horseshit, but you can see her occasionally, as long as she meets her curfew," my father asserted. Frank knew it was the most he could hope for, so he thanked my father and had the good sense to get in his car and drive home.

Thus began a relationship that would span the length of a year, during which Frank O'Connor struggled with the idea of giving up his practice in Southern California but in the end decided he had no choice but to move back to Dubuque, because he couldn't live without me. We were rigorously chaste, because O'Connor knew that I might run given the least infraction of the rules both my father and I had set in place. No sexual intercourse. Kissing and petting were allowed, and we spent hours in the act of love play, teasing at its most heightened and most fraught, hands searching, hands slapped, lips given and forbidden.

Driven by a longing I could neither understand nor share, Frank O'Connor was undeterred and, with a kind of calm determination, flew directly and without apology in the face of convention. He withstood the unrelenting cynicism of my father's remarks, the impish grins of my thoughtless brothers, even my mother's cool, distant appraisal, which may well have been tougher to endure than all the rest. When he came out to the house to pick me up, he was unfailingly polite to both of my parents and returned me to the front doorstep every evening at the stroke of midnight. He was kind, he was decent, but he was head over heels, and this he was powerless to overcome.

Occasionally, in a show of independence and manliness, he would meet my father at a bar in town and spend a few hours drinking with him. This, he knew, would be reported to me, but what he could not have known was that it made everyone in the family smile. It was a relief that he was drinking with my father, and I could be left to criticize and make fun of him with my mother, who thought the whole thing was perverse. My mother believed that I was playing a game, stringing Frank along for the fun of it, that there was no genuine feeling involved. This is what my mother wanted to believe, and it never occurred to me to disabuse her of this notion. Nor did it occur to me to take her into my confidence regarding the reality of my relationship with O'Connor. I couldn't risk incurring her disapproval, and so I sat there in mute accord when, in fact, something was happening that had never happened to me before. I was talking to Frank O'Connor, and he was listening. He would turn his earnest face to mine, those clear blue eyes steady and true, and he would listen to every word out of my runaway mouth, an act which was as intoxicating to a young girl as sex was to a thirty-one-year-old man, the only difference being that young girls aren't aware they're intoxicated until it's too late.

Over time, O'Connor earned my trust, and very slowly the iron will with which I guarded myself began to erode. My parents had instilled in me an almost pathological fear of sex, something O'Connor could understand coming, as he did, from a similar background. Armed with this inherent sympathy, he worked on me in ways another man could not. He was wholly present to me, and when I revealed to him my dream of becoming an actress, it was met with great seriousness, as if I had shared a secret of immeasurable importance. O'Connor's ability to listen translated into a gift unparalleled in my experience. At home, the banter was quick and provocative, the teasing tough and unrelenting, the laughter released in short barks of one-upmanship. My father was a master at reducing his children and could lay waste to a good day faster than anyone I've ever known.

"What the hell's your shoe size, kid?"

"Seven, Dad."

"Jesus Christ, that's not a shoe, it's a ski."

Then, forcing his own smallish feet into my saddle shoes, he'd crow, "Well, I'll be damned. My daughter's a ski foot!"

Most unnerving of all was his unerring ability to know when I was having a private conversation with my mother regarding my future as an actress, at the end of which he would saunter into the kitchen, scotch in hand, and say in a falsetto voice meant to mimic what he perceived to be my affected way of speaking, "My dear, you're so goddam anxious to get out of the gate, you're going to break your neck."

There were no genuine conversations with my father. He was incapable of addressing his children as normal human beings, so that dialogue with him was not only an exercise in futility but a difficult one at that. The constant, unrelenting parry and thrust of our communication wore me down and filled me with frustration. Occasionally, his own fatigue was in evidence, and I could almost sense his longing to give it up, to sit down and face me squarely, father to daughter, but these were uncharted waters and he could not risk losing his way, certainly not with his oldest daughter, whose character confounded him, and so we would retreat to our respective corners until the unspoken sign was given that the games were about to resume.

With Frank O'Connor, there was no threat of punishment. Instead, I was made to understand that, for the first time in my life, I was free to say whatever I liked and there would be no repercussions. This period of grace was not without its shadows, but because I did not anticipate them, I did not fear them. Instead, I talked, and O'Connor received my words as if they mattered. Sometimes, these divulgences were nothing short of cathartic, and I would wrap my arms around O'Connor in relief and gratitude, which would be met with a different kind of seriousness. If I had brought myself to tears, O'Connor would want me to stay in his arms until they had subsided, and only after the storm had passed would he gently disengage himself and, taking me firmly by the chin, draw me into a kiss. The kisses were prolonged, and they made me uncomfortable, but he had listened so beautifully and so intently to my emotional testimonials that I felt it would be unfair of me to deny him something as insignificant as a kiss.

O'Connor must have known he was going to win, that he had the upper hand, that he had had the upper hand all along, but he was old enough and smart enough to bide his time and savor the hunt. Had I accused him of hunting me at the time, he would have reacted almost violently, I think. It would have been cruel of me to so much as imply that he was ruled by such base instincts. Undoubtedly, he would have separated himself from me for a week or so to allow the inappropriateness of my suggestion to sink in, after which we would have slipped back easily into our familiar pattern, and soon enough his mouth would have returned to its work of kissing away my tears.

I went willingly enough. O'Connor had been away on business, and I was eager to feel his pleasure when he scanned me for the first time in almost a week. Dressed in a black turtleneck sweater and camel pleated skirt, my long hair caught in a black satin bow, I paused at the foot of the staircase before turning in to the Good Living Room. It was then that I heard his voice, saying my name, softly. I looked, looked again, caught my breath, and inhaled sharply. When Frank approached me, I gasped and backed away from him. This caused a volley of guffaws from my father, my brothers, and from Frank himself. What they found so amusing escaped me, and only increased the horror I felt as I stared at a Frank O'Connor I did not know but who was, nevertheless, being greeted as an old friend by my family. This Frank O'Connor in no way resembled the Frank of old, with his shoulder-length hair and his clipped mustache. This Frank O'Connor had been shaved clean, his hair cut short and neat, his mouth almost vulgar in its nakedness—and the lips! Thin, vulnerable, gamely attempting a smile, despite my obvious repulsion. My father could not have seen what was so evident to O'Connor, and so the game continued, until we were out the door and heading down the brick path to Frank's car.

"Don't forget your curfew, birthday girl!" my father shouted, lifting his glass in mock salute.

We spoke very little on the way into town, but I could sense Frank's growing alarm. I sat rigidly in the passenger seat, hands clasped tightly in my lap, unable to look at him. The familiar had been replaced by the strange, and for this I could not forgive him. This new face—open, wolfish, ardent—frightened me, and at the same time enraged me. It was unfair, this sudden, inexplicable switch, from something I could count on to something I could not. This face belonged to a younger man, one who felt he could do anything he liked with his face, without giving a moment's thought to how I would react. His jeans were clean and pressed, and he was wearing a new, light blue chambray shirt. As he drove, he glanced at me, again and again, uncomfortable in this silence.

"I have a surprise for you," he said at last, "for your birthday."

"My *seventeenth* birthday," I corrected him.

"Yes."

"Why did you do that to your face?" I asked, petulantly.

"My God, Kate, I didn't have plastic surgery, I shaved my mustache! What's the big deal?"

"It's very strange. You seem like someone else," I said.

"Well, I'm not someone else—I'm me. And I have a nice surprise waiting for you," Frank replied, smiling.

This smile unnerved me, and I felt a sudden, profound disappointment. We were not going to a restaurant, after all. He had a surprise waiting for me, and that could mean only one thing. It was waiting for me at his place.

Fifteen minutes later, we pulled into the paved driveway and O'Connor drove the car around to the back of the house, where he shut off the ignition.

"Come on," he said, "the surprise is inside."

O'Connor did not live in the house, but rented the basement from his landlady, Mrs. Murphy. The basement, like the house itself, was plain, squat, and gray. Gray brick on the outside, gray brick makeshift bookshelves, gray bricks supporting the sheet of glass that served as a coffee table.

On this night, a large bouquet of flowers sat in a glass vase on the coffee table, as well as two wineglasses and a bottle of champagne in a bowl of ice.

"Surprised?" he asked, sheepishly, before crossing to me and taking me in his arms. I immediately pulled away from him.

"What's wrong?" Frank asked, but this was a question he asked often, and just as often I gave him the same answer. Tonight was no different.

"Just give me a minute to get used to everything," I said, stepping back to take in the room.

"Let's have some champagne," he suggested, uncorking the bottle of Korbel and pouring some liberally into our glasses. The foam bubbled over the rim of my glass, and I caught it with my lips.

"Still there," O'Connor said, softly, and brushed my lips with his tongue.

This was my first taste of his new mouth, and I didn't like it. I was accustomed to his mustache, the way it concealed his old mouth and somehow lessened the impact of his ardor. This mouth was glaring, and willful. It was as if he no longer had the decency to hide his hunger, or his years, and was coming at me with a forcefulness that made me jittery.

"Drink up," O'Connor encouraged, pouring another glass of champagne. "I am making you dinner. Rib eye steaks and baked potatoes. What do you say?"

I wanted to say, I'm not hungry, please take me home. But I didn't. I just kept drinking.

Over dinner, seated at the small round dining table on the other side of the gray brick bookshelves, he opened a bottle of red wine. He repeatedly asked if I was having a happy birthday, and I repeatedly said yes.

"But I'm saving your real surprise for dessert," he teased, clinking my glass with his. I suspected it would be something extravagant, something beautiful. A necklace, maybe, or even a ring, something of real value, a token of his true affection.

After dinner, O'Connor excused himself, and I thought, Here it comes! and cautioned myself to maintain my composure, even as he reappeared carrying a plate, upon which sat a small chocolate cupcake sprouting a single lighted candle. I laughed, sure this was merely the prelude.

"Follow me," he instructed, backing up and moving slowly down the short hallway that led to the bedroom. Blushing, I realized that he had strewn roses on the floor. I shook my head as we approached the closed door, but O'Connor took my hand and said, "You have to see your surprise. Just for a minute."

With that, he opened the bedroom door and, as he drew me inside, began to sing "Happy Birthday." The room was full of helium balloons of all shapes and colors, each one inscribed with a salutation or endearment, such as HAPPY BIRTHDAY or I LOVE YOU. The bed was covered with red roses and red carnations, red and white carnations littered the floor, and a blood-red heart-shaped box of chocolates adorned the pillow. O'Connor sat on the bed and, pulling me next to him, reached for the chocolates and said, "You know what this means."

I wanted to giggle but couldn't. It seemed strangely pathetic, and I didn't want to hurt his feelings. I stood and started for the door, but he blocked my way before my fingers reached the handle.

"We don't have to do anything, if you don't want to," he whispered, his face very close to mine. "But please, Kate, come in and lie down with me—just for a minute. I won't hurt you, I promise."

Reluctantly, I sat beside him on the bed. He held my hand, he stroked my hair, he reached for my face and kissed me gently on the mouth. He never stopped promising me that we wouldn't do anything I didn't want to do, even as he laid me down on the bed and his hand found its way beneath my skirt, even as he assured me that he loved me and that he would never hurt me, but that he had waited so long and it had become almost unbearable, and his new mouth pressed itself against mine so that I had to struggle to catch my breath, and his words never for a moment ceased and they were full of love, of adoration, of longing, and he whispered in my ear, even as my satin bow unraveled, loosening my hair, he whispered that he loved me, that he wanted so badly to make me his, oh please, he said, Katy, Katy, let me be the one, don't make me beg, look what you've done to me, and he kissed me again and again and again and soon he was above me, looking down at me, and then he was between my legs and I couldn't believe his strength and I couldn't believe his words because they were so full of love but his arms held me and his legs parted mine and then there was a struggle, brief and frantic, but I didn't cry out because I was with him and hadn't he promised he wouldn't do anything I didn't want to do and hadn't he told me over and over how much he loved me, and then there was a piercing and a thrusting but I couldn't be sure of anything because I didn't know anything, and so we lay there like that, panting hard, and then it was over.

"I need to go to the bathroom," I whispered, sliding out from under him.

"Kate, are you okay? Oh, Kate," O'Connor moaned, but I was out of the bed and in the bathroom before he could get to me. I locked the door and switched on the light. I was naked under the bare overhead bulb and watched in horror as the blood, in a single weak stream, ran slowly down my thigh. Pulling O'Connor's robe from the hook on the back of the door, I covered myself, unlocked the door, and tiptoed into the hallway.

"Kate?" he called.

I hesitated, just outside the bedroom door, and then said, "I need a minute to myself, Frank."

He made a sound like a whimper, and through the door I saw him cover his face with his arm.

It was April, but the Iowa winter had been brutal and even now the ground outside the patio doors was thorny with frost. I pulled open the doors and crept outside. It was late, the house was dark, a full moon illuminated the backyard. In bare feet, I walked out into the middle of the yard, knelt on the hard ground, and prayed to the Virgin Mary to restore my virginity.

I wept and went on weeping through the long night and into the dawn, when O'Connor dropped me off at the stone gates that marked our property. I said nothing, slipped out of the car without saying good-bye, and hoped he would rot in hell for what he had done to me.

I had missed my curfew by a very wide margin and knew that my father would be waiting for me. My mother, too, I supposed, although this prospect was almost too painful to bear. Walking slowly down the driveway, paved with Mulgrew Blacktop, I weighed my options carefully. In the few minutes remaining until the jig was up, I calculated that bravado might be luckier than honesty, and climbed onto my father's forest green tractor, which he kept parked outside the back door. There I sat, in my pleated camel skirt, hair once again tucked neatly into its ribbon, beating my shame into submission.

The back door swung open, banged shut. My father strode down the brick path, pausing only long enough to allow me to feel the full weight of his disgust. He could not bring himself to address me directly but lit a cigarette and, looking off into the timberland, said, "You and I are going to have a talk when I get home tonight. There will be no play practice, you will come home directly after school."

"Dad," I said, "I'm sorry about my curfew, but it was my birthday after all, and then I just wanted to stay up and watch the sun rise."

My father looked at me then, hard, and shook his head. He climbed into his car and sat behind the wheel for a minute, face set and silent, before driving slowly away down the gravel road.

Inside, my mother stood over the kitchen counter, wearing her laminated yellow apron. She turned and glanced at me as I came in, then just as quickly turned away, and bent to her work.

Seldom in all of my seventeen years had my mother not greeted me in the morning with her customary chime of "Kitten Kat Feathers of Joy," but on this morning, when I longed for her greeting as I never had before, I was met with silence and, as I made my way up the front stairs and into my bedroom, I began to understand that there was a price to pay for bearing shame, and that I would be made to pay it for the rest of my life.

❧

MY FATHER GROUNDED me for a year, and Frank O'Connor was banned from the property in perpetuity. Two months later, I looked out my bedroom window and saw O'Connor's car parked in the driveway. He and my father stood a short distance away, their backs to the house, so I couldn't see their expressions. Both looked directly forward, arms crossed in front of them, talking in low voices. Suddenly, I heard O'Connor laugh and watched as he put a hand on my father's shoulder. This gesture seemed to put an end to their conversation. Both men turned and began to walk toward the house. I listened as the front door opened, swung shut. There was silence for a minute and then, from the base of the stairs, I heard O'Connor call my name.

CHAPTER NINE

I have loved you, I thought, looking at my father as he gazed darkly into the fire, but I have not known you. Fathers like you are not to be known, isn't that why you are so loved? If we knew you, as we do our mothers, our criticism would be much harsher. As it is, you are an enigma, and adored. Dear God, I prayed silently, let him go easily. Invoking the name of God, even in my mind, struck me as absurd. What God was I praying to? The same God who would consign him to oblivion, a state that once upon a time he had disdained, just as he had disdained those who did not believe in Jesus Christ. How he had believed! Not just a devout Roman Catholic and a servant of the Church, but a handsome, witty, charming crusader for Christ!

How the women drank you in at Sunday Mass, all those farmers' wives in their washed-out print dresses, their broadening asses concealed beneath the drab cloth, in whose eyes shone the naked hunger of the truly deprived, as they marked your every move once you entered the pew and were safely watchable. Now, this was a Catholic man worth his salt, they said to themselves, standing in rigid submission next to their muscled, sunburnt husbands. We're standing next to our men, they assured themselves, but we're drinking you in, and what a tall drink of water you are, Tom Mulgrew! They feasted on my father, and pitied him his many loudmouthed, ill-mannered brats, all jumbled helter-skelter in the pew, no order, no discipline, and the wife at the other end *reading a book*, for God Almighty's sake. What did Tom Mulgrew do to deserve a family like that? So straight, so trim, so unchanged since his days as a lieutenant in the Army Air Corps. No pretensions in that man, unlike his wife. No, T. J. Mulgrew had a handshake for every man, a kind word for every woman. At Sunday Mass, the women watched with longing and the men with admiration, this much I could see from my vantage point mid-pew, right smack in the middle of the Sacred Drama.

Just as I saw your power then, I can see that now, tonight, you are beginning to be afraid, and that there is nothing to be done about it. Your strength of character, which years of hard drinking and questionable behavior have not significantly diminished, will not allow you to reveal the extent of your fear, and you, yourself, are not at all convinced that this sudden excursion into uncharted waters is an altogether unsatisfactory proposition. I'd say that after as little as one more vodka you'll be looking on the bright side and whispering to yourself that if it has to be hard and fast, then this is the way to go. A few days, a few weeks, a smooth slide into a painless end. You're twitching a little now, too, curious about the pain, wondering how it will come upon you, its intensity, and how it will be alleviated. Now, you glance across the room and your eyes find mine, staring back at you, and you lift your glass in salutation and say to yourself, Thank God for that one, she'll keep me in booze until I don't want it, and then she'll see to it that I don't suffer, but before all of that happens, there's something I want to tell her, something I'm forgetting.

"What is it, Dad?" I asked, leaning forward on the ottoman, sensing a shift and alert, as always, to the dramatic possibilities.

"There's not a goddam thing to do about this, is there?" my father asked, almost wistfully. I saw the shadow of a smile appear at the edges of his mouth and, because it pleased me, I egged him on.

"Not about your condition, no. You made the right decision, Dad," I said, and immediately regretting having said it. He would be onto me in a second if I backpedaled, so I continued.

"You're philosophical about it, aren't you? At the root of it, I think you are."

If this was provocative, or jarring, it was only because the hours were deepening and soon, I knew, we would have to say good night.

My father peered forlornly into his empty glass, which spurred me into action. I crossed the room and, taking his glass firmly in hand, announced that we were going to have a nightcap. Wearily, but not without humor, he shrugged with cavalier acquiescence. What must be, must be, his expression suggested, and if it must be a nightcap, let me endure it with grace.

I refilled our glasses with the last of the Popov and returned to the TV Room. This time, however, I pulled the ottoman across the room, to be closer to my father. I did not want him to strain himself in any way. I wanted the nightcap to soften the inevitability of the evening coming to an end. Much could be said without words, in fact, and although my father had always regarded me as loquacious, tonight we were gathered in sympathy, and we were alone. Tonight, he could not and would not need to tell me to lower my voice, tonight my voice was hushed, our two tidy figures bending toward the fire, and filled with the quiet, and the beauty of all that is, and must remain, unspoken.

"It's a pity, having to become philosophical, especially when it was so good for so long," my father said, and I understood him immediately.

"You mean your relationship with God?"

"Exactly. A real pity about that, particularly under the circumstances. That was a nifty relationship to lean on, when things got tough," he mused.

"But it's been some time, hasn't it?" I asked, crossing one leg over the other, and resting my drink on an upraised knee.

"Since I stopped believing in a personal God? Yes. I clung to the notion of a deity for a long time, even after Tessie died. Hell, I'm still clinging to it, if I'm going to be honest. But *faith* no longer sustains me, as it once did, and that was a beautiful thing. Complete forgiveness, absolved of all my sins, and not only that, but a guaranteed *life after death*. Wow. Pretty terrific. And it worked until I carried my daughter out of here in a casket. That flipped a switch. It ended, just like that. Jesus," my father said tightly, crushing his cigarette into the ashtray, "I courted your mother on the strength of all that—baloney."

He leaned back into the cushion of the couch, resting his head against the long, square pillow. His skin was gray, the growth of his beard uneven and unkempt, the corners of his mouth pulled into a frown. It was then that I glimpsed the magnitude of his exhaustion and realized that he had been in this fight for months, possibly longer, and had never said a word to anyone. Undoubtedly, he had hoped that this sluggishness would pass, this acute longing to stay in bed. His pride was such that he'd forced himself into his khakis every day, pulled his Notre Dame sweatshirt over his head, attempted to brush his teeth, crept down the staircase, holding tight to the banister. There was Lucy to contend with, after all, and his wife was still alive—after a fashion. There was a cup of hot coffee, a soft-boiled egg, a fuss to be made over him as he shuffled from coffeepot to cupboard. There was Lucy's admiration and devotion as she watched him out of the corner of her eye, a spoonful of applesauce on its way to my mother's mouth pausing in midair. There was the beauty of the place, still, and sometimes he'd look out beyond the grape arbor where his youngest daughter had married a Jewish trader, beyond the cornfields that he shared with Gilbert Merritt, a farmer who refused to install plumbing until the school board complained that all of his children had ringworm, beyond the bonfire which stood in a perpetual state of readiness, the logs carefully stacked by his grandson Rory, or maybe his grandson Ryan who, despite a bad heart, loved to carry the wood for his grandfather, beyond the fields and down the long gravel road that wound slowly toward the town, and he would think to himself, Best goddam thing I ever did, buying this place.

The last of the glowing logs, reduced to ember, fell softly in the hearth, waking my father from his brief respite. Sitting up, he registered my presence by cocking an eyebrow and pursing his lips, an expression signifying a slight disappointment in his own inability to stay awake.

"Well, Kitten . . . regrettably, I think I've had enough," he said, eyes drawn to what little remained of the fire.

"Are you all right, Dad? Will you be all right tonight?" I asked.

"You mean, am I afraid of dying?" This question, direct and un-adorned, made me blush. My father had intuited that this was exactly what I'd meant.

He looked away for a moment, as if considering, then fixed his eyes on me and said, "I don't fear death, but I don't welcome it, either."

The sheer simplicity and unexpectedness of this confession filled me with a sudden, terrible pride. It was a sensation that did not demand tears, or even recognition. In this moment, I loved my father intensely.

"I am afraid I'm going to need your assistance up the stairs," he said, and then added, "but I want to ask you to do something for me before we go up."

"Of course, Dad, anything," I responded.

"I want you to look out for your brother Joe. He's a good guy, he's got a tender heart, but he's not as strong as you are," my father said. Not waiting for a response, he rose unsteadily to his feet.

I followed my father as he made his way slowly to the front staircase, where we mounted the steps one by one, until we reached the landing. Here, he paused and drew a long, steadying breath. I took his arm and guided him down the short hallway to his bedroom, where I moved to turn on the bedside lamp.

My father shuffled over to the bed and, placing his hand on the mattress, lowered himself carefully.

"I can manage," he whispered. It was clear that he couldn't manage, but I knew that attempting to undress him would be unacceptable. I knelt down, slipped off his penny loafers, and said, "I'm going to lift your legs now, Dad, so you'll be more comfortable."

As soon as his legs had been settled properly on the bed, he emitted a groan of relief, and when I bent down to kiss his cheek, my father whispered, "I want to thank you for everything you've done for this family."

I stood looking down at him for a moment, and then switched off the light.

CHAPTER TEN

My bedroom was unchanged, but I had the curious sensation that it was beginning to shrink. For a very long time, it had been a high-ceilinged, capacious room, light flooding in through the long windows from every direction. Aunt Jane's four-poster bed, replete with green velvet upholstery and gold tassels, stood where it had always stood, separated from the bathroom by a single porous wall which, for years, had carried all sounds and conversations into my room through an open vent situated directly to the right of the bed, an archaic but extremely effective system of eavesdropping. The cherry wardrobe rested against the western wall, its doors wedged shut with bits of folded cardboard. The armchair and ottoman reclined, like a plump woman dressed in faded pastels, under a warm lamp. The floor-to-ceiling whitewashed bookshelf stood against the wall at the base of the bed, where, depending on one's whim, the eye could rest on a photograph of young Tessie wearing a hat composed of palm fronds, or Viktor Frankl's *Man's Search for Meaning,* or travel upward to the highest shelf, where a small bronze crucifix rested against Will Durant's *The Foundations of Civilization.*

Tonight, the room felt diminished. My suitcase had been placed on the ottoman, but I felt no inclination to open it. Instead, I moved to the window and looked out over the wide lawn, blanketed with snow. The moon was almost full, and silver light illuminated the room, as it had done all my life. My father had thanked me for everything I had done for this family. Those had been his words, formal and composed. Genuine, but detached. Maybe that was what had kept us coming back for more. His distance. The pleasure he seemed to take in withholding.

Looking down, I remembered a snowbound evening two years earlier when Dad, Mother, and I had gathered around a miniature bonfire, just yards from the front door. Javier, Lucy's husband, had shoveled until he carved an ideal spot for us, a perfect circle wherein he had placed a small but beautifully mounted bonfire. Three chairs had been arranged around the fire, each covered with a heavy blanket, and Lucy had provided a picnic consisting of cheese and crackers, ham sandwiches, and a bottle of Jameson.

We gathered around the fire as I filled our glasses with whiskey. Both of my parents were relaxed, and this state, I knew, could provoke mischief in both of them. A winter picnic appealed to their sense of whimsy, their love of the unexpected. I watched them sitting side by side in the glow of the fire, and it was as if they'd made the mutual decision to put all of their troubles aside and submit completely to the moment.

My mother, wrapped in her checked blanket, legs crossed, was full of a girlish confidence I had forgotten she once possessed utterly. She reveled in the moonlight, the fire, the heat of the whiskey. She loved the novelty of it, as well as the freedom. We were having an adventure, and she was thoroughly immersed in it. She was the central character in this vignette and, like the best actresses, moved to dispel that notion at every turn. She proffered her glass for more whiskey, she winked at me as I poured, she reached out and half-batted, half-stroked my father's cheek, she gazed at the moon. A part of her knew it was unlikely that she would experience such a night again, and so she allowed herself to be ravished by it.

Next to her in his green down jacket, my father sat upright in his chair, a blanket draped over his knees. Raising his glass, he blew a kiss to the moon with his free hand and said, "Just beautiful." In the light of the bonfire, I saw deep pleasure in his eyes, an inward look that told me this was enough. His wife at his side, the whiskey warming them both, his daughter across the way, looking on. He talked of the things that gave him satisfaction, and my mother, in her silence, concurred. They relished the cold night, the sting of the whiskey in their throats, the broad and exquisite vista above them. They would not talk then, or ever, of affliction. It did not suit them. It did not become them. It was not their way. Theirs was the way of a cold night lit by an Iowa moon, of laughter, and of irreverence. They shared a profound unwillingness to let go of the moment, and so we sat for hours in the chill and the quiet of that moonlit night, until the whiskey ran dry and the fire burned to embers, whereupon we all rose to our feet in unison, proclaimed it a damn good night and, looking upward once again, shook our heads in amazement.

I want to thank you for everything you've done for this family. How is it that words so longed for can hit and miss with equal acuity? Perhaps this was my father's secret weapon, to withdraw at exactly the moment of greatest accord, a skill he had deployed with such cleverness over the years that I had failed until now to recognize that he had been doing it all along.

CHAPTER ELEVEN

In the dead of night, it began. The first bubbles of amusement reached me like tiny balloons that had traveled from my mother's mouth, through the slightly ajar master bedroom door, beneath the crack of my own door, and finally to the folds of my eight-year-old ears, where they settled gently and then softly burst. I sensed, with prepubescent acuity, that something highly unusual was afoot, and slipped from my bed with the dexterity of a child long accustomed to eavesdropping.

Across the hall, where they slept, the light was still on. Although their bedroom door was ajar, it was not generously ajar, and I knew I would need to steal myself for some serious sleuthing if my efforts were to be rewarded. I crept across the hall on tiptoe, stopping every foot or so to reassure myself that I had not been discovered. No, they were far too engaged in whatever it was they were doing to give me a second thought. My mother's infectious laughter made me feel anxious, and I was shocked to find myself alone on the upstairs landing, since such laughter was fit only for the daytime, and would surely awaken my siblings and call them to arms. No one else, evidently, could be bothered, or else they had fallen into such deep slumber that even an incident as remarkable and disturbing as this could not rouse them. *This is why I am different*, I thought, plastering myself to the wall adjacent to my parents' bedroom door, and ceasing to breathe. With exquisite slowness, I turned my head and, finding a vantage point through the crack of their door, adjusted my gaze so that I could have an unhampered view of the crime scene.

In the bed, my parents lay together. My father's bedside lamp was on, illuminating the drama. I had only to raise myself on the highest of tiptoes to gain a perfect view. I proceeded to do this, while clinging to the wall with lizard-like fingers, damp and splayed. Silently, voraciously, I studied them. My father lay on his side, dressed only in his light blue boxer shorts. This was startling, since I seldom saw my father in his underwear, let alone in his underwear in bed with my mother. Bare-chested and grinning slyly, he had caught my mother's hand with his own, and appeared to be speaking to each of my mother's fingers individually, which effectively sent her into paroxysms of hysteria. When he had finished talking to a finger, he folded it gently but firmly back into my mother's hand. If she allowed the digit to reemerge, he would look sharply at her and, shaking his head, he would spank the tip of the errant finger with his own bossy finger, causing my mother to scream with delight. They lay facing each other, he in his boxers, she in her white flannel nightgown, her face suffused with merriment, his with pleasure, when suddenly I felt the blood rush to my cheeks, and my heart began to pound so loudly I was afraid they would hear it and turn to find me spying on them. At exactly this moment my father leaned into my mother and, hidden by the tall walnut footboard, disappeared from my view.

⊱⊰

"I THINK IT might be time," I said softly, leaning on the footboard of my parents' bed, wearing my mother's handmade apron, and wondering what to serve for dinner that night. It had been two weeks since my father's diagnosis, and my siblings had arrived to keep vigil, both those who lived in town and those who came from far away. Everyone needed to be fed. Cocktails would be poured around six, my brother's jazz CDs slid into sentience, and familiar bodies would begin to saunter in and out of the kitchen, looking for comfort.

"Not yet. Christ, it hasn't even been two hours," Joe said, unpleasantly.

"They told us to look for the grimace. Well, there it is, Bo. That's a grimace. He's in pain," I responded, curbing my anger. This exchange had occurred every day, sometimes more than once, since hospice had taken over. Joe had agreed to hospice when it became obvious that Dad would not be emerging from his coma. The endgame, he knew very well, was also the game of mercy. This meant the administration of morphine.

Joe and I were straightforward with each other. I did not feel the need to be careful with him as some of my other siblings did, and yet his stubbornness prickled me. It seemed to me willful and petulant to withhold the drug simply because of an arbitrary timetable, one rec-ommended by women who were skilled in the business of death and what it does to people who are unwilling or unable to face it.

"What the fuck is your rush? He'll die soon enough," Joe said, bitingly.

"Don't lash out at me, Joe," I warned, slipping a chill into my voice. "I'm on your side."

My brother's words stung because I suspected that they were, in part, true. Wrapped in my mother's apron, serving dishes from my mother's oven, commandeering the sickbed and the old man in it, I knew that my thinly veiled arrogance often masqueraded as self-righteousness. Time to get the dinner on, time for hospice, time for the morphine, time for the sponge bath, time for a break. As long as I kept moving, and moving briskly, all would be well. Up and down the stairs ten times a day, checking the coffeepot, checking the laundry, writing the market list, simmering the sauce, staying constantly, irreproachably busy.

In that way, I could walk the plank and at the same time count my-self among the most stoic. Certainly, one of the most organized. The trick was to keep life going at a real clip, so as not to feel the plunge into emotion too keenly. To not feel at all, if possible. The objective was to trip over the death of my father with only a very slight bruising to the heart. As for my father himself, I wanted him to disappear quickly. I almost wanted him to surprise us.

The fact that I wished for such an end for my father did not sit well with Joe. He had his own ideas about the getting of oblivion and being surprised was not one of them. Joined as we were by this morbid need to assist our father in the act of dying, we were divided in our opinions as to how death should come. My brother clung to the idea that my father would want to die naturally, that he would choose to forgo palliative drugs. Attached to my father was a stoicism based, I could only conclude, on his reticence. Where others spoke, my father had retreated into a hard stillness, the veneer of which frightened everyone away. This ongoing taciturnity had endowed my father with an unassailable authority and cowed the more voluble among us into whispers. As the years unfolded, my father had sought the confines of his self-imposed hermitage with increasing determination. The mere prospect of having to be within twenty feet of an animated conversation between two women vexed my father so much that, as a matter of course, I would swing shut the door linking the TV Room to the kitchen. Even then, Mother and I modulated our voices, so as not to nettle my father who, sufficiently incensed, might stalk in and, shaking his head, say, "Jesus H Christ." If this made me laugh, he would pause on his way to the coffeepot and hold his right hand aloft, bringing his fingers rapidly together in a code well known to mean "the incessant chatter of women is intolerable."

Why then, I wondered, would my brother assume that our father, so near death, might yearn for the very sounds that only a month earlier had driven him crazy? Was the incessant chatter of women more palatable from the depths of a coma? Would that noise, which had so clearly offended him, transform itself into music, simply because he was dying? How very odd and strangely amusing to think that this man, who had disdained any form of idle conversation outside of the drunken, might suddenly long to hear the raised voices of his womenfolk, mixed with the darker tones of his male progeny, and even more curious was the suggestion from our hospice nurses that our voices might have a salubrious effect on our father. It was a well-known fact, they assured us, that hearing was the last sense to go.

It made me nervous to think of my father straining, as if from a too-great distance, to catch the threads of our deathbed conversation. All of the women instinctively lowered their voices upon entering the master bedroom and, if the talk was too impersonal, subdued them still further until a conversation about something as mundane as a bad hair job reduced them to tones so hushed as to be indecipherable. If it was true that hearing was the last sense to abandon the corporeal ship, why then did everyone immediately slip into muted cadences when they walked into the room? Even those who moved directly to my father's side, where they often knelt, spoke slowly and softly into his ear. It never occurred to me that their questions might be reaching my father and, even if this were remotely possible, that my father might consider these questions answerable. From the depths of a cancer-induced coma, I simply could not imagine that a query as perfunctory as "How are you doing today, T. J.?" might elicit a response. I imagined the inquiry would have to travel like a tiny bee through wads of cotton wool, which would absolutely dement my father. By the time the bee stung, he would wish himself well and truly dead.

Joe considered the liberal use of morphine a kind of aiding and abetting, and counseled discipline. What felt like anger coming from him was, in fact, sheer frustration. The thought of our father in pain caused him great anguish, but even more disturbing to my brother was the thought of our father trying to communicate and failing because he was completely narcotized. The prospect of a last-minute reprieve, from which our father might rouse himself to speak, was something my brother wished for until the end. I wanted our father succored with efficiency, mourned with dignity, and buried quickly. Joe wanted words, a gesture, a look. One last moment of connection, during which love would be conveyed and understood. In this way, he could bid his father good-bye, and go on living.

"Okay, Bo, have it your way. We'll look at him after dinner," I said, knowing that this suggestion would alarm my brother, signifying, as it did, a long cocktail hour followed by an even longer dinner, at the end of which time our father might very well be in agony. Joe's love for our father rose swiftly to the surface as he pushed the little blue packet into my hands and said, "You better hope it's a fucking grimace."

As I withdrew the small syringe from its nesting place inside the cushioned kit, my heart sank. What if my brother was right and I was wrong? What if, after all was said and done, our father *could* hear what was being said and, even more distressingly, *wanted* to hear? What if, at the end of this journey, he longed for the last vestiges of human sound to ease his way?

"Can you hear me, Dad?" I asked, removing the small cap from the tip of the syringe. The hospice nurse had shown me how to administer the drug, by pressing the syringe into the flesh of my father's cheek and waiting until the small barrel had been completely emptied. I knelt beside my father's bed and studied his face. Although I had not yet given him the morphine, the grimace appeared less extreme than it had only moments before and, looking around for verification, I was startled to find I was alone. Joe had left; he didn't like to watch as the grimace relaxed, leaving our father's face as smooth and blank as a mask.

My father did not respond to me, although I had hoped he would. Like my brother, I held out hope that I would be the one he could not resist. "Take me out of this, Kitten," he might say to me or, better yet, "Good girl, give me more." But my father said none of these things, and I knelt there for some minutes deliberating as to whether the severity of his grimace warranted a dose of the drug. As the voices of my siblings rose from below, hungry and restless, I knew that they would soon be expecting their dinner. I heard the distant tinkle of ice in glasses, the cool, brassy strains of Miles Davis, someone's laughter.

"I don't think so, Dad. I don't think you can hear me," I said and, gently opening my father's mouth, inserted the small plunger into the flesh of his cheek.

When I withdrew the syringe, I looked at my father in consternation. The grimace was still there.

CHAPTER TWELVE

A Thursday afternoon in the middle of January in a midwestern town is, at best, bleak. The sterile fields, covered with snow, stretch for miles in every direction. Occasionally, a farmer will leave a tractor or a thresher standing in the barnyard, as if in defiance of the laws of nature. These are oversights, however, because the people of Iowa understand that January is essentially a month of hibernation. In January, time stands still. The farmers see to their livestock, but spend most of their time indoors, checking the weather forecast, adjusting the thermostat. The farmers' wives, otherwise so busy in their vegetable gardens, so prolific with their pies and breads, are forced to share their husbands' solitude, which creates an atmosphere of tension. While the fields lie fallow, the men and women whose livelihoods depend on them resign themselves to the inevitable, and burrow in for a long winter of waiting.

Waiting, I thought, as I pressed my nose against the tall, frosted window in the dining room, is something I know a lot about. As an actress, I understood the nature of being forced to do nothing for extended periods of time, so I could sympathize with the farmers, but this sympathy was limited because I knew that the farmers, despite the long winter, could anticipate the arrival of spring. For actors, there is no springtime, there is only the telephone. There is only, ever, the job. Between commitments, an actor is rendered helpless by her own uselessness, so she learns very early in her career how to hibernate. She determines a routine from which she dares not deviate, lest anxiety rear its ugly head. Much like the farmers of Iowa, the actresses of New York learn to accept long periods of suspension, during which it is crucial to remain as composed and hidden as possible. They stock up on books, they listen to music, they take yoga classes. They retreat.

Their lovers, if they have them, may or may not be allowed to join them during these periods of imposed exile. It is of little consequence, the devotion of the lover, and can often be unduly annoying. An actress can do little with the lover's ardent embrace because she is not, in fact, present. She is peering over the lover's shoulder at the bedside table, upon which sits her mobile phone in its sleek protective jacket, black and silent as a spider. Should it ring in the middle of lovemaking, the actress knows she will disentangle herself from any erotic entwining faster than anyone would think humanly possible. The lover, dazed and disgruntled, will be left to wrangle with a snarl of empty sheets while the actress paces the entire length of her apartment, speaking in loud and often vibrant tones to the person at the other end of the phone. That magical being, capable of usurping a lover in less than a second is, of course, the agent.

This person, much less capable of devotion than the lover, is none-theless more desirable to the actress than any lover could ever hope to be, and this is because the agent signifies the possible end to what has become an excruciating period of waiting. The agent, like an audible shot of prednisone, instantly restores the actress to a state of strength and vigor. In the time it takes to abandon her lover and retrieve her phone, leaping out of bed with the agility of an acrobat, she has already begun to reclaim her sense of purpose. As her voice fills the apartment with sounds of barely contained excitement, the lover wonders for the zillionth time what in hell he is doing in this woman's bed, and why he always returns to it. But that is neither here nor there, because the lover's period of agonized waiting does not concern the actress. What is important is that the actress's period of waiting has come to an end.

As I climbed the stairs bearing a tray on which rested a glass of ice, a washcloth, and a can of Ensure, I realized that my father's im-minent death had filled me with a purpose not unlike the two-hour one-woman show I had been performing for more than a year. The process was surprisingly similar: both were physically as well as emotionally challenging, both called on certain unique skills, and both promised a closing. I could address my father's dying with the same concentration I brought to playing a difficult role, a discipline acquired over many years of practice. Most important, the waiting was ameliorated by the intensity of my daily workload, self-imposed or otherwise. My siblings, while perhaps not understanding this on a conscious level, had nonetheless conspired to give me a principal role in this real-life drama.

I entered my father's bedroom and, as I crossed to his bedside, emitted a small gasp of surprise when I realized that my sister Laura was sitting quietly in the armchair next to the tall, partially shuttered window on the far side of the room. I had thought I was alone and felt momentarily as if my thoughts had been caught red-handed. Laura had the ability to unsettle me.

She arrived nearly every afternoon around two and, after visiting Mother in the Good Living Room, made her way upstairs to our father's bedroom. Once inside, she would move to his bedside and stand there for a few minutes, looking down at him. She didn't touch him, nor did she make any attempt to care for him. She did not smooth the covers, she did not soothe his brow with a cool cloth, she did not bring ice chips to his lips. She stood and observed him. Then, satisfied, she withdrew to a corner of the room and situated herself in my mother's faded yellow armchair. Often, she sat there for hours, disturbing no one, saying nothing.

Unlike my other siblings, who announced themselves with chronic politeness, Laura felt no such compulsion. She had come, she had taken a seat, she was holding vigil. She felt no need to explain her actions and was, if anything, slightly amused when I turned and said, "Jesus, Laura, you scared the shit out of me!"

"How ya doin', Bate?" Laura asked, as softly as she could. After years of smoking and drinking, my sister's voice had become rough and flat, devoid of nuance. Yet there was a gentleness in her manner when she asked me how I was doing, and the fact that she had addressed me as Bate indicated that she was in a forgiving mood. I cannot now remember why each of us had been reduced to the attachment of a nickname beginning with the letter *B,* an adjustment we found inexplicably hilarious. In stunningly short order, Tom had become Bom, I became Bate, Joe was Bo, and so on down the line, with variations on some names so as to avoid hurt feelings. Laura somehow lacked the desired rhythm as Bora, and so she was soon transformed into Bore or, in happier circumstances, Borley. Tess was Bess, a good, if lateral, move. Only the Smalls, Jenny and Sam, escaped the torturous alliteration and were nicknamed, respectively, Wren and Buck.

Curiously, I could never bring myself to call Laura "Borley" and, on the odd occasion when I attempted to do so, I felt awkward and affected. The others had no such difficulty, and I had grown accustomed to Joe and Tom referring to Laura almost exclusively as Borley. This, I knew, was meant with real affection, and yet I couldn't bring myself to do it. Ours was a more formal relationship.

"I'm good, Laura. How long have you been sitting there?" I asked, scooping ice chips into a cotton handkerchief.

"Oh, I don't know. Awhile, I guess," my sister replied.

It was midafternoon, and the sky was gunmetal gray, but I could see my sister clearly from where I stood. Small and whippet-thin, her ash-blond hair curled close to her small head, she wore a pink polyester athletic jacket over black leggings, her narrow feet concealed in ankle-high brown boots. I felt her eyes on me as I attempted to moisten my father's lips, and was suddenly acutely conscious of my mother's apron, tied snugly around my waist.

"You're good to come every day," I continued, regretting the stiffness of the words as soon as they escaped my lips. Dialogue did not flow easily between Laura and me. I felt self-conscious in her presence, and always had. It was as if she could see something the others could not.

"Well, he *is* my father, ya know," she responded with a short, derisive chuckle.

"Did you have a chance to spend any time with him before he got sick?" I asked, looking at her across the room.

"Not really, Bate, because he just *got* sick, didn't he?" Laura answered, again laughing drily. I interpreted this as a criticism, although of what I wasn't entirely sure.

"I mean, did you spend any time with him *before?*"

Laura relaxed back into the armchair and smiled.

"Jeez, it's too bad we can't smoke in here," she said. "I could really do with a smoke."

"Go outside," I suggested. "He'll be here when you get back."

"Nah, it's all right. Stupid habit. I should quit," my sister said, crossing her legs. "After all, look what it did to him."

"He liked his drugs," I quipped, thoughtlessly.

There was a brief silence in the room, during which I wondered if my sister had heard me or not.

"I didn't know him very well, but I loved him. I sure *respected* the man, I can tell ya that. But we didn't have a deep relationship, if that's what you're asking," Laura explained, rising to her feet and approaching the base of the bed.

"Who did?" I asked, rhetorically.

"Well, Bo for sure had a friendship with Dad. And Bom, too. Dad loved the boys, always loved the boys," she said, as if apprising me of this reality.

I lifted my father's head gently and readjusted his pillow.

"He never really liked us girls," Laura continued. "Bess, I guess, he loved her. Yeah, he loved Bess. But he wasn't a daughter kinda guy, didn't know how to relate to girls. Well, Jesus, Bate, *you* know what I'm talkin' about."

This was an ample mouthful for Laura, but her expression remained inscrutable. Each sentence was layered, and each had a secret meaning. The key to unlocking the secrets would be impossible to find.

Maybe she doesn't need to understand everything she says, I thought, again busying myself with the bedclothes. Maybe it's enough to come and sit with him in the stillness of the afternoon, maybe that's as close as she wants to get.

My sister had moved to the other side of the bed, so that we were now facing each other. Her large blue-gray eyes were fixed on my father's face, her fingertips resting gently on top of the duvet. I longed to say something to her, but I had no idea what that might be. Ours was a bond without resilience. We had not fought for a friendship, we had not suffered because of the lack of one. We had taken wildly divergent paths and, in so doing, we had lost each other.

"Why did you name her Laura?" I had asked my father, one night long ago, sitting out under the stars.

My father's eyes softened, he held his cigarette to one side, and he began to sing. "'Laura, that face in the misty light. Footsteps that you hear down the hall. The laugh that floats on a summer night . . .' Hmm. Nice lyrics. Beautiful broad, Gene Tierney."

"That's your explanation? You named her after a song because you liked the lyrics?"

"Why not? Your sister was—what? Number four, number five? Your mother was at the hospital, in labor, and I was stationed at my post, waiting for the nurse to call. Killing time."

"What post would that have been?" I demanded, rolling my eyes.

"My customary post at the tavern located two blocks from Mercy Hospital. The nurse would call the tavern, the bartender would hand me the phone, and bingo! Drinks on the house. Hell, I think that song may have been playing on the jukebox at precisely the moment the phone rang. Laura."

It was a name in a dream. Undoubtedly, my father would have finished his drink, thrown down some money, and found his way to my mother's bedside in the maternity ward. Equally unquestionably, my mother would have been asleep. A plump, imperturbable nurse would have directed my father to the nursery, where she would have pointed to a cot wherein lay a tiny figure, swathed in blankets and sporting a pink cotton cap.

"What are ya gonna name this one, T. J.?" the nurse would have inquired, smiling wryly.

My father, lost in the jukebox dream, would have looked at the cot and whispered, "Laura."

Then, when the nurse had turned and walked away down the hall, my father would have pressed his nose to the glass. He would have stared for a moment at his fifth-born.

"Hiya, sugar," he would have said. And then, buttoning his coat and flipping the collar up, he would have winked, and sauntered away.

Laura's enigmatic expression, as she stood across from me looking down at our father, had not changed, and it suddenly occurred to me that our father had very likely never shared this story with the daughter who had inspired it. In the intimate ambience of our father's room, I considered telling my sister how she had come to be named Laura, but at the last minute decided against it.

CHAPTER THIRTEEN

The time had come to give my father a bath. Days had elapsed since he had slipped into a coma, and the perfunctory sponge bath was no longer sufficient. The hospice nurse, in her neat blue cotton top, looked at my father and said, "We're gonna get you fresh as a daisy, Tom." I blinked, surprised, and cut my eyes to see what Jenny was doing. My little sister stood at the base of the bed, her chin in her hands, elbows balanced precariously on the footboard. Jenny was drawn to the drama of this dying, and found moments such as these intensely interesting.

"I'd like to bathe him, if that's all right," I said, whereupon Jenny gasped. The idea of bathing her own father alarmed my youngest sister and provoked a sudden fit of embarrassment.

"Are you actually going to *do* that?" she hissed, trying to stay out of the hospice nurse's earshot.

"Yes, I am. Are you going to help me?" I asked, easily, attempting to provoke her.

Jenny waved her hands in front of her and whispered frantically, "No, for Christ's sake, no! Are you *kidding*?"

Then, just as quickly, she gripped the footboard with her hands and whispered, "But I'll watch. Can I watch?"

I nodded my head and, turning to the hospice nurse, said, "Okay, Wanda, if you'll bring up some hot water and fresh washcloths and towels, I'll take it from here."

Wanda, taken aback, did not respond warmly to this suggestion. She was clearly surprised, perhaps even a little shocked, by my willingness to undertake the task. In her experience, this was not something the next of kin was inclined to do. On the contrary, in fact. Now, here she was facing off with the oldest daughter, a bossy enough contender under the best of circumstances. God only knows why this woman, this *actress*, would want to strip her poor father naked, rub him all over with soap and water, and dress him up again. *Weird*, Wanda must have concluded, but quickly reminded herself that as a nurse, and more important, as a Christian, who was she to judge?

"You sure? 'Cause it can be, you know, kinda strange if you haven't done it before," she offered, standing vigilantly next to my father.

"Well, this may come as a surprise, Wanda, but I have actually bathed people before. Many, in fact. I have children, and I have younger siblings, and I've had, *you know*, a variety of bathing experiences," I explained.

Jenny chuckled inappropriately from the base of the bed.

"My little sister is laughing because she's uncomfortable, not because she's an idiot," I assured Wanda, who smiled gamely.

"I guess it's your decision. I mean, he is your father, isn't he?" Wanda asked.

"Allegedly," I replied, which elicited no response.

Wanda reluctantly left the room in search of the necessary articles, and I readied myself to remove my father's clothing. I could feel Jenny inching her way across the footboard, availing herself of the best possible view.

"I don't know how you can do this, but I know I'm not leaving," she whispered, with barely concealed excitement.

Wanda reappeared bearing a large basin of warm water, a pile of clean washcloths and towels, and a fresh bar of soap. She placed these items at the end of the bed, just beyond my father's feet, and stood back. I glanced at her, smiled with modest confidence, and said, "You can go now, Wanda. If you don't mind. I think we'd like this to be private."

The hospice nurse is a remarkable and unique creature, but she is still human. I watched as she silently battled with her own instincts before she submitted with grace and decided to accept that I was going to perform these ablutions, with or without her approval. For a moment, I saw the entire argument play out across her features. Resistance, followed by resentment, then a kind of perverse admiration and, finally, resignation. This was a first but, then again, it was also a last, and she was not about to introduce conflict into a situation that did not warrant it. Instead, she showed herself to be of true hospice stripe, and stood aside. After having assisted at the deathbeds of hundreds of people, she understood that even more crucial than the letting go is the giving up. The last bath is a relinquishment of the physical, every bit as much as it is a reclamation.

After Wanda had left the room and closed the door behind her, I folded back the blankets. My father lay there, very still. His breathing had become irregular, and often a deep inhalation was followed by a protracted silence, which was nerve-racking. We waited, hardly breathing ourselves, until he released air through a long, shuddering exhalation. His face betrayed nothing, aside from the now permanent grimace signifying a level of pain none of us could understand. In his worn striped pajamas, he looked old and tired. *Tired unto death*, I thought, as I began to unbutton his pajama top. It was easy enough to remove the top, and surprisingly uncomplicated to remove the bottoms. I simply pulled gently from the cuffs, and off they came.

Naked except for a pair of woolen socks, my father's body looked like that of a young man. His torso was smooth and virtually unwrinkled, his limbs were fine and strong, there was not a mark on him. Unscathed, this body was, despite its eighty-three years of hard living. Seeing my father's naked body for the first time in my life did not unnerve me, nor did it sadden me. His body was surprisingly youthful. I took pride in his corporeal beauty and, if I did not look at his ravaged face, it was almost as if I were bathing my son.

When I pulled off the socks the hospice nurse had insisted would keep him warm, I stopped. The sight of his feet, untended for weeks, shocked me. His toenails, coarse and yellowed, had grown so long that they curled over the tops of his toes. This sight was extremely unsettling, and I felt my father's humiliation as keenly as I might have had he been conscious. This negligence, more than any other single indicator, revealed to me the extent of my father's helplessness. Never would he have allowed this, so great was his personal vanity. He would have hated having his oldest daughter witness this final act of betrayal. When did it happen that he knew he could no longer take care of himself? One morning, overcome with fatigue, he must have looked at his unkempt feet and said to himself, Who gives a damn? Did he sit there for a moment, realizing what this meant? My father was a proud man, very careful with his appearance, and it disturbed me deeply to think that he had deliberately hidden his unsightly toes and said to himself, This is the beginning of the end, and by the time my negligence has been discovered, I will be long past caring.

"Look at his feet," I said to my sister, who was watching between slatted fingers.

"Oh my God," Jenny whispered. "Why didn't he tell somebody?"

"Too vain, too tired, too sick," I replied, drawing the warm washcloth over my father's chest.

"Jesus, Kate. Promise me you won't let my feet get like that," my sister pleaded. "I don't think I could bear that."

"You won't have to bear it, you'll be dead," I said, taking my father's hand in mine, and gently cleaning between the fingers. He had managed to maintain his beautiful hands. This effort, however laborious, he had made on a regular basis because the nails were trimmed and neat. Hands he himself must have recognized as unusually attractive. Without question, they had been admired. These he had protected from shame until the last moment.

"Just make sure you hire someone to take care of my appendages," Jenny whispered, watching intently as the washcloth traveled over my father's body. I lifted each arm by the wrist and washed his underarms.

I washed his penis, I washed his belly, I washed his knees. I carefully bathed his feet, his toes with the monstrously overgrown nails, and experienced a sudden wave of pity so strong that I had to stop for a moment.

"What's wrong?" my sister asked, frightened.

"I can't look after your appendages because I'll already be dead," I said, dipping a fresh washcloth into the basin and bringing it to my father's face.

The face was ready for death. Ashen, drawn, cool to the touch, none of my father's features would ever relax into themselves again. The cloth moved across his forehead, his eyes, his cheeks. His beard was sparse but still growing, another one of the indignities of dying, I thought. I was not going to shave him, that would be pointless. Something to do when there is nothing left to be done.

"You don't know that you're going to die first," Jenny said, pulling her hands from her eyes and placing them over her mouth, as if uncertain of what might emerge from it next.

No, I don't know that I'm going to die first, I can only hope, I thought, gently drying my father's body with a worn terry-cloth towel.

"Wren, get me a clean pair of pajamas, will you?" I asked, putting the washbasin on top of my father's bureau. For many years, he had emptied his trouser pockets and thrown loose change on this bureau at the end of the day, nickels and dimes and quarters, and if one of us dared to creep into his room in the dead of night to filch a coin or two, our father's eyes would suddenly fly open and from the darkness of the bed he would roar, "*Out*, you little thief!"

Jenny handed me a pair of carefully pressed blue pajamas, and I said, "Now, you can help me put them on him."

My sister stood there, frozen.

"But I bore *witness*," she said, defensively.

"Knock it off, will you? Just give me a hand," I demanded.

Together, we dressed him in his immaculate pajamas, and pulled fresh socks over his feet. We lifted the blankets and folded them carefully over our father's inert form. I took a small black comb from his bedside table and ran it gently through his white hair, startled by its softness.

"All done," I said and, leaning in, kissed my father's cheek.

"Wow," Jenny said, "I'm glad we did that."

"Wren, do me a favor and take the basin and towels downstairs, would you? I'll be down to start dinner in a minute," I assured her, knowing that she was unlikely to leave of her own volition.

Reluctantly, Jenny gathered the dirty pajamas and rolled them into the bath towel. These articles she put into the still-full washbasin and, noting my expression, said, "Don't worry, I'll throw it all into the washing machine. But first," she added, sighing heavily, "I need a smoke."

I wanted a cigarette badly myself but had begun the difficult process of quitting, and often played games with myself to strengthen my resolve. Nothing, I instructed my weaker self, could be more important than being completely present to this moment. Sitting on the bedside next to my father, I allowed my eyes to wander slowly around the room, taking in the neglected objects of a fifty-year marriage: my mother's chest of drawers and vanity mirror, unused for decades, pushed into a corner to make way for the large table my father used as a desk; a whitewashed bookshelf featuring a framed photograph of me taken when I had won a poetry contest in the eighth grade; a beautiful oak chest covered with frayed blankets and old newspapers; books littering every available surface; a long, narrow mirror nailed to the wall; the incongruously lush forest green carpet laid wall to wall lo, those many years ago, when such an addition would have been considered luxurious.

The bedside table had been reordered, and now the paraphernalia of a terminal illness had usurped the items so familiar to a child's eye— the pack of Pall Malls, the ashtray, the lighter, the library book. This table contained a small drawer, one which had long been off-limits. My father had never stated that it was, in fact, forbidden, but this is the mystery I attached to that drawer, and so had never known its secret contents. I glanced at my father, then pulled the drawer open. The small enclosure was untidy, clearly intended as a receptacle for afterthoughts. An old silver lighter rested on its back next to a faded black-and-white photograph of Tessie. Beyond the photograph, gathering dust in the nether regions of the drawer, lay an old passport. Eagerly, I fished it out and flipped it open. Astounded, I saw my own face staring back at me. Looking at the expiration date, I searched my memory until, with an exclamation of surprise, I recalled the reason for the discarded passport. I was twenty-one years old and had been visiting home for a weekend before I had to leave to shoot a film in Ireland. At some point over that weekend, I had opened my bag and realized, to my horror, that my passport had expired.

Frantically, I had beseeched my father to prevail upon his friend Chuck Murphy who, as the postmaster, could issue a temporary passport in time for me to make my flight to Dublin. My father had sought this favor from his friend, and the next day I had driven down to the post office, where, to his growing discomfort, the postmaster had been made to listen to the extravagant effusions of gratitude that only a twenty-one-year-old actress who had narrowly escaped disaster can offer.

What I could not explain to myself was why my father had kept the passport. This was puzzling to me, and I longed to solve the mystery. Did the postmaster return the expired passport to my father one day, over drinks at their customary haunt? Did Mr. Murphy perhaps intimate, throwing the document on the bar counter, that he found it both amusing and intriguing that his pal T. J.'s daughter needed a passport renewal in order to get to Ireland in time to make a movie? Did my father, then, insist on buying a round of drinks, over which he downplayed the entire episode? She's a piece of work, all right, an oddball like her mother, he might have suggested, smiling. Yes, but, T. J., let's face it, Mr. Murphy may have responded, your oddball kid's got a first-class ticket to Dublin to star in a movie with Richard Burton. My father, accepting his first drink of the day from the bartender, may have lifted his glass to Mr. Murphy and said, That may be true, but she wasn't going anywhere without your help, pal. They would have touched glasses, father to father and friend to friend, and that would have been the end of that.

I think some feeling must have swelled in him, seated at the bar, that day, and that is why he tucked the passport into his jacket pocket until, sitting on the edge of his bed that night—just as I was doing now—he had recalled the words of his friend Chuck Murphy and, crossing the room to retrieve the passport from his jacket pocket, he had looked at it, chuckled softly, opened his bedside drawer, and tossed it inside.

CHAPTER FOURTEEN

The Mexican approach to death is level, unfettered by sentimentality.

"When?" Lucy wanted to know.

We sat across from each other at the kitchen table, drinking coffee. Lucy made coffee just as I'd taught her twenty years earlier, with freshly ground beans and a touch of cinnamon. The house had not yet stirred. I knew enough not to pull any punches with Lucy but, at the same time, I needed to protect my brother. This would be a fine dance, given the natural antipathy between them.

"Soon," I answered, "maybe even today. But I don't have a crystal ball, so it's impossible to predict exactly when."

Lucy nodded, and rose to get the coffeepot. As she poured the coffee into my cup, she said, "I visit el señor last night, after I put Beanie to bed. He no look so good. Maybe he ready. He in a lot of pain, señora."

"We're on top of that," I assured her.

"How you on top?" Lucy demanded, pushing the creamer in my direction.

"We're giving him the morphine every few hours, we're watching his pain."

"You can tell when el señor need the morphine?" she asked, pointedly.

Not wanting to sound defensive, I told her the truth.

"He's dying, Lucy, we're certain of that. His days are numbered—maybe his hours are numbered. We're keeping him as comfortable as possible."

"I no understand what that mean, señora. The señor, he tell you

himself he uncomfortable? He ask for the drug? No, he don't speak.
Just the look on his face, señora. That tell the story," Lucy said.

"And I am watching his face very carefully," I countered, not without an edge.

"I think you watch el señor's face but you *wait* until is okay with the
nurses. Until is okay with Joe," Lucy said, her dark eyes flashing.

Defeated, I put my head in my hands. This was a battle I did not
want to engage in, given the willfulness of the adversaries involved.
Joe and Lucy shared an antipathy born out of an intuitive and mutual
distrust, a dynamic that confounded the rest of us and one that, despite
our best efforts, we were unable to rectify.

"I can't win, Luce, no matter what I do. I just can't win," I complained, fatigue getting the better of me.

"You can win, señora. You a strong woman," Lucy stated, already
moving to the sink. As she pulled on yellow rubber gloves, the back
door swung open and Joe walked in. He allowed the screen door
to bang shut but stayed in the back room, stamping his feet on the
doormat.

"How bad outside?" I asked my brother.

"Colder than a witch's tit," he replied, unzipping his down jacket.

"Have a cup of coffee," I suggested, indicating the chair opposite me.

"I don't drink coffee, Kate," my brother explained, as if to a small
child. "I drink tea. How many times do I have to tell people that?"

"As many times as it takes to get a cup of tea, I guess," I replied,
rising to put the kettle on.

"Thanks, Bate," Joe mumbled, crossing to the chair without acknowledging Lucy. A high-wire act could have been performed on the
line of tension between them.

"You get any sleep last night?" I asked, knowing the answer.

My brother shrugged as if to say, What does it matter?

"How's Dad? Any change?" Joe had asked this question every

morning for the past week, and every morning I had delivered a short update on our father's decline.

"His breathing is completely erratic," I said. "The grimace is pronounced."

Joe sighed, just as his father had sighed; heavily, accompanied by a sound of tremendous fatigue.

"That fucking grimace trumps everything, doesn't it?"

My brother had not started the day well, had probably slept little the night before, and knew that the hours about to unfold would do so with agonizing slowness.

I did not respond, but went about the business of making him a cup of tea.

"How about some eggs?" I urged, standing at the stove.

"Christ, no," Joe replied, emphatically.

Soon, we would make our way up the front stairs and into my father's bedroom. Soon, but not yet. There was time enough for a hot drink, a word, before it began all over again, this exacting process of seeing our father to his death. My patience with the life force was wearing thin, although I didn't dare to openly admit it. If I scratched at the surface of this anxiety, the truth would soon be revealed, and I would be forced to acknowledge it.

My father had captured it so effortlessly: *I don't fear death, but I don't welcome it, either.* Death did not frighten him, or so he had said two weeks earlier, fortified by many drinks. To be finished with life, one needs to be utterly exhausted, and worn out by heartache. The loss of Maggie at three months followed thirteen years later by the death of Tessie had swung savagely at my father's well-being, crippling his confidence. His failing asphalt business, his compromised health, his increasing need for drink, all of this contributed to my father's passive appraisal of death, where once he would have fought like a lion. It was this transformation from lion into a creature he could no longer identify that led my father to his own demise. This man, who had once loved passionately, fought fiercely, laughed often, now spent his days in an empty room doing crossword puzzles.

It is any man's choice to do crossword puzzles or not and is not in itself diminishing. What eroded my father's pride more than anything was the bitterness he had promised himself as a young man would never get the better of him. Observing his own father's behavior, he had sworn to be a different kind of man, and so he believed he was when he met and wooed my mother. My mother had the artist's inner sight, however, and that is why she resisted him for so long. She knew that somewhere in my father's character, somewhere as yet hidden to her, there existed a terrible wound, and that one day, because of this damage, he would be forced to abandon her. Not physically, of course, but in the far more effective way of disappearing through emotional escape. When it became clear to my father that he had lost his wife's regard, he decided to make for himself a new way of life, one that demanded only a modicum of communication. As my mother's disappointment deepened, my father drank with increasing abandon. In this way, he neither acknowledged nor felt the pain that, with exquisite denigration, reduced him to a man who had traded companionship for crossword puzzles.

There is a slim chance that my father did not recognize that he had substituted someone else for himself, but only a very slim chance. After all, he was unusually adroit at crossword puzzles and had spent his years of idleness becoming a master wordsmith. He knew the significance of things. He knew that his days no longer constituted a meaningful life, at least not as he had once understood a meaningful life to be. He knew that he had succumbed to his father's weakness, and this alone was enough to separate him from his own life, and the person in it whom he had loved unconditionally. It is little wonder, then, that he could wax philosophical about death. Whatever else he would be made to endure in this life, he knew would be reasonably quick, and that the suffering that had come to define him would soon be over.

Trudging up the stairs, I felt again a surge of tenderness for my brother, whose love for his father was virtually unstained. I envied him this innocence and wanted to protect him from the loss of it, but at the same time I found the daily inching toward death almost intolerable. Grief manifests itself in many ways and is often perverse. In me, it whipped up an intense longing to see my father at peace, safely removed from the prying eyes of the excellent hospice nurses, the expressions of morbid curiosity on the faces of the children, the fraying nerves of those keeping the protracted vigil.

Joe's love for our father was not like my love. His was a love without criticism, without judgment. If anything, his love for our father was purer than any other love he had experienced. Even his passion for a wild, blond Irish gypsy who would bear him three children could not surpass the devotion he felt for his father. His childhood, his youth, his manhood, and all of his dreams were somehow made right by this love. It was the one relationship that had both defined and sustained him. He did not want his father to die.

In the bedroom, we assessed the situation. Our father's breathing had become ragged, his inhalations profoundly disturbing, as if he had been held underwater and could break the surface only after protracted periods of submersion. It was torture to watch his chest expand, his rib bones stretching the skin of his torso in a desperate attempt to take in oxygen. Equally torturous were the periods of stillness that followed, and the terrible uncertainty of what that stillness meant.

Joe gazed at his father's face with the expression of a young boy who knew he had come to a primal, unavoidable rite of passage but who, nonetheless, longed to turn back time, if only for a week.

Undeniably, the grimace had deepened, forming angry clefts in my father's brow. I put my arm around my brother's shoulder and said, "He's clearly in severe discomfort, Bo. We need to do something about it."

My brother looked at our father and then, without a word, turned and left the room.

I waited. No one else was present, the day had just begun. Within minutes, Joe returned and, walking over to me, extended his hand. In it, lay the small blue packet containing the syringes of morphine. He did not meet my eyes, but transferred the packet to me abruptly, with barely concealed disgust.

"You do it," he whispered. In these three words, fury, contempt, and despair were unmasked.

Joe did not linger, but walked quickly out of the room, leaving the door ajar.

I stood at the foot of the bed for a moment, holding the blue packet. It did not occur to me to close the door. Instead, I waited until my father drew another breath, and then I moved to his side. Sitting on the bed, I placed the packet on the bedside table. Inching closer to my father, I lowered my head until my mouth reached his ear.

"If you can hear me, Dad, I want you to listen. It's time to let go. I love you, we all love you, but we don't want you to suffer anymore. It's enough. I'm going to give you something that will put you to sleep, and that will be all. Okay?"

Pulling back, I searched my father's face for any sign of response. There was none; not in the eyes, motionless beneath blue lids, not in the pale lips, not in the coarsely veined nose. No pulse struggled in the darkening throat.

I took the packet and unzipped it. Inside, six syringes of morphine were arranged in tiny cots. Withdrawing a single syringe, I gently opened my father's mouth. Inserting the syringe into his cheek, I held it there until I was certain the drug had been absorbed. I continued to do this until only one syringe remained.

My brother was pacing downstairs, but his grief reached me upstairs, sitting by our father's side. I stroked my father's face, his white hair. Holding the last syringe, I put my lips to my father's ear and said, "I love you, Dad. I love you. Let go now." Carefully, I moved the syringe into the flesh of my father's cheek, and as I did this, I thought I discerned some movement in my father's face. For a brief, unnerving moment, I had the idea that he was attempting to shake his head, but the movement was so slight, so far away, as to be almost imperceptible. Still, I returned the empty syringe to its cot and sat there, scrutinizing my father's face.

There had been no movement, of course. Such an effort far exceeded my father's capacity. It had been a figment of my imagination, nothing more.

The only movement I would recollect in years to come was the suddenness with which my father's grimace disappeared. It was as if it had never existed at all.

CHAPTER FIFTEEN

Sitting on my father's bed, waiting for him to die, I took my time before calling down to Joe. I wanted to be alone with my father, I wanted to rest with him. I studied his face for what I knew would be the last time and felt as I had always felt when my father slept; that he was never really completely asleep but only waiting to be disturbed by the rude noises of children, his wife playing Chopin badly on the piano, a car full of friends pulling into the driveway, a daughter across the hall packing her suitcase, cursing the insufficiency of her wardrobe.

He had been eager for me to leave the nest. This was something I felt acutely, and consequently I had moved in that direction with preternatural focus. Why he was so anxious for me to get out of the house and into the world remains a mystery, and one that will never be solved. The evidence, however, suggests that he was self-centered and maybe a little jealous. He was tired of watching me monopolize my mother's time and attention and was further frustrated by her obvious pride in me. She had always championed me and, in an act of deliberate perverseness, my father took the opposite approach. Perhaps he thought he was preparing me for the harsh realities of the world, or perhaps he didn't give a damn. I'm inclined to believe that he didn't really care what I did or where I went, as long as I got the hell out of his hair. In fairness, I think he felt this way about all of us. What had begun as a romantic ideal had ended in weariness and grief. This was the result of producing too many children at too rapid a rate and then, out of a general sense of indifference, leaving them to grow up essentially unsupervised.

My father saw me perform exactly twice over the course of thirty years. The first time was when I played Tamora in a very fraught production of *Titus Andronicus* at the Delacorte Theater in Central Park. Sitting in my underground dressing room, shared by all of my fellow actresses, I heard my father's voice rising above the din: "When the hell is halftime?"

Many years later, my father escorted me to a screening of an independent film I'd shot in Ireland with Richard Burton. He agreed to do this because the film was being shown at a theater in Dubuque, Iowa, to help raise funds for a local charitable institution. When it was over, I leaned in and asked him what he'd thought of it, to which he immediately responded, "Couldn't understand a goddam word."

Curmudgeonly and critical though he may have been, at the root of it he simply couldn't be bothered. He knew enough about my career to take his jabs with precision. Kitten, a nickname I loved, was more and more often replaced by sobriquets such as Hollywood or Big Shot and, though he made it clear this was all in jest, it always stung. I was careful to conceal this from my father, who was extremely intolerant of petulance and whose response to hurt feelings was to further belittle the victim. If he was unpredictable as a young father, he was seldom cruel. It was only after Tessie died and he'd sold his business that he became increasingly solitary but, when his solitude was threatened, he could move with the lightning speed of a scorpion. We cannot escape our DNA, and as my father advanced into old age he withdrew into himself rather than become the brute his father had been. As for his mother, none of us was encouraged to come home for her funeral. "Don't bother," my father had said to me on the phone, "she's dead as a doornail."

And yet. I never ceased to long for his approval, for a warm glance, a wink. I had, after all, danced on his shoes when I was five, and according to him it was I who drove him to drink when, at the age of six months, I discovered the unutterable delights of solid food and expressed this unbridled passion by dumping whole jars of pureed bananas on my head.

It was not disappointment but rather heartbreak I experienced when, at the age of seven, I felt myself being lifted into my father's arms and heard him say, "This is the last time I carry this one up the stairs. Jesus, she's all there, isn't she?"

He could convert himself into a frighteningly perfect gorilla, and would chase us through the house until, screaming for mercy, we threw ourselves at his feet. He could roll up the rug and transform the dining room into a dance floor, if he had a mind to. For a long time, he made my mother laugh until she cried, and for many years he carried himself with aplomb. When his beauty eroded, he accepted it with apparent grace, and went about the business of growing old with discretion and dignity. It's true, he was a terrible miser, and for this he cannot be forgiven, but even this was overlooked when he'd accept a drink, a head rub, or a soft-boiled egg and, looking at you, say, "You're aces in my book, sugar."

He had, for me, a charisma that remained undimmed by time. In his presence, there was always the possibility of love. It hovered ever near and, though it seldom showed itself, it was distinctly real. Occasionally, finding myself alone with my father in the living room, I would sense the distance between us softly closing, and something else opening up. It was more than the need for a drink, or the sudden impulse for company. It was a silent bridge that we acknowledged, a bridge that ran between us, one that we saw and felt but somehow could not cross. He would glance up, then, as if surprised to find me there and, in that moment, I would read in his eyes what he could not say, and I understood that in this withholding lay all of the sorrows of his life, and all of the regret.

CHAPTER SIXTEEN

At twenty, I'd had some minor success on television and wanted to show off, so I stepped off the plane wearing a navy double-breasted merino coat that fell midcalf, and a matching deep blue beret. My mother usually started waving from inside baggage claim as soon as the plane touched down. Neither a frantic nor a friendly wave, hers was a very singular greeting, both arms fully extended and raised high above her head. In those days, the Dubuque Regional Airport was not much bigger than an old-fashioned wraparound porch, and as we approached the gate I could always make out her trim figure behind the glass pane. This time, she was nowhere to be seen. She must be late, I thought, or she might be parking, although neither of these possibilities seemed plausible. My mother was never late, and the rules of parking eluded her altogether. She simply pulled into any spot that could accommodate her car, turned off the ignition, and left.

I descended the steps of the twin turboprop plane, crossed the postage stamp of a tarmac, and quickly made my way into the terminal. Having fully expected my mother to pick me up, I was at first surprised and then bewildered to find my father standing on the far side of the small baggage carousel. My father had never, in all the years I'd been flying home, collected me at the airport. According to him, this was a duty reserved for my mother, and so it should be, allowing mother and daughter to work off some of that heady separation steam that kept the two of them locked in a world of their own for what often seemed like days. Yet here he was, wearing a forest green windbreaker and his Timberland work boots, one hand lightly tucked inside the pocket of his khaki pants, the other holding a cigarette low to his side. From the tone of his getup, I concluded that he had taken a break from whatever road he was currently blacktopping and had told my mother that it would not be inconvenient to pick me up. Undoubtedly, she had been both surprised and perplexed by this offer, but my mother was not one to fight a good impulse, and so she had said, "That's a novel idea," and he had probably replied, "Might be a couple of hours," which had startled my mother into a brief silence. "Well, don't be late picking her up, Tom," she'd cautioned him, as he walked out the back door. "I'm never late, and neither is Kitten!"

It was clear my father was not about to move toward me, so I crossed the room with a broad smile and said, "Dad! What a surprise! Did you come to get me?"

"No, just thought I'd take a drive, check out the beautiful Dubuque International Airport," he said.

"Ever dazzling," I agreed, and leaned in to kiss his cheek. The cheek was smooth, freshly shaven, and smelled of Old Spice.

"Don't be a smart-ass," he said.

While we waited for my suitcase to arrive on the carousel, my father fielded greetings from many people. People I had never seen before approached my father with an ease and cordiality that never ceased to amaze me. They came up to him and shook his hand and said, "How are you, T. J.? Haven't seen you around much. This your daughter?"

Airports allow for a familiarity that other venues discourage. My father answered each of these strangers in turn, introducing me as he did so, until finally my little valise emerged through the mysterious black flaps behind which all luggage exists in a kind of limbo, eliciting a small shriek of joy from me. It was always a crapshoot, sending my bag to Dubuque from New York through Chicago. A fifty-fifty shot, I'd say, and when it didn't make it there was almost a sense of relief. I knew, then, that I could wear my mother's funky cotton pajamas with impunity, perhaps adding one of her soiled sweatshirts to ward off the chill. This was the preferred ensemble and one I did not alter until the day of my departure, when I reassembled myself into the snappy girl who lived in New York City.

A pleasant, portly man in his fifties came up and, looking at me, said to my father, "Well I'll be damned, T. J.! This the girl who went off to seek her fortune in New York?"

"Allegedly," my father answered drily, setting the stocky man off into chortles of approval. To this man, my father was not only successful, good-looking, and personable, but he was also one of the wittiest men in town. Hard to be witty and get away with it in Dubuque County, but my father had the gift, and it was appreciated. When my father introduced me to this man, he shot me a stern look, warning me to be polite and, if remotely possible, gracious. I instantly flipped the internal switch that regulated my attitude, took the man's hand, and smiled at him warmly.

On our way to the car, I again expressed surprise that he had come to get me, to which my father responded, "The work site is nearby, and it's almost lunchtime. Thought I'd save your mother the trouble." He looked at me, checking my face for signs of disappointment. He found none.

"How about a bite at the Coach House before I take you home?"

This invitation, following so hard on the heels of his apparent pleasure in picking me up at the airport, gave me pause. Invitations to the Coach House were so rare as to be almost nonexistent. This was my father's club, insofar as a vintage roadside tavern off Highway 20 could impersonate a club, ideally situated, as it was, between his office and his home. He went to the Coach House for lunch, and more nights than not stopped for a drink on his way home. Clearly, this explained my father's almost perpetual absence from the dinner table. In this habit, he was not alone. His cronies, too, enjoyed a long liquid lunch and a quick stop-by before returning to their respective houses, wherein lurked a danger so palpable that none of these men were able to confront it without fortification. By this, I mean their wives, and their ever-growing broods of children. The danger lay not in the women and children per se, but in what might happen to the men were they to arrive in their kitchens unprepared to greet the discomfiting sight of so many ravenous mouths, crudely devouring whatever facsimile of meat loaf the wife, attired in sweatpants and greasy apron, her hair flattened with sweat and stinking of beef chuck and onion, had managed to place on the table before falling into her chair and succumbing to a sinking spell. "Sinking spells," a form of modern-day midwestern neurasthenia, were very common among mothers when I was growing up, and my mother was no exception. After struggling with his responsibility as a father for perhaps a minute as he left his office and headed in the direction of his home, my father concluded that his time and goodwill were better spent among people who were more appreciative of his natural talents. Thus, around six o'clock his car would turn off Highway 20 into the small gravel parking lot outside the Coach House, and my father would enter the environment that had become his home away from home.

Naturally, it was an establishment that strongly discouraged the presence of children. Even wives, caught in the middle of a domestic emergency, were frowned upon. Should a woman suddenly appear tableside, it was considered unseemly, as if she had walked in on them all naked. She'd frantically communicate the nature of the catastrophe to her husband and, in what usually involved a brusque and irritable transaction of funds, he would then dismiss his wife by lifting his glass and shouting to the bartender, "One for the road, Mary!" It was seldom one for the road, however, what with this one buying this round, and that one buying another, and all of it drunkenly elliptical in its rules and regulations.

The Coach House had a mystique and an allure that was incontrovertible. Of course, I questioned my father's motives in wanting to take me to lunch on a Friday, after I had just arrived from New York. Was there something he wanted to tell me? He hadn't seen me in almost a year, during which time I'd landed a big part on a new soap opera and was living in a high-rise on Central Park West. My father did not mention the soap opera, not once during the time it took us to get to the Coach House from the airport. This struck me as odd, as it was his dearest wish to see us all completely independent and self-sufficient. However, experience had taught me to take his indifference in stride. I asked him how business was, he said fine, not getting as many bids as he'd like, but it was steady. And Mother, I inquired, how's Mother doing?

"Your mother is fine," he replied. His words were measured, and implicit in them was the warning not to come at him too hard about Tessie. My sister had died a year earlier of an astrocytoma brain tumor. She was fourteen years old, and her death had fractured the family.

"She's got her goofy coterie of pals. Mother Columba, her painter friends, the priest out there, what's his name?"

"William," I said. "Father William, he's the chaplain."

"Right. And she's got her studio—she's in there all the time. Don't know what the hell she's doing in there for hours at a stretch."

"She's *working*, Dad," I responded, incredulously. "She's an artist. What do you think she's doing in there?"

"How the hell would I know? That goofy music she has turned up so loud you can hear it all over the damn house. Door locked. Death masks, for Christ's sake. What the hell is a death mask?" This was clearly a rhetorical question. He didn't want to know why my mother was sculpting death masks, or what it meant. In the silence that fell between us as we approached the old tavern, there existed everything that could not be said without a drink. Even with a drink, my father was unlikely to share his deepest feelings with me. Certainly not the grief that leeched the life out of him after Tessie died. He did with his sorrow what he did with his love—he hid it. Intense feelings were better off compartmentalized, allowing life to go on, at least on the face of it.

We pulled off the road and onto the narrow strip of gravel that served as a parking lot. The Coach House was banked just off the highway, a nondescript single-level structure composed of dark wood and a metal-framed front door. To my surprise, my father came around and opened the passenger door, indicating that I was to precede him into the tavern.

I had seen the interior only a few times in my life, and a kind of awe washed over me when I walked through the front door. It took a moment to adjust to the darkness, having come in from a bright October day, but once I did I saw immediately that nothing had changed. The room opened in front of me, as it had when I was a young girl, with the tension of a suspense novel. Directly before me was the long dark oak bar running the length of the main room, before which were situated a number of high-backed swivel chairs. There were four or five men populating these chairs, all sipping tall steins of beer. The proprietress, whose name was Mary, bustled to and fro behind the bar, although at a fairly easy pace. She was a short, stout, middle-aged woman with teased gray hair and kind eyes, and she was never in a hurry. When the door opened, she looked to see who had come in and said, in a tone both measured and pleased, "Hi there, T. J., how are ya?"

"Just fine, Mary, how are you?"

"Can't complain. Who's that you got with ya, Tom?"

Steering me toward the bar, my father made a formal introduction. "This is my daughter Kate. Kitten, you remember Mary."

I extended my hand and said, "Nice to see you again, Mary."

"Well, you're all grown up, aren't ya? Where do ya live now?"

"I live in New York City."

"That's right, I heard about that. How's that goin' for ya?"

I laughed and said, "It's going well. I'm very happy there."

Mary nodded her head and, smiling, said, "I'll bet you are."

As I removed my coat, my father indicated the coatrack on the far side of the room, close to the kitchen. I could smell the hot oil while

French fries popped in the deep fryer and the unmistakable, mouth-watering fat of Iowa beef burgers, sizzling on the grill. As I made my way to the coatrack, my father stopped at a large round table in the center of the room. This table, I knew, indicated premium membership in the home-away-from-home club. I hung up my coat and, as I turned, was startled to find several pairs of hooded eyes examining me as if I were an ocelot.

Each member of this exclusive club had children my age and, though they knew I was T. J.'s oldest daughter, most of them did not know my name. I was another in a long line of children, albeit an adult child wearing a long coat and a striking blue cap, and one who appeared undaunted by the presence of such a distinguished assemblage. My father's brother, Uncle Bob, half rose to greet me, but I spared him the full effort by stepping lightly to his side and landing a quick kiss on his cheek. He and my father had formed a partnership and built a business many years ago and, whereas Uncle Bob was closer to my father than any other human being, he remained a complete enigma to me. In all the years I'd known him, I'd seen him speak directly to his wife, my aunt Lou, only twice. He disdained speech the way my father disdained food, and yet managed to convey a gravitas that defied explanation. I was a little afraid of him.

"Katy, nice to see you," he said, in a voice suggesting that I had done something wrong. He made me bristle, as if he secretly thought I was full of myself and that he might use this against me if I were to overstep my bounds. Those bounds, like everything else about Uncle Bob, were known to him alone. You never quite knew where you stood with him, so I stood apart, and smiled. He lifted his preferred cocktail, Bacardi and Coke, to his lips, and settled back into silence.

The rest of this collective I recognized as creatures from a familiar if overextended fairy tale; bigger than life, important, and formidable. Mr. Crane, Mr. Murphy, Mr. Conlon, and Mr. Glab sat there and appraised me, Tom's young daughter home for a visit from New York

City, and what they saw will remain a mystery. These men were not flatterers, they lacked hyperbole and scorned politesse but curiously, instead of detracting from their power, these characteristics only enhanced it. Whereas it could hardly be said that they were delighted to see me, one or two of them half rose from their seats and extended a hand, acknowledging that I appeared to have grown up and deserved the respect that attended such a precarious process. An invitation to join them was not forthcoming, nor was it expected. An ocelot should never dine with sleeping dogs.

"Well, gentlemen, if you'll excuse us, we're going to grab a bite to eat," my father announced, rather formally. The men nodded slowly, as if slightly disgruntled at having had their conclave interrupted and uncertain as to where exactly, in the interstices of the protracted silence they considered conversation, they'd left off.

At a small table close to the bar, but in full view of everyone in the room, my father came around and held my chair while I settled into it. The tavern was divided into two areas: one with a bar, and one without. The tables were adorned with red tablecloths, white cloth napkins, and glasses of ice water. The ambience was relaxed and friendly, particularly on a Friday afternoon when the October sun, mellow and still warm, promised a weekend of good weather. Nothing made the people of Iowa happier than fine weather, except maybe the opportunity to celebrate that weather in their favorite bar. Many of the tables were occupied, and raucous laughter emanated from the back room, where a long table was crowded with people enjoying an extended lunch.

A waitress approached our table, a woman of about forty, worn but still pretty, with long black hair caught up in a frosted silver clip. In contrast to Mary, this woman was heavily made up, her eyes outlined with kohl, her mouth a cantaloupe orange, her earlobes adorned with multiple silver hoops. The way she stood, one hand on her hip, her left leg taking most of her body weight, told me that she probably had young children at home and thoroughly enjoyed spending her afternoons inside the relative comfort of a well-run establishment like the Coach House.

"What'll you have, T. J.?" she asked, pad in hand.

My father looked at me and raised an eyebrow.

"I'd like a cheeseburger, please, medium," I said.

"Basket or plate?" she demanded, cocking her head to one side, as if it were a trick question.

"If by basket you mean burger and fries, then by all means, the basket, please. I'm not dead yet," I declared, satisfied with the unseemliness of my choice.

"Honey, you ain't *close* to dead," the waitress opined.

My father emitted a subtle groan, as if the very idea of watching me consume a basket heaving with greasy fries was the punishment he deserved for offering to take me to lunch in the first place.

"I'll have a dry martini—"

"And a plain hamburger medium, no bun, with a sliced tomato on the side," the waitress interrupted, finishing his order.

"Roger that, sweetheart," my father agreed, relieved to be spared the discomfort of having to vocally enumerate food items.

"And I'd like a glass of white wine," I said, casually.

Our waitress pursed her lips and looked heavenward, as if pondering the weight of my request.

"We got some, but it's only the one kind. That okay?"

"That's perfect," I replied.

"I don't know about perfect, but that's what you're gonna get," she said, snapping her pad into her hand and tucking it neatly into the pocket of her black nylon apron.

Keeping my eyes on the waitress as she leaned over the far end of the bar and barked her drinks order to Mary, I asked my father if he liked my beret.

"Nifty," he replied, a response I was not expecting. Suddenly, the beret assumed a chicness it had not possessed when I bought it.

"Bought a new hat, a new coat, and moved into a new apartment in less than a week. Not bad, huh?" I asked, efficiently filling my father in on the movements of my life.

"That's a lot of dough to throw around in a few days, isn't it?"

He could not bring himself to ask me directly about my career but would vigorously engage in any conversation concerning money.

"I'm doing pretty well on the soap. The more shows I do, the more I make, and I'm doing a lot of shows. My character is very popular," I said.

At that moment our drinks arrived. Two olives on a tasseled toothpick adorned my father's frosted martini, which he picked up rather gingerly and lifted in a toast.

"Cheers," he said.

"Cheers to you for picking me up at the airport," I declared, causing him to shake his head and smile wryly.

"So, what do they pay you for this—whatever you call it—serial?" my father asked, his curiosity piqued.

"That's better than *soap opera*, Dad. More dignified. But really, everyone in show business calls a soap opera what it is—a soap," I stated definitively, showing off my expertise.

"Everyone needs soap, is that it?"

"Exactly! I'm paid $350 a show, and if I do a minimum of five shows a week, which is typical, I can bring in $1,750, but if I do two shows in one day, which is increasingly the case because my character is so popular, I can make as much as $2,500 a week. That's not chopped liver," I said, taking a sip of my wine.

My father emitted a low whistle and conceded that such a salary was far from chopped liver, that to the contrary, it was a honeypot.

"Yeah, I'm lucky. They like me on this show. And the city is so expensive! I can throw away fifty bucks without blinking in New York. A taxi, a movie, a couple of drinks—bang! Gone."

This kind of information both fascinated and repulsed my father, who studied his martini with a curious intensity. He sat facing the imperial members of the home-away-from-home club, a vulnerable position and one that demanded subtlety of expression.

"Why the hell are you blowing your money like that? Complete extravagance. Don't you have suitors lined up to buy you a drink, a bite, a blue beret?"

Since I'd left home, my father had rarely expressed an interest in my private life—he considered the subject essentially distasteful—but now I marveled at his ability to dig into the topic as a sign of his earnest protectiveness regarding my newly acquired fortune.

"I try to limit the suitors to one at a time—two, if I'm feeling frisky," I divulged, a truth masquerading as a joke. My father raised an eyebrow, sipped, and looked at me suspiciously.

"No, no, I'm kidding. I have a boyfriend. He's very handsome, very smart, a theater director. He's Jewish," I said, "and he's broke most of the time."

"Jesus," my father muttered, then lifted his empty glass to Mary, indicating that he'd like another. I did the same.

"What the hell is a broad like you doing with a guy who can't afford to buy you a drink?" he demanded. "Doesn't make any sense."

"What do you mean, a broad like me?" I was intensely curious to divine his meaning and, in that moment, could have rolled the dice either way.

"A knockout is what I mean," my father declared, accepting his second martini with a wink at our waitress.

I busied myself by handing the waitress my depleted wineglass and receiving the replenished one. There was no hiding from my father's comment, no pretending I hadn't heard it. It reverberated in my head like a bell. Suddenly, I was overcome with a shyness I'd never experienced in my father's company, and before I knew what was happening, my cheeks had turned pink.

"What's the attraction?" he asked. "What's this guy got that some-body with a steady paycheck hasn't?"

Composing myself, I took a breath and fixed my father with a look that warned him I was about to take a chance. He was familiar with this expression, and a small smile tugged at the corners of his mouth.

"He's quiet, he's deep, and he's a wonderful kisser," I explained, try-ing hard to keep my gaze steady, despite the magnetic pull of the earth, which threatened to open beneath me.

Slowly, deliberately, and very gracefully my father lifted his glass and held it there until I brought my glass up to join his. We clinked.

"Arguably the only currency superior to money," he observed, his eyes full of mischief.

We toasted to superior currency and, just as our waitress arrived bearing a basket containing what I knew was going to be the tastiest meal I'd had in ages, I looked at my father and said, "You know, Dad, even a lady can have fun."

He considered me, then snapped his napkin sharply before placing it on his lap.

"Sounds like a line from this soap opera you're doing," he remarked.

Startled, I glanced at my father, my attention momentarily diverted from the basket of French fries in front of me. It seemed incredible to me that he had forgotten the words he'd said to me the night before I'd left for New York to study acting at NYU, four years earlier. In his bedroom, he had looked at me closely and told me to enjoy myself. He had suggested that Catholicism was not always the path to enlighten-ment, and could put a fork in romance, if I let it get in the way. *You can have fun and still be a lady, Kitten,* he had said. *Remember that.*

Delicately lifting his fork, my father paused for a moment as he ex-amined the hamburger on his plate.

"Tell your writers they need to work on their material," he said.

CHAPTER SEVENTEEN

I f I step back a little, I can see it clearly. The house, beckoning from within its copse of trees, a mystery. The figures within, light-footed and laughing, running up and down the stairs. That's not entirely true. My father did not run up the stairs, it wasn't in his character, but my mother could not do otherwise, and so I suppose he was always chasing her. Into that room at the far end of the upstairs hallway, always dimly but warmly lit by table lamps. It was sacrilegious to turn on a ceiling light. Only farmers did that, and their houses were stark and grim, their rooms flooded with false light. In my house, the house of my childhood, the evenings were shaped toward charm, and I see golden light, someone with mischievous eyes putting a long match to the kindling and newspaper in the dining room fireplace. Doors swing open to a busy kitchen, stutter shut on a burlap bag full of library books.

Upstairs, chaos, and sometimes a silence inscrutable and thrilling. Never, never is the door to their bedroom tightly shut. It is always slightly ajar. If she is inside alone, we enter softly but with confidence. If he is with her, we do not enter at all. It has never been forbidden, it simply is not done. We step away, we stand apart, almost happier that we are not included. If they are in there together, and there is the occasional sound of laughter, and if that laughter is my mother's, we are content to do without. Their mystery is so much greater than anything we might offer, and infinitely more powerful. It is intensely clear to me that this is where my father most likes to be, in this bedroom with my mother. She may be trapped, caught in those bedclothes, but still she laughs, so there is no need to be afraid. He is the king, in that bed. I see him there, one arm behind his head, ankles crossed, smoking. His languor doesn't fool me. He is wide awake, every nerve alert, waiting. He is waiting for her.

Time shifts, and I am many years older. The room is the same room of my childhood, only now it is cramped and full of people. In the bed, my father still waits for her. It cannot end until she comes. Slowly, she is led in by Lucy, who has prepared her for this visit. My mother has been bathed, her white hair shampooed and brushed, her thin lips animated with pink gloss. Lucy looks at me expectantly, and I accept this as the cue to take my mother's arm and lead her to the bedside. One of my brothers quickly reaches for a chair and places it as close to my father as possible. My mother is uncertain, but I assure her that she is fine, and that she should sit down. I take her hand and place it on my father's chest.

"This is your husband, Mother," I say. "This is Tom. Your husband."

Again, my mother hesitates, and withdraws her hand. She plucks at the blanket drawn neatly over my father's body. Her eyes dart about the room but settle on nothing. Suddenly, she begins to hum. I kneel next to her and say, "Mummy, this is your husband. Tom. Don't you want to say good-bye to him? I think it's time to say good-bye." My mother looks at me, unseeing, but the humming ceases and she seems to relax. Her gaze falls upon my father's face and she is still. She cocks her head slightly to one side, as if trying to ascertain the nature of this puzzle. The task is too demanding, however, and she gives up. She does not know if she has failed or succeeded, only that it doesn't matter.

When the tuneless humming begins again, there is a palpable tension in the room. We have gathered for this moment, and we cannot proceed without this, the smallest of miracles. We cannot finish this until my mother unlocks her mind for a split second and in that particle of time lets her husband go. It is a senseless wish, and yet we are collectively bound by it. All of her children, her grandchildren, and her great-grandchildren are riveted to her; it is a cathedral, and we are watching her as she awaits benediction at this strange altar. Suddenly, my mother lifts her hand and, resting it on my father's brow, begins to drum her fingers very lightly on his forehead. There is the nuance of a smile, the memory of a smile, and she leans in closely, as if studying a palimpsest. What she utters is unmistakable. Still drumming her fingers on my father's forehead, in the voice of a girl my mother says, "Adiós, el señor."

After a silence, in which the irony of this final parting is not acknowledged, the room comes to life. There is music to honor my father, the music he loved. Frank Sinatra sings "Summer Wind" from a boom box set atop the bureau which was once, and for so long, the treasure chest of a mighty king. My older brother, Tom, catches my eye, and we are captured in the same lens, a brief transcendence. We, my father's progeny, celebrate transubstantiation in the manner he would have preferred. Trays bearing glasses of Irish whiskey are passed around, and my father is toasted, first by Tom and then by all. In the air, in the dust that films the sheer curtains, in the whiskey-brightened cheeks of the young, in the long mirror's reflection, in this room where so many began, in the waning light of this January day, there is empirical evidence of love.

The whiskey and rising emotion of the crowd hold actual grief in abeyance. That will come later, much later. Bodies sway together and around the figure whose dominion is without question, even as my mother is led out of the room and down the stairs to a quieter place. This place is far from quiet. Children, despite the too-still figure lying on the bed, have begun to dance, some of the women are still weeping, the young male cousins are gathered in a corner recounting memories and drinking freely from their small chalices, and I am still standing at the foot of the bed.

When someone dies, time changes, and so it was that day. It seemed as if the afternoon had been preternaturally extended, the will of God on an otherwise bleak midwinter day. How like the caprice of nature to shift from the celebration of death over a long day into a night so sudden that I was incredulous when the men came through the bedroom door, recognizing them instantly as strangers. The men from the funeral home, come to take my father. Joe backed away from the door, as if he'd been struck. There must have been words of acquiescence, although I've long forgotten them, because these men moved swiftly and smoothly to my father's side and without words or explanation of any kind, transferred his inert form into a long black bag, zipped it up, and began to carry him from the room. There was an audible gasp from the group, because it was terrible in its suddenness, and we knew that my father's wish was to be cremated and therefore we would never see him again as we had known him. The weeping intensified as the men withdrew from the bedroom, as the women urged the children to stay behind, not to follow. But I followed and so did Joe, down the staircase so familiar to my father's step, out through the front door into the blackness, down the brick path my father had laid so many years ago, past the swing he had hung from the maple tree, under a brilliant canopy of stars, and into the back of a hearse, where we struggled to touch one last time his feet, his head, and Joe blocked the shutting of the door until one of the men put out a hand and rested it on his shoulder.

The hearse drove off, and I knew I would never see my father again in this lifetime, so I stood there until the vehicle had passed through the old stone gates and started its journey down the gravel road. I watched until the headlights were no longer visible, and then I turned, expecting to find Joe beside me. I'd felt him near me in the darkness all along, and even now I was sure he must be there, standing somewhere in the shadows, not wanting to be seen.

CHAPTER EIGHTEEN

When my father died, we held the wake at Derby Grange. The event was not traditionally Irish, his body was not displayed in an open casket so "that he might face the rising sun." His body had been incinerated and the ashes placed in a lovely wooden box. Everyone understood that the ashes given to us were an amalgamation of ashes scooped out of the crematory at the end of the day. Still, we accepted the box as the bones of our father, and spread the ashes over the front yard, in the bonfire, at the bases of trees that had been planted commemorating the birth of each grandchild. Lucy, when the box was passed to her, dipped her fingers in the ashes, made the sign of the cross, and put the ashes into her mouth. It was a striking gesture, one very foreign to the rest of us, and starkly moving on that gray winter's morning.

The wake was a proper party, which is what we'd anticipated, the house quickly filling with people we'd known for many years. Jenny and I applied our makeup in the upstairs bathroom, sharing the only well-lit mirror in the house. We laughed because we couldn't help it, as if this were just another great Derby Grange party, as if our mother weren't lying twenty feet away, in her old bed, in my childhood room, staring at the ceiling and thinking nothing. Lucy had seen to it that our mother had been safely ensconced in her old bedroom earlier in the day. With agonizing slowness, supported by Lucy on her left and me on her right, we had climbed the stairs, and when we reached the bedroom, my mother had immediately lain down. She would soon be asleep, her eyes would close suddenly, an unsettling transition from blank wakefulness to complete inertia. There would be no struggle to find sleep, no fluttering of the eyelids, no tossing and turning.

The party had all the elements of old: plenty of booze, good music, laughter rising and falling, a paucity of food. My father would have approved. I moved from one room to the next, greeting people I hadn't seen in years, listening to insignificant chatter and watching as the gathering gained animation, and voices were raised high above the din, some to the point of shouting. I heard, from across the dining room, "Katy Mulgrew, come over here! Come and see an old friend of yours!" The pitch and familiarity of this greeting struck me as vulgar, and I wanted nothing more than to retreat, but first I threaded my way through the throng of people and submitted to the embrace of a woman who, I knew, would not otherwise leave calmly. The banter was loud, inebriated, and clumsy. When my father was mentioned, it was with astounding gracelessness.

"Oh, you know we all loved T. J.! Jesus, he was one helluva guy! Are you still living in *New York*? Christ, how do you stand the *noise*?"

If my father had not died the day before, and if I had had one instead of three whiskeys, I'm sure I would have been able to exercise tolerance, but under the circumstances I found the woman's behavior appalling and couldn't wait to get out of there. When she turned away to talk to someone else she hadn't seen in ages, I slipped out of the room and ran up the front stairs and down the hall to where my mother lay sleeping. Quietly, I opened the door to the bedroom.

Lucy sat in the yellow damask armchair against the far wall, her feet on the ottoman, a table lamp illuminating the room with soft light. I put my finger to my lips and whispered, "Go to bed, Luce—I'll stay with her."

"You sure, señora?" Lucy asked, rising from the chair.

"Absolutely. I'm exhausted. Just going to crawl in next to her and pass out," I replied, removing my heels.

When Lucy had closed the door behind her, I slipped out of my dress and, finding an old nightgown in the closet, put it on and got into bed beside my mother. The lamplight infused the room with warmth.

I lay on my side, facing my mother, who slept as if she had been painted there, without movement, without sound. Muted laughter and conversation from downstairs floated up, emerging through the wall vent like sounds from an old radio show.

As very often happens when we are consumed with the busyness of life, a condition exacerbated by the occasion of death, we are shaken when, at last, we find ourselves useless. Some vestige of the hypervigilance I had practiced for two weeks remained with me as I lay in that bed with my mother, turning over in my mind the events that had led to my father's wake. Notwithstanding the disease that had hastened his death, what had caused my father to so categorically renounce his life? He deliberately chose not to fight, there was no passionate pronouncement of regret, he exhibited none of the steely reserve that in the past had characterized willfulness. He had accepted his imminent death with grace and quiet stoicism. At no time did my father show fear or resist that which was clearly inevitable. Instead, he allowed his guard to drop, revealing a man whose vulnerability would not now be judged, whose endurance would be honored. For two weeks, he had lain in his bed, listening to the chatter of his children, powerless to resist their ministrations. He responded to nothing, not with so much as the hint of a smile, and yet I felt his presence, and knew that he was there. Even as he slipped into unconsciousness, I had had the uneasy but unshakable impression that he was waiting for something.

Looking at my mother's face—vacant, masklike—I suddenly stiffened. My parents had had no closure, and it was for this that my father must have waited, hoping that my mother's last words to him would in some way validate the fifty years of their union. This, of course, was not to be. She had studied her husband for a moment, but she had not been perplexed when she drummed her fingers on his forehead and said, "Adiós, el señor." Everyone standing vigil had smiled at the strange idiosyncrasies of my mother's affliction, but not for a moment had anyone regarded her words as the death knell, and yet, that is what they were. If he was not already gone, those words ushered my father into oblivion.

How he must have resented those final years! Crossword puzzles, vodka, and a wife, whom he had once adored, slowly and inexorably losing her mind. Propping myself up on an elbow, I searched my mother's face for signs of stored secrets. Nothing to suggest disquiet in the unfurrowed brow, the set mouth, the closed eyes behind which no dreams stirred. She would not have been aware of it, had my father crept into her bedroom one night when, after a long day, Lucy had gone to bed and my mother was alone. She would not have known that he had stood looking down at her, glass in hand, slowly shaking his head, sure that he had been right about this thing and everyone else had been deluded, impulsive, moving with unforgivable speed and efficiency to consign his wife to madness.

If they'd just left her the hell alone, it would have worked itself out, he may have thought. Or maybe not. Having harbored similar feelings about Tessie, he understood the way of pernicious illness, and yet, this wasn't a helpless child with an inoperable brain tumor, this was Jicky, his *wife*, the girl with copper hair and intellectual chutzpah challenging him from atop a barstool, the slim, surprising, nimble mother of eight children, the passionate artist with open disdain for his love of drink, the partner who amused, the woman full of laughter and play, so essentially and incurably naughty, who lay before him immobile and utterly impassive. How could this be? my father must have thought. Or, worse, silently pleaded with her, C'mon, Jick, wake up!

The more likely scenario, and the one that expedited his demise, would have featured my father in a profoundly resigned and bitter state of mind, wherein every surge of resentment, every flush of impotence, every grief was vigorously, impatiently suppressed, and the glass brought hastily to his lips to vanquish the last drop of self-pity.

He never left the couch, never ventured beyond the confines of the TV Room, never once considered taking her with him. He never said good-bye, and maybe that's why the day he shattered his glasses wasn't one he considered altogether unlucky, but was instead the beginning of his escape from under this bell jar, this untenable and agonizing place where from one day to the next he was made to bear witness to the many creeping horrors that preyed on his wife's mind, stealing in a single hour her smile, the turn of her head, her step on the stair.

His only defense was resistance, a powerful exercise of the will that enabled him to defy Dr. Fortson, to scorn and belittle science, to withdraw entirely behind a façade of impregnable self-righteousness. His retreat from my mother's affliction was one of tremendous strategy and strength, almost equal in proportion to the depth of his love. But not quite. When the opportunity presented itself, he moved quickly. He measured his chances against hers and took the fast track. This way, at least, he could stop playing the game of pretense that left him utterly depleted by three o'clock in the afternoon, waiting only for the first drink, marking the threshold of a relief that would continue to elude him. This way, he would be vindicated, because she could not blame him. She would not know. She would never know.

I would like to think it is a mystery why my mother did not immediately confide in my father that certain doubts had begun to plague her, that she was feeling slightly off-balance and that occasionally whole thoughts were wiped from her mind by a swift, invisible authority that unsettled her and forced an unnatural silence, but it is not a mystery. This behavior subscribed to the unspoken tenets of their relationship, which held as its mandate that they should never be emotionally vulnerable to each other, that such exposure could only lead to trouble and, besides, it wasn't as attractive as the high road. They valued courage and honor above devotion, and withdrawal above displays of emotion or affection. They did not weep, they did not howl, they did not fight, they did not complain.

Whatever burned within each of them burned deeply and fiercely, but they were not the type to roar. The drama of their joined lives was made manifest in the stoicism of their grief, the contagion of their laughter, his hyperalertness to her presence, her willingness to persevere. They were never confidants, they never paraded as intimates, and yet their sheer tenacity in the face of difficulties, their remarkable ability to rise above the nearly unbearable, their patrician pride, and their respective minds—supple, witty, unorthodox—announced to anyone who had eyes to see that they were bound to each other, and that the arrangement would remain undisturbed.

In the end, she did not wish to disappoint, and he did not wish to be disappointed. A silence grew between them that may have been construed as a bridge, in the way of plodding sufferers everywhere, immersed in commiseration but lacking all empathy, but this interpretation would have been false.

My parents said good-bye to each other in much the same way they had said hello, those many years ago outside a Catholic church on a rainy day in Chicago, when they were as yet unknown one to the other.

PART TWO

My Mother

I have always known

That at last I would

Take this road, but yesterday

I did not know that it would be today.

ARIWARA NO NARIHIRA

CHAPTER NINETEEN

He was uxorious, my maternal grandfather. "What does that mean?" I'd asked my mother. I was twelve years old, and she'd fixed me with a look that stopped me cold.

"A man who loves his wife too much," she'd answered, and refused to say anything more.

I could not have understood then what I understand now, and it's a good thing, too. It would have prevented me from having even a semblance of the relationship I shared with my maternal grandfather who, when I was a young aspiring actress in New York City, would come in from New Jersey and take me and my friends out on the town. There was always a flower in his buttonhole and a kerchief in his jacket pocket, and I thought he was dapper, charming, and ebullient. Frank Kiernan spoke loudly and quickly and had a pronounced New Jersey accent. "Katy Mulgrew!" he'd shout, when I appeared at the designated meeting place, which was either Sign of the Dove on the Upper East Side or the Russian Tea Room on West Fifty-Seventh Street. There was a third place, a real joint in midtown, which he loved because it had a piano bar and low-hanging fringed lamps and an atmosphere of perpetual gaiety. We'd sit at the piano bar and order drinks and shrimp cocktails and laugh over the music and the noise and Grandpa Kiernan would ask about my mother.

"How's Joanie?" he'd yell, even though I was sitting right next to him, perched high on my barstool. He always referred to my mother as Joanie, something that didn't sit right, but who was I to argue? My grandfather must have thought that Joan Virginia was a good name for a Catholic girl born to a fairly affluent family in Upper Montclair,

New Jersey, in 1927. Secretly, I thought it didn't suit my mother at all. Too dull, too square. I'd answer politely enough, though, eager to get on with the business of eating and drinking, knowing I wouldn't get another meal like this for a long time. I tried to be engaging, bellowing anecdotes above the din, and Grandpa Kiernan in turn showed genuine interest in my passion, which was, of course, the theater. Having loved the circus all his life, he felt that the craft of acting was something shared by all people in the entertainment business: elegant ladies atop elephants, dwarves popping out of tiny cars, strong-torsoed men on the flying trapeze—weren't they performers, too? Wasn't it all the same magical world of make-believe? Although I took issue with this conflation of two very different worlds, I nodded and let my grandfather believe that he and I were, indeed, cut from the same cloth.

This period, during which I saw my grandfather every few months for lunch or dinner, was a challenging one for me. I was trying hard to become an actress, and life was not easy. While I did not think of him as particularly intuitive, Grandpa Kiernan called one day when I was really at my wit's end, and said he was coming into the city and that I should put on a pretty dress, he was taking me to lunch at the Russian Tea Room. I'd been there with him once before and leapt at the invitation. The Russian Tea Room was everything my life was not and allowed me to forget that in just a few hours' time I'd be back at Friar Tuck's Inn, zipped into a too-tight nylon uniform and flirting with old men in the desperate hope that they'd be moved by my extreme youth and pale prettiness and would, out of pity, leave me a generous tip. It was dark at Friar Tuck's, loud and chaotic and full of aspiring young actresses like me, waiting tables to make enough money to pay the monthly rent for a five-floor walk-up just south of the Bronx.

The Russian Tea Room, however, was a world unsurpassed in order and beauty, where waiters dressed like Cossacks dazzled the crowd bearing silver trays upon which sat crystal shot glasses of vodka or flutes of champagne or delicate china plates ornamented with caviar blinis. The booths were upholstered in red leather, the tables were draped in starched linen cloths, and the maître d' preceded me into the room with a stateliness and dignity that belied my rather questionable appearance. Anyone looking closely could see that I was wearing a costume, one that had been worn too many times and for far too many auditions: gray wool pleated skirt, white silk blouse, tailored double-breasted black jacket, and a pair of black classic Ferragamo pumps. I had coveted those shoes, had saved up for weeks in order to afford them, but after six months of hard walking in weather conditions that changed with startling regularity, they lacked any resemblance to what they once were. These were my audition shoes, my good luck slippers, and it was devastating to see them fail me.

Nothing daunted my grandfather, however, neither shabby shoes nor dampened spirits. Everything about the Russian Tea Room was evanescent, sublime, and we were to honor this exceptional ambience by sitting up straight, laughing delightedly, and cooing extravagantly over the chicken Kiev. My grandfather had long, white teeth, which he showed often and happily. It struck me, sitting there, that while there was a clear physical resemblance, I could find no other similarities between my grandfather and my mother. My mother was not loud, she did not bray, her smile was subtle.

Maybe this is what an uxorious man is like, I said to myself, observing my grandfather as he covered his lap with an oversize linen napkin.

"How is Natalie?" I inquired, referring to his current wife, a wife who never left New Jersey and seldom, if ever, ventured outside their condo in Upper Montclair.

"Oh, you know Natly!" my grandfather shouted, expertly reducing his wife's name to two syllables.

"Actually, Grandpa, I don't know her very well, but I'm curious about something. Why doesn't she ever come into the city with you? Doesn't she like New York?"

My grandfather slurped a forkful of beef Stroganoff, smacked his lips, and answered, "Oh, you know Natly! She likes her cards, she likes the club, she's a homebody!"

I'd met Natalie only a few times, and it was not hard to accept this explanation. She was a soft-spoken, simple woman who was content to while away her days watching television, playing cards, or having her hair done at the beauty salon conveniently located in the lobby of the high-rise where they lived. It was my impression that she was an indolent woman, and that she was in no way embarrassed to lie on her couch all day nibbling peanuts and leafing through beauty magazines. On the rare occasions in which we'd had what amounted to a conversation, she'd looked at me as if I belonged to another species.

How curious, I thought, glancing at my grandfather as I consumed a large piece of chicken dripping with warm butter, that he is what my mother calls uxorious, and yet his wife is neither fascinating nor beautiful. Natalie was Grandpa's third wife, and it was hard for me to square uxoriousness with the lethargic creature I'd met in their uniformly beige, shag-carpeted living room. Didn't uxoriousness imply desire? I wondered if perhaps uxoriousness really meant a kind of insatiable need, the need a certain type of man has to satisfy in order to call himself a man. It crossed my mind that any woman would do, as long as she was essentially dull and affable. Then another thought followed, one that confounded this possibility. Grandpa's wife before Natalie, a woman called Alfreda, was neither dull nor affable. Not only that, but she was, by all accounts, a very attractive woman. Lithe and soigné, she wore her frosted silver hair in a chignon, her features were made of ice, and in her heart there was very little room for anything that did not please her. It was possible Grandpa had married her before he had a chance to assess her character, but it was equally possible that he had no intention of examining her character beyond the need that presented itself to him, immediately and insistently. The need to have her as his wife.

"You never talk about Alfreda, Grandpa," I remarked, sipping from my champagne flute. "I'd love to know more about her. I mean, she was my mother's stepmother, wasn't she? She was important."

"Katy Mulgrew! You're just like Joanie! My God, could that kid ask questions! All the time. What about this, what about that? So many questions! How's your chicken Kiev?" he asked, wiping his mouth with the linen napkin in a gesture signifying that the end of the meal was near.

I knew it was pointless to persist, that in his mind Alfreda had vaporized into the mists of lore and was therefore no longer meaningful. I knew, too, that Alfreda was of singular importance to my mother and that my grandfather had conveniently compartmentalized the events of the past in order to make sense of the present. When children are very small, however, they are incapable of compartmentalizing, and so the incidents that shape them and the people who discard them are forever fresh. Alfreda met my grandfather shortly after he had lost his first wife, Florence, who had died giving birth to her third child. Frank Kiernan was too young and too untried to be considered uxorious in those years, years leading up to the Great War, and too flush and ambitious afterward as he careened into the Roaring Twenties. All he recognized was his own helplessness, and a paralyzing fear that he would fail as a father. It was in this interstice of intense anxiety and uncertainty that my grandfather met Alfreda and knew instantly that he would make her his bride, if she would have him. Alfreda had smiled coolly at him and said why yes, she'd be delighted to come for lunch and meet his children. Would this Sunday be too soon? my grandfather had asked.

Looking at the three small children, who were not much more than toddlers, Alfreda grew thoughtful. Frank, Joanie, and little Tony stood upright in their cribs and stared at her, their tiny faces sprinkled with freckles, their blue eyes alert and watchful. They were good children, attractive children, and Alfreda could see at a glance that intelligence shone in their eyes. Even the copper mops on their heads could be considered becoming, although the little girl's cap of red curls was a bit too vivid for Alfreda's taste.

The future stepmother calculated that she would have to endure no more than a few years of unpleasantness, by which time she would have Frank Kiernan so completely in her thrall that he'd do anything to please her. This is exactly what came to pass, and one day the children were told that they were no longer babies, that they needed a proper education, and that separating them would encourage independence. Therefore, my grandfather had explained, Frank would go to an uncle in Florida, Tony to relatives across town, and Joanie, the only daughter, would have the privilege of attending Sacred Heart Boarding School for Girls in Reading, Pennsylvania.

My mother went willingly. She had never trusted the stepmother with the frosted hair and ice blue eyes who had cast a spell on her father. Stoically, she walked away from the house of her childhood and into a world that would teach her how to forget.

During holidays, my mother would return to the large Queen Anne style house in Upper Montclair, over which Alfreda presided with an authority that embarrassed my mother. At the dinner table, she sat and watched as her father openly fawned over the woman he adored. The woman for whom he had discarded his children.

As soon as politeness allowed, my mother would excuse herself from the table and go to her room, which Alfreda had kept as it had always been, thinking this would soften my mother's heart. My mother was completely indifferent to Alfreda's intention, which was to win her over, and would have openly scorned this exercise in coercion were it not for the fact that Alfreda had failed to remove from her bedroom the one item that my mother coveted above all others. It was a photograph of my mother's real mother, Florence, taken shortly before her marriage to my grandfather. In the photograph she is in her bathing suit and her hair is still wet from the sea. She gazes at the photographer (whom one assumes must have been my grandfather) with the look of one very much in love. She is not conventionally pretty, yet she is wonderful to behold. There is nothing elegant or fragile about Florence, her bathing clothes are mismatched and her wet suit bottom clings to her ample thighs, about which she appears to be completely unconcerned. There is laughter in her eyes, and shyness, but in her high forehead and strong chin there is mettle and determination. She is unassuming and vital. My grandfather had seen in her what anyone who looks at the photograph can see clearly: she was authentic and would have considered any display of uxoriousness not only silly, but wasteful.

My mother would have sat on her childhood bed, holding the photograph, straining to remember her mother's voice, her touch, her smell. She had been three years old when Florence died, and her impressionable mind would perhaps have convinced itself of a memory and clung to it fiercely as a way to give meaning to the image she now held in her hands.

My mother would have lain back on the narrow bed, closed her eyes, and reached deep into the recesses of her memory until she was sure she could recall that night, the night before her mother went to the hospital to have Tony. The door to her room would have been half open, and her mother would have entered, her stomach huge with the baby soon to be born. Something in my mother's face, some perplexity, would have made Florence laugh, and she would have approached my mother's crib and lifted my mother into her arms and she would have told her that she loved her.

Florence did not return home. Very little was said. There was suddenly a vacuum where before there had been a mother. How frightening that shadow must have felt, falling across my little mother's life. How long, I wonder, did she wait for her mother to return? And how did she make sense of the sudden, awful disappearance of the only person in her world who really mattered?

My mother never did make sense of this first, terrible grief. It was never processed, it was never understood, and it was certainly never explained. The years passed, and my grandfather married Alfreda, who unwittingly did my mother a great service by sending her to a boarding school where she made friends, discovered God, and kept her sorrows to herself.

This beginning did not augur well for my mother. Her capacity to put her grief in cold storage was a device, not a solution. She would spend the rest of her life searching for her mother, and she would never find a suitable replacement because, of course, there can be no replacement for the real mother. This unfulfilled yearning could not be contained, it was bigger than my mother's stoicism, it undid her stiff upper lip and began to abrade her reason, but so slowly and with such deftness that it revealed itself as nothing more than eccentricity, a quality I could no sooner disassociate from my mother's personality than I could her love of art, her love of God, or her love of me.

CHAPTER TWENTY

We lived on Langworthy Avenue, I was three years old, and I remember:

The bright, hot sun on my naked, sturdy little body, the concrete sidewalk beneath my little feet, those feet pattering along at what I thought was a furious pace, turning to look behind me every few seconds, trying not to stumble. An injustice involving my mother had whipped me into a rage and I was on the lam. Stripping off my clothing and leaving my belongings behind, I had made my way out the front door and onto the sidewalk before she knew I was missing. I was filled with a sense of invincibility and believed that my legs were carrying me with great power and speed, and that she would see this and admire it. So complete was this sense of newfound independence that I almost felt sorry for her, sorry that it was necessary to part in this way. Still, I carried on, my cropped, feather-like hair lifted by the breeze, my face purple with indignation, my spirit rebellious. This time, I knew, she would be properly punished. My disappearance would put an end to the harsh rules imposed on me daily, and she would have her comeuppance.

Suddenly, I heard her calling my name, and my heart raced. I determined to run even faster, and felt myself tearing down the block, my feet hardly touching the ground. She called again: "Katy Kitten Kat Mulgrew, come back here!" Something in her voice was choked with emotion and, despite an effort at coolness, I was struck by it. Dare I turn my head for a second to see that she was not crying? Would my feet continue to land on the concrete if I attempted such a trick? Again, a garbled cry, this time even stronger, and I began to worry that maybe she would fall down, in her grief, and hurt herself.

I decided to risk it and slowed down just enough to turn my head and take a quick look behind me. My mother was not far away, but she had stopped still and was bent over, holding her stomach. I, too, stopped, afraid that she might be dying, and it was then that I saw my mother's eyes filled with tears and, in that moment, I forgave her everything, even as she offered a half-eaten banana with one hand and, with the other, clutched her side as she sank to her knees on the sidewalk. I waited.

Sobbing with laughter, my mother lay doubled over on the hot concrete. This sight infuriated me. Suffused with resentment and not entirely certain I had the upper hand, I planted my hands on my hips and decided to "rise above it." This was an oft-used phrase in the house on Langworthy Avenue and one I had come to believe meant something grown-up, and good. With careful, deliberate steps, I walked back down the street toward the house and, just as I passed my mother, turned my face away from her in a gesture of cool detachment. Having half risen to greet me, she again collapsed, shrieking with laughter.

When I reached the house, I paused to look at her, crumpled on the sidewalk in the midday sun, then walked through the open front door and closed it behind me.

CHAPTER TWENTY-ONE

Whenever my mother had a miscarriage, and according to her she had eighteen, a migraine was sure to follow. On at least two occasions, she called for me to bear witness as she baptized the fetal matter floating in the toilet.

"I baptize you in the name of the Father, and of the Son, and of the Holy Spirit, Amen," she'd say, then hold the handle down to make sure all the bits of bloody tissue made it down the drain and into the sewer. We had only one upstairs toilet and perpetually faulty plumbing, so the john was constantly backing up and overflowing, which was bad enough when trying to eradicate human waste but decidedly awful when a fragmented fetus kept reemerging.

This distressing ritual had no apparent emotional or physical repercussions, other than the predictable migraine headache, and even this affliction was borne with singular stoicism. My mother would start walking toward her bedroom and without turning would say to me, softly, "I'm having a sinking spell, Kitten. Get me a cold cloth and a ginger ale, would you, dear? And don't forget the bucket."

My feet could not carry me fast enough, as I somehow intuited that the cold cloth and ginger ale were the only effective palliatives in an otherwise dark vortex of pain. When I entered her bedroom, carrying a tray on which sat a small bowl of ice water, a washcloth, and a ginger ale, a metal pail hanging from my arm, my mother was already under the covers, her face barely visible in the late afternoon light. I knew not to turn on the lamp, or to move too quickly, or to speak too loudly. The cloth was to be thoroughly saturated with cold water, carefully wrung, then gently laid across her forehead. Following this, I needed to help my mother hold her head up while she sipped from the glass of ginger ale. This was tricky because any movement, however careful, could cause a sudden wave of nausea, which demanded a hypervigilance on my part, as it was imperative that I switch out the glass of ginger ale for the bucket before she threw up all over the bed. If I were successful in this endeavor, I would stand vigil over my mother and wait quietly until her groans subsided and she had fallen into what she called a "twilight sleep," which wasn't a sleep at all but rather a reckoning with pain so exquisite that she needed to concentrate her whole will on remaining as still as possible. She would suffer in this way for two to three days, emerging at last looking extremely pale and drawn.

It was then a race to the kitchen to see that the girl who worked for us had begun to prepare the only repast my mother could hold down: a soft-boiled egg accompanied by buttered toast and a cup of coffee with milk. This girl, whom we referred to as a "mother's helper," was invariably too slow at her task, and I would become increasingly agitated until, fed up, I would say, "It's okay, Doris, let me do it. You go and take care of the babies and make sure they don't come into the kitchen because Mother can't take any noise, all right?" Doris was a well-meaning girl, and she was actually quite helpful around the house and with the little ones, but any kind of drama threw her for a loop. She was in awe of my mother, and when these episodes occurred, she did not know how to react.

A place was set at the booth in the kitchen, and my mother would sit on the cushion and, taking the cup of coffee in her thin hands, would look at me over the rim and say, "You know, Kitten, you go blind when you have a migraine. That's why it needs to be dark. Any light is painful—it sears through the brain."

I knew I should not ask questions, that what she needed more than anything was food and quiet, and yet I could not resist.

"Is it unbearable?" I asked, handing her a piece of toast.

My mother nibbled at the edge of the toast then, dipping it into the soft yoke of the egg, said, "It is absolute agony."

There never seemed to be any acknowledgment of the miscarriages, despite the attendant migraines. In those years, my mother accepted pregnancy as the will of God, a will made manifest by my father's libido. Acceptance and appreciation are two entirely different states of mind, however, and in the evening, when his car was heard coming down the gravel road, my mother moved like lightning. If she was reading a book, she threw it on the coffee table; if she was working on a painting, she abandoned it; if she was with me, she'd whisper as she ran out through the kitchen on her way upstairs, "Tell your father I'm having a terrible sinking spell and I've gone to bed!"

Confronting my father with this reality was scary, and I needed to brace myself before delivering the bad news. He'd come through the back door, allowing the screen door to bang shut, and look into the kitchen expectantly. When he did not immediately see my mother, he'd hang up his coat, fix himself a drink, and then stand in the middle of the kitchen for a moment before asking, "Where's your mother?"

I'd look up as casually as possible from my book and answer, "She had to go to bed—she was having a sinking spell."

My father would allow his eyes to stay on me a fraction too long, and then he would go into the TV Room, where he had a view of the upstairs master bedroom through the small window on top of the TV Room door. He might stand there for a good two or three minutes, during which time he may well have seen the sliver of light coming from the master bedroom suddenly snuffed out, thereby precluding any possibility of enjoying his wife's company that night.

In the morning, my mother would be up early and busy in the kitchen preparing breakfast. What this meal consisted of I cannot now remember, as I have no recollection of ever having been served a normal breakfast. Breakfast was simply not an important meal and we learned young not to expect it. There might have been the odd piece of cold-buttered toast, and once she unwittingly bought a box of Pop-Tarts, which threw us into a frenzy so extreme that within minutes we were at each other's throats over possession of the unheard-of treat.

"You see?" she said, regarding us with disgust. "Not worth it."

When my father walked into the kitchen, adjusting his tie and looking very handsome, we all paused to assess his mood. My mother did not look up from her position at the stove but asked him if he wanted a cup of coffee.

"I'll get it," my father replied, gruffly.

The atmosphere in the room was suddenly unpredictable, as if a line of tension had been drawn between my father pouring coffee and my mother at the stove. They didn't look at each other, nothing was said, but we sensed our father's obvious displeasure as acutely as we did our mother's apparent indifference. Moments of sustained silence would pass during which we would try to pretend nothing was wrong, and yet found ourselves mysteriously reduced to whispers and sign language.

After my father had left, placing his coffee cup too loudly in the basin of the sink, my mother would visibly relax, and into the pan on the stove she'd add a tablespoon of butter, a handful of sliced onion, and a piece of liver, which she would sear and subsequently devour. I'd wrinkle my nose and groan at the sight of the slippery brown organ meat covered with onions. My mother would smile and say, "You don't know what's good."

"Yes, I do, and it's definitely not that putrid stuff! Why do you like it so much?" I'd ask, genuinely perplexed.

"I crave it because I have an iron deficiency and because I know it is the one thing you kids won't touch. Heaven," she'd say, smacking her lips lightly.

After she'd driven me to school, she'd put the car into park and looking out the window, as if lost in thought, would suddenly whisper conspiratorially, "Why don't you go to the nurse's office after lunch, tell her you're sick, and I'll pick you up and we'll go to the movies?"

This suggestion was always met with an exclamation of delight, regardless of what my scholastic obligations may have been, and my mother would be waiting for me in her station wagon at the appointed hour.

The afternoon would be spent sitting in a near-empty darkened movie theater in downtown Dubuque, riveted for hours to whatever film my mother wanted to see.

If it was *Doctor Zhivago,* she'd say afterward, "Adultery in Siberia—ghastly."

If it was *The Sound of Music,* she'd say, "I hope Christopher Plummer was nicer to Julie Andrews than he was to Tammy Grimes."

If it was *Butch Cassidy and the Sundance Kid,* she'd say, "You know, you look like Katharine Ross, only prettier."

And if it was *Gone with the Wind,* she'd look at me penetratingly and challenge me to tell her who the real heroine of the movie was. Then, without waiting for my response, she'd declare, "Melanie, of course! Completely selfless."

Treats were never allowed because, as she often stated with conviction, "Eating in the movies is strictly for losers."

Instead, we would drive to Long John Silver's, my mother's preferred fast-food establishment, and tuck into baskets of fried cod and shrimp, accompanied by generous portions of French fries. She'd lean across the table and whisper, "You know and I know it's really catfish, but who cares? Anything deep fried is divine."

Her spirits restored, we would drive home discussing the merits and flaws of the movie we'd seen, with the implicit understanding that no one would ever know about our stolen afternoon. My mother at no time warned me to keep it a secret, as such a direct order would have been demeaning to both of us. She'd had a miscarriage, she'd had a migraine, this was her reward for having overcome them both, and who better to share it with than her oldest daughter, the one whom she had asked to bear witness.

CHAPTER TWENTY-TWO

It began when I was still very young, far too young to attach any great importance to it, and yet even then the faraway look in my mother's eyes unsettled me. I see her standing over the kitchen sink, in the gray afternoon light, wearing her soiled apron and pretending to do the dishes. She despised doing the dishes, and therefore she washed them with a carelessness that stopped just short of sloppiness. The glass would be dipped in the murky water, then lifted and placed negligently on the sideboard, no cleaner than it had been before. She would handle the dirty dishes robotically, never looking at them, never with a view to improving them, her slender hands moving in and out of the water, her simple gold wedding band glinting on her ring finger.

If I were coming into the kitchen with the intention of talking to my mother, the sight of her standing over the sink would stop me short. She was there, and yet she was not there. I sensed this as a deviation from the normal and would hide myself where I could watch her unobserved, stepping onto the base of the back staircase, leaning quietly against the wall. My mother's gaze would be fixed on the view outside the kitchen window, on the cornfields and the apple orchard and the line of evergreen trees that led to a small grove, in the middle of which stood a statue of St. Francis. She gazed, but she did not focus. Hers was an inward turning, producing almost a trancelike state. It was not the stillness of her form or the stepping away from reality that so unnerved me, but the vacancy in her eyes. It was clear that she saw nothing, that her mind was at a standstill, and that whatever was causing this torpor was as powerful as a drug. My mother was inert, unresponsive to her surroundings, and lost entirely in another world.

From the vantage point of my hiding place, I studied her face with intense curiosity, and the longer I looked the more anxious I became. Her blue-gray eyes appeared spiritless to me, no sign of life flickered in them. A fear crept over me, one that I experienced as a coldness in my hands and feet, and one that also defined the physical distance between my mother and myself as unbridgeable, existing, as we did in that moment, in two completely disparate realities. Strangest of all was the profound sadness I felt at witnessing my mother in this state, and I somehow grasped that she, too, was filled with an ineffable sense of loss. Most disturbing of all was her extreme detachment. It was as if she were someone I had never known. I desperately wanted to wrench her from this state, to restore her to the mother I knew, and yet, I couldn't move. I was transfixed.

When waiting for my mother to return to herself became unbearable, the time of her absence too attenuated, I would step lightly into the kitchen and, standing behind her, whisper, "Mom, what are you doing?"

She never jumped, my interruptions never startled her, she would immediately return to the present, but she would retain a thoughtfulness that continued to bother me. I yearned to know where she had gone, what had pulled her so far away, and yet, standing in the kitchen alone with my mother, I did not ask, and she offered no explanation. Instead, she would drop the glass she was pretending to wash into the water, as if she couldn't bear to hold it for another second. The dishes were often left like this, piled in a basin half filled with cloudy water, a dirty gray washcloth floating amid the debris.

Turning, my mother would acknowledge me, but give no indication that I may have caught her in the act of doing something strange. From her perspective, she had been daydreaming over dirty dishes, enjoying a brief respite from the endless responsibilities of motherhood. Still, I knew that what she had been engaged in was not mere daydreaming, nor had she been lost in thought. My mother had truly gone away, disappearing behind eyes that no longer saw the fields outside the window, into a shadow-world where perhaps nothing existed at all.

As disconcerting as these episodes were, they were dispelled by the usual bedlam at dinner, over which my mother presided with an air of tired resignation. Tucking into my portion of jambalaya, I would steal glances at her, worried that she might be considering another disappearance. I wondered if my mother's trances were brought on by a disappointment she may have felt, a longing for something she once had that now completely eluded her grasp. Most of all, I worried that wherever she had gone, she had gone without me. I resolved to bring my mother into the present, so that I would not be left alone again, exiled to a place where I could see her, but where she could not and would not see me.

A very effective way of pulling my mother into the present was to suggest that she have a dinner party. Although my mother was a terrible housekeeper, neither this nor her pauper's budget deterred her from throwing dinner parties.

Food was the least of her concerns, as she laid the large oval table in the dining room with mismatched china plates and twisted half-burned candles into the pockets of a silver candelabra. She was a skilled seamstress, and the dinner table was always adorned with a colorful tablecloth and napkins. If she were in a particularly festive mood, she would place the napkins into the wineglasses and tug them into bloom. It was an artist's table, and by the time the guests sat down to eat, the drama was well under way, and my mother had already begun to show signs of weariness. She resisted this impulse with bravado and would initiate an argument with the guest on her right, who was invariably a priest, a painter, or a con man. If he was a con man, the argument ended in laughter. If he was a painter, it ended in mutual admiration. And if he was a tall, strapping Irishman wearing a Roman collar, it ended in romance.

Love affairs percolated in the house all the time; it was a heady, boozy place full of low light and music, with children underfoot, a fire crackling beneath the marble mantel over which hung an enormous gilt-framed mirror, reflecting all the people at the table who, illuminated by candlelight, appeared lovelier and more sensuous than they ever could in the cold light of day. These evenings unfolded in stages, each one of which provided a stepping-stone to the next until, at last, my mother would slip from her chair and steal away, never saying good night, never saying good-bye. Again, she had disappeared so artfully that it was some time before her absence was noticed, and by then the remaining guests would have been lost in worlds of their own, with the possible exception of the Irish priest who, while noting my mother's disappearance, nonetheless rose and moved to the other end of the table, where he pulled up a chair next to my father and helped himself to another glass of wine.

CHAPTER TWENTY-THREE

Children born into large families have a curious habit. When asked if we have siblings, we are inclined to answer in an almost military fashion and, not without a sense of pride, we call out those who have shared our upbringing. We are wont to count those who have died, as well as those who have survived. Tom, Kate, Joe, Maggie, Laura, Tess, Sam, Jenny. There's rhythm in that lineup, if you like jazz. We never had the full lineup at once, which is a palpable regret. Tess, Sam, and Jenny never knew Maggie, and little Maggie, given only a few months to live, knew no one at all. In the Catholic community where I grew up, bewildering sorrows like Maggie proliferated, but were not considered unusual. Babies died for all kinds of mysterious reasons, were buried in tiny caskets in the family plot, and life went on.

My father bought a small nineteenth-century estate on the outskirts of town, which we called Derby Grange. In that verdant place, on those forty acres of land, we thrived. We were allowed to run free, almost virtually without supervision. My brother Tom, older than me by a year, naturally assumed leadership and often led expeditions which, in hindsight, came perilously close to real danger. It delighted him if we were lost, he was amused by our helplessness, and for some unaccountable reason he always emerged from these harrowing adventures unscathed and undaunted. When we returned home to find our mother hunched over the kitchen table, thoroughly engaged in sculpting a miniature clay figurine, she'd say, "Don't bother me. I'm working on Jesus."

"But we're hungry," Joe would retort, tired and irritable after having endured yet another journey into the snake-infested timberland, where Tom had convinced us that spearing frogs was imperative in case we were permanently lost and faced starvation.

"Go outside and pull some rhubarb out of the patch," our mother advised, intent on the microscopic head of Christ.

In the singular dynamic shared by siblings very close in age, we were bound to one another whether we wanted to be or not. Tom's easy personality was the perfect antidote to Joe's pugnacity, and both of them exulted in making fun of me and did so continually until I turned on them with dire warnings of what would happen to them if they did not stop. Teasing was by far the most effective means of communication, and we developed it into a fine art. We tested one another, we shaped one another, and we depended on one another. We were the three oldest, and therefore we were entitled to form a collective that stood apart from the rest and removed us from exercising too much responsibility over our younger brothers and sisters, whom we referred to as the Smalls.

It's not that we didn't like the Smalls. They were necessary to our ongoing sense of superiority and were often amusing in their own right. Laura, who was two years younger than Joe, was neither a Big nor a Small, falling, as she did, in the middle. She stood alone, and very early on developed an independence that separated her from the rest of us. As a result, her accomplishments were more unexpected; we marveled at her double-jointedness, her acrobatics, and her dazzling dance steps. She was a natural athlete, and we regarded this as both a gift and a curiosity.

Therese Louise followed Laura, and she, too, quickly revealed a personality that was not typical. Neither Laura nor Tessie looked like the rest of us, but in entirely different ways. Whereas Laura was slim and pale, her head a mass of ash blond curls, her large blue-gray eyes fringed with light lashes, Tessie was strong-limbed and green-eyed, her olive complexion an exception in this otherwise fair-skinned, freckled family. She had a muscular little body, and supple limbs, and it was not uncommon to find her climbing tall trees. It was even less surprising to find that she could scale walls if she climbed quickly enough, plopping to the ground on her bottom, her sturdy legs splayed in a wide V. Climbing was her sport, and her object of affection was my father, who pretended impatience with her hijinks but laughed when she sprang onto his shoulders, clinging to tufts of his thick black hair. He nicknamed her Creature, but we knew we were not to use that name ourselves. This was a special nickname which my father alone was entitled to use and, although it singled Tessie out and may even have been interpreted as a sign of favor, none of us seemed to mind.

While Laura danced, and Tessie crawled, the two youngest were relegated to another world entirely. Sam and Jenny were the babies of the family; small, curious, and unkempt, they toddled around the house in a perpetual hunt for forbidden treasure, which could mean anything from my mother's attention to a dead mouse fossilized under the couch. Very early on, it became apparent that although they may have resembled each other physically, there was no such similarity in their personalities. Whether extroverted by nature or by necessity, Jenny soon became outspoken and strong-willed, demanding my mother's attention and defiant if she did not get it. Very often she did not get it, and this advanced a gene that might otherwise have lain dormant. Jenny was smart and observant and quickly ascertained that a sure way to our mother's heart was to entertain her. My sister became an expert mimic and learned to impersonate all of us, which delighted my mother and earned Jenny a place at the dining room table.

Sam was the outlier. Although a year older than Jenny, he showed none of her aggressiveness. Instead, he was remarkably self-contained and spent hours in his own company. Sam's happiest day came when Mother took him to see *Jeremiah Johnson*, a movie he loved featuring a character with whom he so identified that for months afterward he took to stalking the grounds wearing an oversize cowboy hat, a long blade of grass sticking out of his mouth. We called him Buck because he had a rather unfortunate overbite, a flaw made less and less apparent by his transformation into a quiet, questing cowboy, alone on the Grange.

There was a time of grace, when my mother started painting in earnest, and the house simmered with life. Though she was far from a skilled pianist, when she sat and played in the early evening I stopped whatever I was doing to listen. Her fingers, long and slender, falling lightly on the keys, promised safety. Her dinner parties, more extravagant than ever and more bountiful, stretched into the early morning hours. My father grudgingly attended these parties and was always reluctant to see them end. He and my mother went away for a long weekend to Aspen, where my father could spend his days on the ski slopes and my mother could amuse herself going to art galleries. When they returned, my mother seemed distracted and nervous, but I put this down to her disappointment at having to return to the domestic grind.

Over a period of weeks, perhaps months, something had begun to happen to Tessie. We weren't paying attention, we were busy living our own lives, so we didn't find out until much later. We were a robust family, and ours were parents who tended to ignore complaints of constant, throbbing headaches, who did not find crossed eyes amusing, and who considered tears cloying. In our world, it was impossible to imagine that, behind Tessie's dancing green eyes, something pernicious and indestructible had taken root.

CHAPTER TWENTY-FOUR

In the months before Tessie was diagnosed with an inoperable brain tumor, my mother and I were busy attending to my future. We agreed that high school was a waste of time, so if I was late for a class or skipped one altogether in order to sit at the kitchen table absorbing my mother's counsel, it was accepted as necessary. If I had been a more attentive student, and my mother had been a stronger disciplinarian, it is likely I would have had a very different future. In my early quest to become an actress, these late morning or early afternoon conclaves became imperative, and we would gather at the kitchen table, heads together, animatedly discussing our shared goal.

"You'll need to be classically trained, if you want to be a serious actress, and if you want to be a great actress you better get started on the Shakespearean canon. Apply to the Cherub program at Northwestern University, or the Guthrie Theater in Minneapolis—they must have a summer program for kids! Get going! Whatever you do don't give up your job at the coffee shop and take double shifts at the Holiday Inn because you know, and I know, that Daddy is not going to spring for this."

At fourteen, I was a short-order cook at Pete's coffee shop on the weekends and worked Friday and Saturday nights serving cocktails at the Holiday Inn, where no one ever thought to ask how old I was.

"Come on, Mother, Dad will give me *something*, won't he?"

"Don't count on it. Your father has never subscribed to the theory that work is happiness. And by the way, Daphne darling, watch your figure," my mother said, using the name of a character she'd found in a Mitford novel, one that allowed her to send important messages in the guise of playfulness.

"Nobody," she added, "likes a fat leading lady."

Occasionally, we would be interrupted by the phone ringing. Mother would jump as if spooked and, looking at me, would frantically mime that I should answer it. Unaccountably, since the phone was still ringing, and we were alone in the kitchen, I would mime back *why?* in response to which she would lift her hand and draw it slowly across her throat. I was baffled. Why did my mother regard the phone ringing as a prelude to her execution? Nonetheless, I did her bidding, only to hear Father O'Byrne's voice on the other line.

"Oh, hi, Father O'Byrne, how are you?" I'd ask, which was all that was needed to send my mother flying. She was up and out of her chair in seconds, pausing only to mouth *"Not home"* before running from the kitchen into the dining room, where she evidently felt she could eavesdrop with impunity.

When the phone call had ended, my mother reappeared and sat on the edge of her chair, looking at me intently.

"What did that jerk have to say?" she asked, to my astonishment.

"Jeez, Mother, take it easy. He's a priest, you know, and they don't like being called jerks. But since we're on the subject, *why* do you think he's a jerk?" I asked, rising to refill our coffee cups.

"He's so full of himself it's unbearable. God's gift to Catholic mothers everywhere," she scoffed, looking out the window.

I poured a dollop of milk in my mother's cup and waited for her to speak. When she turned back to me, her expression had changed completely. Not ten seconds earlier, she'd clearly been furious, but now, lifting the coffee to her lips, she suddenly appeared very young and very vulnerable. She looked into my eyes as if searching for something, then dropped her gaze and whispered, "I must be out of my mind."

Instinctively, I pulled back. I wasn't at all sure that I wanted to know why she must be out of her mind. The entire episode, brief as it had been, had a chilling effect on me, and I knew that our conversation about my future as an actress was over.

When it happened again, two weeks later, the same pantomime was repeated, only this time I was annoyed and let her know it.

"You're acting sort of childishly, Mother, you know," I said, when she again emerged from the dining room and again sat gingerly on the edge of her chair. "What's going on?" I demanded.

My mother lowered her head and shook it rapidly from side to side, as if trying to dislodge a sharp hairpin.

"I don't know, Kitten, but it's awful."

"How awful?" I persisted, despite her evident distress.

It was then that she looked at me directly and a shift took place, one in which she decided to take a risk.

"I don't know how it happened," my mother whispered.

"How *what* happened, Mom?" I asked, my own voice dropping.

"Oh, Kitten, you *know* what I'm talking about. It's agony. Like a sickness."

It suddenly struck me that Father O'Byrne had visited the house a lot more in the past year than he ever had before. Everyone understood that he was a very important priest and in demand at Catholic seminars and conferences all over the country. Tall and imposing, Kevin O'Byrne was a well-traveled and sophisticated priest, one who drank easily with my father, and laughed heartily. It was obvious that my father admired him, and that is why the priest was given entrée to the house at any time, and why he was so graciously received. My father's veneration for Father O'Byrne allowed the priest every privilege, and though these privileges appeared innocent on the face of it, they were, as it turned out, very dangerous. O'Byrne and my mother under the maple tree, my father inside making drinks, leaving them undisturbed. O'Byrne and my mother walking slowly down the gravel road, alone. O'Byrne and my father, heads thrown back in mirth, and my mother's face, white as chalk. O'Byrne approaching the front door, and my mother, seeing him, taking to the stairs but caught by my father's

voice calling, "Jick, O'Byrne is here—come on, let's have a drink!"
O'Byrne and my mother embracing in the orchard during a summer
party, the kitchen full of noise, the house crammed with people, and
Joe crashing through the back door, shocked and livid with rage.

"I'd give my right hand never to have met him," my mother said,
and I believed her. From that moment forward, I was complicit in a
love affair I didn't fully understand, nor did I want to. I was intuitive
enough to sense that this entanglement was harrowing for my mother,
and that the shame it fomented ate at the very core of her being, but I
was too young to understand it on a deeper level. My mother longed
to believe, if only for a few years, that she was understood and adored,
and that having a love affair with a priest was somehow the price one
paid for such an unfathomable need.

Over the following months, we devised a shorthand when referring
to Father O'Byrne, one that allowed us to talk about the situation without taking it too seriously. It was my mother's way of managing something over which she had no control, a tool she had needed to learn as
a young girl and one that protected her from the intolerable nature of
the truth.

"He thinks he's a big star, you know—big star of the diocese, with
his golf tournaments and dinner invitations and every woman in town
fawning all over him. When he's on the altar, it's nothing but a big
show," she said, working herself into a lather.

"You don't know that, Mother," I countered, attempting to salvage
some semblance of propriety.

"I know what goes on in the sacristy, and I can promise you, he's
full of it." She spat out the words. Her feelings were strung on a live
wire, and I was frightened.

"Maybe that's what we should call him," I suggested, pretending
indifference.

"What?" my mother demanded. "What should we call him?"

"Star!" I declared, triumphantly.

My mother laughed and then clapped her hand over her mouth like a girl, as if she'd been caught in the middle of a prank.

"That is perfection," she said, a glint in her eye, a half sob mangled in her throat. "From now on, he will be known as Star."

My mother gave me the impression that she wanted desperately to be rid of O'Byrne, but this was hard to square with her ongoing, passionate response to him, one that was both physical and emotional. She expressed to me her great wish that she'd never met him and, for the most part, I believed her, but there was a part of me that found her desire for him not only bewildering, but repugnant. While I could understand my father's deficiencies and how they might dampen my mother's enthusiasm for the marriage, I could not justify her ardor for a Roman Catholic priest. It occurred to me, only much later, that she had been seduced by the very thing that was most forbidden in her world, and perhaps this was the ultimate allure. An unheard-of secret that she alone possessed but could not quite bear to shoulder all by herself led her to seek vindication in her fifteen-year-old daughter's eyes. As was true of most of her deeper yearnings, she was incapable of dabbling, so she continued with the priest until the day she found Tessie curled into a ball at the base of the stairs, grasping her head with both hands, tears streaming down her cheeks.

When my mother learned that Tessie had a tumor the size of a grapefruit in her brain, and that it could not be removed without permanent damage, that this malignancy was, in fact, called a "butterfly" tumor because of the insidious way in which it had spread its wings throughout the matter within the very organ that had, only weeks before, inspired my sister to leap onto my father's shoulders—when all of this had been explained and a death sentence guaranteed, my mother cast O'Byrne out and began to prepare for the crucible from which she would emerge indelibly changed.

CHAPTER TWENTY-FIVE

It lasted a long time. My mother had to endure the unraveling of her beautiful twelve-year-old daughter. Each week, something new and impossible to let go of was sacrificed, and it was my mother who served as Tessie's guide across this minefield. She watched as the headaches increased in intensity, causing my sister to weep, and then as her vision became affected, one green eye moving fractionally, relentlessly to the right. She watched as her daughter's mobility became impaired to such an extent that Tessie needed to be taken out of school because the other children were beginning to make fun of her unpredictable pratfalls, and this deprivation was the hardest of all because then she was consigned to home, to the isolation that sickness imposes, to the abominable acceptance that there was no way out.

On the face of it, life went on. There were still three other young children at home, and they needed to be cared for. The three oldest—Tom, Joe, and me—made plans hard and fast, and moved on them as quickly as we could. I left home early, having graduated from high school at the end of my junior year, and moved to New York, where I attended New York University and studied acting at the Stella Adler Studio. My brothers went off to college, Tom to McGill in Montreal, and Joe to Assumption College in Worcester, Massachusetts. Laura, Sam, and Jenny were still in grade school, a time when children are most impressionable and in need of a mother's care. Of this crucial element there was a distinct paucity, but because my siblings loved their sister, they did not complain. Whatever frustration, resentment, or anger they harbored (and I now believe they must have battled these feelings daily), they treated Tessie with unflagging tenderness.

Still. Within the walls of a house that had at one time resounded with laughter, where life had for so long been lived audaciously, there suddenly existed a new and unsettling delicacy. A strange, inarticulable decorum was imposed on the young ones as a result of Tessie's sickness, and this must have frightened them more than anything else. Though they longed for their mother, at the same time they must have resigned themselves to her absence, a conflict that undoubtedly compromised all three of them.

There was, of course, a succession of mother's helpers to assist with the chores, and friends were attentive and generous with their time. The disease followed a wayward course, during which there were periods of stability. Conversely, there were weeks when Tessie had been completely immobilized and would suddenly appear in the dining room as we ate, a specter floating from chair to chair as we watched in astonishment. The tumor wending its way upward in her brain controlled my mother's actions, as well as Tessie's. Initially, my mother tried her best to live with the death sentence that had been imposed on her daughter, but ultimately the terror of what was to come, combined with the memory of what once was, worked to abrade my mother's nerves, and over time she developed a detachment that filled us with a new kind of fear. The two of them were linked, my mother and my sister, and they would go together.

On my visits home, which, admittedly, were insufficient to in any way help my mother or ease her pain, I would nevertheless try to steal her away from Tessie's bedside for an hour or two for a heart-to-heart. At twenty, I had become a professional actress, and Tessie's battle with cancer had lasted for more than two years. I tried to entertain my mother with anecdotes about my life in New York, but very soon the subject would lose its flavor, and her eyes would assume the old vacancy that frightened me so much.

"What are you thinking about, Mums?" I asked, putting my hand over hers. We were sitting at the kitchen table having coffee, as had been our habit for years.

Almost wistfully, my mother looked at me and said, "I'm thinking that if your father goes into Tessie's bedroom, I'll kill him."

By this time, my mother and Tessie had moved into what we called The Addition, a partition that had been built onto the back of the original house when my father reached the limits of his patience, and wanted the chaos of laundry, garbage, winter coats, and cartons of empty beer bottles to be confined to one area, so that guests entering through the front door would not be assaulted by the sight of such mayhem. The Addition was a narrow, dreary room lined with a grimy linoleum floor, on which rested a washing machine and dryer, my mother's old-fashioned sewing table, an ironing board, a refrigerator, a table that ran almost the entire length of the space, and a bulletin board attached to a wall that separated the bathroom, which my father had grudgingly installed, from the bedroom. On that bulletin board, my mother often tacked quotes, the favorite of which had been written in her distinctive, looping hand: *Never resist a good impulse.* This is where my mother settled herself and her daughter in the final months of Tessie's life.

The vitriol with which my mother spoke these words alarmed me deeply, and I realized that she had chosen my father as the receptacle for all of her impotent rage. He was the only person she felt she could blame with impunity—after all, he was the one who had wooed her with such tenacity, with such assuredness, whose countless letters showed a single-mindedness: *I can't offer you the easiest life in the world—you know that. But it'll be fun and, because our love will be based on love of God, I feel confident that He'll see us through the rough spots. If He won't, I will. Either way you're covered. You might as well hang up your spikes, sugar—this is the McCoy.*

He had not made good on his promise, life was not fun, and God was not seeing them through the rough spots. My father had been tried and found guilty. To compound this growing alienation, my father sold his asphalt business and, having nothing to do and nowhere to go, consigned himself to mowing the lawn for hours every day. Despite his loneliness, my mother would not speak to him, nor would she permit him access to the back room unless it had been planned in advance, and even then, these visits with his dying daughter were tightly controlled.

In the evenings, my father poured himself a drink and settled into his place on the couch in the TV Room. Several more drinks would follow, until he felt the first wave of deliverance from the guilt that had gnawed at him all day. As midnight struck, he would stumble upstairs and fall onto the bed he had once shared with his wife, slipping into a torpor so profound that he did not wake until ten o'clock the following morning, when he knew, even before he opened his eyes, that the nightmare was destined to begin all over again.

On a hot July morning, my mother opened the window in the back bedroom so that she and Tessie could listen to the birds singing in the orchard. It is doubtful that, in the last moments of my sister's life, she was capable of hearing anything, but it is certain that my mother heard them, as she sat on the narrow twin bed and stared at her fourteen-year-old daughter. My mother watched as the tumor pushed its way through Tessie's eyes, a struggle that lasted nearly two hours, and during this struggle my mother understood that the birds outside had stopped singing, and that something terrifying and unbidden was about to overwhelm her.

CHAPTER TWENTY-SIX

Immediately following Tessie's funeral service in the front yard, my mother went upstairs to her room and locked the door. When she did not soon reappear, my father climbed the staircase and called to her. She did not respond.

"Jick," my father said, quietly approaching the closed bedroom door, "we've got to go to the cemetery now. It's time."

From within, there was silence. My father began to plead.

"Come on, Jick, we have to do this together. I can't do it without you."

Minutes passed. My father rested his forehead against the hard wood of my mother's bedroom door. His hand, placed flat against the door, was trembling.

"Please, Jick," he pleaded.

As the minutes passed, my father's anxiety turned to resignation and, turning from my mother's door, he made his way down the front stairs and walked slowly to the driveway, where Tessie's coffin was waiting for him.

My mother waited until the last car had driven away. Then she pushed herself up from the floor, where she had been laying, and moved toward the closet. Without thinking, she pulled a few items from hangers, and stuffed them into a faded red duffel bag. Opening the bedroom door, she paused. Hearing no movement downstairs, she descended the stairs and made her way through the dining room, the kitchen, until she arrived in The Addition, where her daughter had died only the day before.

Standing at the door of the bedroom where Tessie and my mother had spent so many weeks was a tall, dark-haired woman whose face had once been pretty. This woman, whose name I will not mention, had loved my father for many years, but whether theirs was a realized love is immaterial. What is important is that this woman, with her elegant, worn features, had immediately forsaken my father when she learned that Tessie was going to die, and had turned her allegiance to my mother. For many months, she had assisted my mother, and the two women had worked together to make my sister's final months as tender and painless as possible. It is perhaps fortunate that neither woman could have imagined the grotesquerie of Tessie's last hours.

Unsurprised, my mother looked at the woman, and put her hand on the doorknob. When she opened the door, she felt the woman's hand on her arm, and allowed herself to be led down the short brick path to her car. Opening the car door, the woman who had once loved my father kissed my mother's cheek and said, "Good-bye, Joan. Be careful."

On that sunny July day, while Tessie was being interred at Asbury cemetery, my mother drove away from Derby Grange and kept driving until she arrived at Our Lady of the Mississippi Valley Abbey, where Mother Columba stood waiting for her at the top of Abbey Hill Lane.

WEEKS LATER, WHEN my mother returned home, I found myself pacing back and forth in the kitchen. When I heard her car pull up, the pacing stopped, and I waited. Moments later, my mother walked into the kitchen, carrying her red duffel bag. She was gaunt, and very pale. Around her head she had wrapped a large red kerchief, of the kind my father habitually tucked in his trouser pocket. The kerchief rode low on her brow and, when she had finally been coaxed to sit down and a cup of coffee placed in her hands, I knelt beside her and gently pushed the kerchief back from her forehead. Reflexively, I gasped. Her forehead was kneaded with bruises, the abrasions purple and raised.

Seeing the expression on my face, my mother looked at me and smiled, a smile of inexpressible weariness, and said, "Oh, Kitten, don't you know? That's what happens when you beat your head against a wall."

CHAPTER TWENTY-SEVEN

My first husband was a theater director, and I sobbed violently as we drove through the stone gates of Derby Grange the day after our wedding, down that long gravel road and into a new life. My mother stood in the middle of the driveway, her right hand held high, her expression inscrutable. Was she thinking, It's about time, she's twenty-seven years old, or was she perhaps reading in the tea leaves of her imagination that two months later I would be on the phone shrieking, "I'm pregnant, can you believe it? Jesus, I just got married!"

Three months later, after my beautiful towheaded son was born, I flew to Dubuque to show him off to my mother. She was unimpressed, which I found deeply perplexing, but worse than this was her appraisal of my body.

"You're looking rather hefty, Daphne darling," she said, and lightly swatted my hip.

"But don't you think he's absolutely *divine*?" I demanded, holding my perfect baby aloft.

"He's a serious little thing, isn't he?" she responded, studying Ian's face.

Ian looked back at her, deadpan, which seemed to trigger a moment of elucidation.

"Watch out! He's smart. He's very smart, and very robust. He might be interesting when he's twenty," she declared.

Ten months later, I brought her a second exquisite son, and her response to this one was in keeping with the first, if slightly less dry.

"Big boy," she said, patting his head. "Let's hope there's something going on in there.

"And as for you," she continued, again raking her eyes over my figure," I see that you may need to have your jaw wired shut."

My mother showed little interest in my babies, and even less interest in my husband. She maintained this coolness for many years, and only once openly expressed admiration for him. He had directed me in a production of Ibsen's *Hedda Gabler* and at the party afterward, she leaned into my husband and said, "You've created a beautiful valentine to my daughter. Congratulations."

As the years of my marriage unfolded, I often sought my mother's advice. She parsed her counsel regarding the vicissitudes of matrimony by presenting me with anecdotes bearing incontrovertible evidence that the institution had long since lost its credibility, at least as far as she was concerned.

"Case in point," my mother would say animatedly, demanding my attention.

"A seventy-year-old woman from Georgia filed for divorce after fifty years of marriage. The judge asked her if she were suing for adultery. 'No, Your Honor.' Domestic abuse? 'No, Your Honor.' Irreconcilable differences? 'No, Your Honor.' 'Then on what possible terms, my good woman, do you wish to sue for divorce?' 'He bores me to tears, Your Honor.' The judge looked at her, then slammed his gavel down and said, 'Divorce granted! Case dismissed!'"

A pattern of sequestration had been established early in our relationship. When I was young, and her secrets were as yet unrealized, my mother conceived of sequestration as a way in which to reward herself. It also allowed her to steady herself. Our long heart-to-hearts at the kitchen table, or in my bedroom, always evolved with an urgency followed by immediate action.

"Kitten and I are having a talk and do not wish to be disturbed," she'd announce to anyone present, then she'd take her coffee and quickly precede me through the dining room and up the front stairs. Looking back, I can see Jenny's little face as she stood frozen in the dining room, dismissed and banished. With the crook of a beckoning finger, I could have filled my little sister with joy, with a sense of belonging, but I never did this because the imperative was so clear. My mother wanted my company, and mine alone.

What did we talk about that was so important it demanded complete exclusivity? Everything and nothing. She was escaping the drudgeries of life. She was locking herself in her room, away from her stepmother, she was hiding in the chapel with her first real friend at boarding school, she was putting off yet another inevitable encounter with her husband, she was unlocking secrets about Star, she was running from the memory of Tessie, she was trying to find a way to lift herself up. She was desperately seeking comfort. In me, she found a channel, as well as an excuse. She even regarded me as a possible substitute for the one person who was, quite simply, irreplaceable.

Many years earlier, we had been stationed at our usual places at the kitchen table, and my mother had looked at me strangely, as if recognizing something for the first time. I was fourteen years old and had dramatically risen to my feet, rhapsodically painting a picture of my future in the theater when suddenly my mother interrupted me and said, "You should be my mother."

"What?" I laughed, thinking she was bored with my histrionics.

"I mean it. You know, Kitten, my mother died when I was very little, and that opened a terrible gap that I have never been able to fill. You can't get over never having had a mother, it's an impossible thing. I'm always looking for her," my mother said, softly, "and, of course, I'll never find her. But *you* could be my mother. You're capable and sturdy and kind and strong, all the things a mother needs to be. I think things got mixed up, don't you? So, let's just keep this between us, but from now on, you'll be the mother. What do you say?" At that, she lifted her coffee cup and I lifted mine, and we clinked. It was done.

These were secrets that were shared in the spirit of the moment and, although I recognized them as preposterous, they did not resonate that way. We may have laughed at the patent absurdity of this proposal, and I may have shaken my head at her incorrigible eccentricity, but as the weeks passed into months, I realized that my mother was urging me to leave, with the unspoken understanding that I was to send for her as soon as possible.

CHAPTER TWENTY-EIGHT

There were times when I thought she was putting it on. Delightfully putting it on, but still. The oddness of her humor, its unpredictability and distinct theatricality, had the curious effect of drawing us closer together. Many of her more outrageous quips were so clearly said for effect that all we could do was shake our heads, smile indulgently, and wonder at the eccentricity of such a mother. Despite the uncontrollable laughter her aphorisms provoked, she was not an affectionate mother in the conventional sense of the word. There were no warm embraces, no fond patting of the cheek, no idle stroking of the hair. If you were a daughter, you might be pulled down next to her on the couch and your head carefully examined for cuts, a nervous habit as much as an expression of tenderness. I never saw her do this with any of my brothers, it would have been too intimate a gesture.

She was a strangely formal woman who had made up a set of rules for herself that allowed her to persevere within the confines of her circumstances. This formality was in itself unusual, because my mother was a lively, intelligent creature who could conduct herself with confidence in any situation. She was not afraid of life, she traveled widely, her curiosity was insatiable, but she was not a conventional mother, and we grew up knowing this. Some of us accepted it, others had a harder time. If Jenny was complaining loudly about some privation or other, Mother would turn and declare, "You should be thankful—you were born in wedlock, you're an American citizen, and you live on dry land." If there was chaos in the kitchen and we were all buzzing around her like flies, impatient for her attention, demanding she name the ones she loved best, she would delicately sip her coffee and say, "I love all of you, but I like some of you better than others. You know who you are."

She disdained linking arms and stated unequivocally that walking three abreast was for losers. She preferred striding off on her own. If this happened in New York, as was often the case, I would catch up with her only to find her immersed in conversation with a stranger. If she was talking to a black man, she'd ask, "Why do you love your mother so much?" If it was a white man, she'd ask, "Why do black men love their mothers more than white men?" Her target was seldom, if ever, a woman. My mother preferred the male of the species and, when pressed, would assert that men are more interesting than women.

There was nothing remotely politically correct about my mother, and she categorically refused to be hamstrung by convention. If she were forced to be polite to someone who might not otherwise understand her, she would last about two minutes and then, turning to shield her face, would make the square sign followed by an exaggerated yawn, which signified that she was close to dying of boredom. Snobbishness was a learned trait, and one she was openly proud of. Above all, she both despised and feared mediocrity, and spent the better part of her mothering years warning us against the unending perils of the "herd mentality." In this way, she infused us all with a perverse love of solitude, and nurtured in each of us, if not a longing for greatness, then certainly a need to distinguish ourselves from the crowd, and the best way to do that was to step outside it.

She did this herself quite effectively when she moved to Dubuque, Iowa. The very qualities that did not necessarily set her apart in New York blazed in Dubuque. In a way, she was saved by this extraordinary turn of events. In the East, where her pedigree was not considered exceptional, she may have struggled for years, and almost certainly would not have married to her satisfaction. But in Iowa, where her intellectual curiosity shone like a veritable beacon in the darkness, she was instantly and inarguably raised to a new and exceptional station. Circumstances abetted her movement. The remoteness of Derby Grange provided a distinctly different lifestyle, one over which she reigned supreme, albeit in unlikely and unexpected ways. My mother had no interest in the well-to-do families in Dubuque, and asserted that most of them were professional Catholics, singularly lacking in dimension. Instead, she attracted personalities who were drawn to the vividness of her spirit, who shared her passion for the arts, her thirst for mysticism, her decidedly off-key sense of humor. My mother spent her time with the abbess of the Trappistine convent, Mother Columba; with the dynamic painter Francesco Licciardi; with the renegade Christian B. J. Weber; and with her outlandish friend Peggy Ludescher, whose very voice set my father's nerves on edge and whose death sent my mother into a depression unlike any she had suffered before. Stupefied with grief, my mother could not come to grips with the fact that Peggy had been cremated and repeated tonelessly, "They turned my friend into ashes."

All of her closest friends overlooked the fact that my mother was an abysmal housekeeper, that laundry proliferated unnaturally on top of the washing machine, that there was never enough toilet paper or soap, that children eavesdropped at ventilators and behind doors, and that dinner was necessarily mysterious. Unlike the liquid, bawdy dinner parties over which my father presided, he was seldom, if ever, invited to these intimate soirées. It was not for the food they came, or for the children, or for my father's company, but to sit at my mother's uniquely composed table and talk about God, death, sex, and art. Their conversation was reckless, passionate, and ribald, their laughter rising with increasing abandon in the dining room.

As children we knew that the house was, as my mother put it, a disaster area. This in no way deterred us from inviting an unending stream of friends to share in the adventure; many of them stayed for days, sometimes weeks, at a time. My mother was aware of their presence, if only tangentially, but never encouraged untoward demands. If she were approached with complaints of severe hunger or dehydration, she would round on us and say, "Never become an indentured servant," or, less effectively, "This place is surrounded by farms. Use your imagination."

This idiosyncrasy was most in evidence when my mother wished to detach herself. On the occasions that called for serious focus, when one of us had done something she considered reprehensible, she brought to bear on the moment all of her hidden mettle and unleashed a part of her personality that was both startling and intimidating. Gone was the laughter, the lightness, the mischief. My mother could not tolerate a liar and mortified those guilty of this transgression by summarily withdrawing her affection. This was a misunderstood and misguided punishment, but it proved to be inordinately effective. Equally, she despised indolence, greed, and any kind of depravity. Although she loved nothing more than a good talk about sexual intimacy, when it came to her children, especially her daughters, she was profoundly disturbed to think that they could bring such shame upon themselves. The learning curve wobbled, but when necessary she fashioned it into a scythe.

Over the course of seventeen years, she instilled in me values that have proven immutable. Whereas I am constitutionally hyperbolic, I am incapable of lying. My table manners, despite a savage and insatiable hunger I have never been able to mitigate, are impeccable. Children are wonderful to look at, but I prefer the company of old women and young men. My greatest drive and pleasure in life has always been work and, although I enjoy a lifestyle that is unquestionably comfortable, I would relinquish all of it if I could not share it with those I love.

And of those I loved, I loved my mother more.

CHAPTER TWENTY-NINE

I sent for my mother as soon as I could afford to pay for a round-trip ticket. All things considered, she didn't have long to wait. *Ryan's Hope*, the soap opera I was starring in, enabled me to present my mother with this gift, the gift she had anticipated for so long, the gift that promised her freedom. She came immediately, establishing a pattern that did not change for more than thirty years. My good fortune was my father's bad luck, acting, as it did, as an agent of separation and, although my father never said as much, he resented her leaving him. Even if it was no more than a four-day visit, it was four days without her presence, and my father felt her absence keenly. More than her absence itself, the urgent, excited way in which she left hurt my father. He mourned, then he seethed, then he got even, in the most expedient way possible.

Meanwhile, my mother would have arrived at my apartment building at 80 Central Park West and, leaping from the taxi, thrown out her arms and cried, "Kitten Kat Feathers of Joy!" She loved everything about New York, not least the fact that her best friend lived there. Jean Kennedy Smith and my mother had first bonded at the Sacred Heart Boarding School for Girls, and the attachment had deepened over the years into one of enduring friendship. The Kennedys were a possessive lot, and Jean would have monopolized my mother's time entirely had I not put my foot down. We went to the theater, on Broadway and off, spent hours in subterranean art houses watching obscure foreign films, dined on linguine alle vongole at Paolucci's in Little Italy where, after the dinner crowd had thinned out, Danny Paolucci pushed the chairs aside and created a dance floor where we sometimes danced for hours, finishing the evening with glasses of sambuca and amaretti cookies wrapped in delicate tissue which, once ignited, floated magically to the ceiling. We walked tirelessly through the neighborhoods of New York, exploring boutique bookstores, bringing afternoons to an end over manhattans at the Oak Bar. Often, my mother preferred to stay with Jean at her elegant townhouse on the Upper East Side, and I didn't mind this. After all, my newly acquired apartment was furnished with only a couch and a glass-topped dining table, and at night frequently featured a handsome young man with inky black hair and sullen brown eyes. My mother did not like my boyfriend. She thought he was surly.

"You're very quiet for someone in the theater," my mother would remark, appraising him. "Has it occurred to you that you might be clinically depressed?"

Likewise, my mother showed little respect for the job that had provided me with the means to buy her a plane ticket.

"Kitten, I really don't understand why you're doing a *soap opera,*" she'd say, dramatically lowering her voice. "Why don't you do movies instead? Then we could see them together."

Her costume never varied. Whatever the country, the climate, or the circumstances, my mother never forsook the ensemble she had so carefully selected from the limitless racks of the Goodwill thrift shop. She would never betray the emporium that had allowed her to travel in style and comfort and often shook her head pityingly when we questioned her taste in venue.

"Judge not! You couldn't buy this outfit for less than a thousand bucks in New York," she would argue. "And the raincoat is terrific. It may not have a label, but it is a classic trench coat and *I,* in case you haven't noticed, am a classic traveler. I like to pack with an eye to the next adventure, and I like to pack light, so your father can't catch me."

That ubiquitous raincoat: in the mist of a West Cork dawn, in the frigid, unrelenting rain of Seattle in winter, in the immutable heat and chaos of LAX, in the lavender coolness of a Florentine sunset, in the darkness of a Chicago bar, in the midday bustle of the Spice Bazaar in Istanbul, in every quadrant of New York City, and at every conceivable time of year, in the ruins of the Pallatine, in the afternoon shadows of the Via Dolorosa, and on an early May morning in 1998, in the gray light of a London hotel room where she sat on her bed, waiting.

"What are you doing, darling?" I asked, so quietly I was afraid she may not have heard me.

"I'm waiting," my mother replied, blinking behind her thick-lensed glasses.

"But what are you waiting for, darling? It's five-thirty in the morning," I said, moving slowly down the stairs into her bedroom.

My mother hesitated, clutched the handle of her purse, looked away.

"Jenny," she whispered.

"Oh, Mummy, Jenny won't be here for hours," I explained, as gently as I could. My sister was living in Kensington with her husband, whose bank had temporarily transferred him to London, and Mother and I had decided to make this visit our last stop before returning home. After almost ten days in Turkey, on the Seabourn cruise up the coast of the Aegean Sea, followed by nearly a week in Israel, we had, at last, arrived in London.

The moment snagged, hung suspended.

"Why don't we take off your coat?" I urged, reaching for her hand.

My mother looked at me expectantly, then withdrew her hand.

"No," she answered. "No. I'm waiting for Jenny."

When, three hours later, Jenny finally waddled into the suite at the Royal Garden Hotel, her advanced pregnancy announcing itself loudly as she came through the door, my mother stood up, smiling.

"There you are!" she said. "Let's go!"

The three of us set forth, out the door and onto the streets of London, whose denizens walked hurriedly in no particular pattern, so that I continually found myself bumping into people. My sister took my arm and said, "The Brits have no sense of personal space. Let's get Mother off the street."

Jenny was bubbling with ideas as to how we should spend the day.

"Later we'll have high tea at the Milestone, which is supposed to be fabulous, but first, a stroll through Kensington Park!"

My mother paused, looked at Jenny curiously, and said, "Why would I want to walk in a park? I *live* in a park!"

Jenny and I laughed and continued walking, but when we turned back we saw that our mother was no longer behind us. She had wandered off the sidewalk into the park after all, and appeared to be fascinated by something she saw on the ground. As we approached, our mother leaned down and plucked an object from the gravel.

As the three of us resumed walking down Kensington High Street, our mother slightly in the lead, my sister nudged me and whispered, "Look at her left sleeve." Peering closely, I saw two long, gray feathers protruding from the sleeve of our mother's silver knit sweater. Jenny and I exchanged a look that felt a little like a betrayal but was, in fact, a confidence—a confidence we both understood we would not be sharing with our mother.

CHAPTER THIRTY

Kitten?"

A Saturday morning in Brentwood, the breakfast room flooded with Southern California light. The year was 2000, we were nearing the end of the sixth season of *Star Trek: Voyager*, and I had filmed very late the night before. Irritably, I scraped strands of tangled hair from my eyes and lowered my head, pressing the receiver to my ear.

"Mother, is that you?"

A long pause, then the voice returned, each word strained as if through a fine sieve.

"I think something's wrong," she said. Again, she lapsed into silence.

"Mother, listen to me," I commanded, intuitively using a voice both firm and gentle. "You need to tell me what has happened. Take your time. I'm here."

There was a moment on the other end of the line that opened like a void, dropping my mother into a confusion so palpable that I wondered if I had lost her.

"I think I may have had a series of small strokes," the voice at last responded, small and hesitant.

"What do you mean? Tell me exactly what happened, Mother, as clearly as you can."

"I fell out of bed and my glasses broke."

"Why do you think you had a series of small strokes?"

"It felt like electricity zapped my brain six or seven times, and then I fell out of bed."

"What do you mean, electricity zapped your brain?"

"I was reading and then currents—like bolts of lightning, or strobes—flashed in my brain. Very powerful, very quick. So strong it knocked my glasses off, and now they're broken."

Another long pause, during which I processed this information and my mother attempted to compose herself. But she was distant, her voice tremulous, and even as we spoke, I felt her slipping away from me.

"How are you feeling now?" I asked. "Mother?"

"I think something came out of the wallpaper."

My pulse quickened.

I lowered my voice, steadied it.

"What came out of the wallpaper, Mother? Can you tell me?"

Then a groan, stifled as it rose in her throat.

"What was it, Mother? What came out of the wallpaper?"

"Spiders," she whispered. "Black spiders."

My turn to be silent. She meant every word, I knew this. The phone call must have demanded extraordinary effort. She was terrified, and worse, she was disoriented.

"Where are you now, Mother?" I asked, scribbling the words *spiders* and *hallucination* on a scratch pad.

"Upstairs," she replied, and I envisioned her in her blue cotton pajamas, standing next to the small oak table in the upstairs hallway where the phone sat, clutching her damaged glasses in one hand, staring back through the open door of her bedroom.

"Mother, have you told Dad?"

A whimper, one of anxiety.

"Mother? Are you there?"

I sensed that she was giving up, failing, that the conversation would soon overwhelm her, so I pressed on.

"Mother, I think you should tell Dad."

Again, that sound caught in her throat, unable to escape. A long pause.

"Oh, no, dear. No," she said at last, and then I knew that it was only a matter of seconds before I lost her.

"I'll come, darling, so don't worry, all right? I'll come as soon as I can."
There was a dropping off, a fumbling, and then the line went dead.

SPIDERS WERE HER friends, something she had made clear one day
years earlier when I sat down beside her at the kitchen table and found
her once again lost in thought, staring out the window.

"Mother, do you think we might have a conversation?" I demanded,
reaching across her for the small pitcher of cream.

"Shhhhhh! Don't be rude, be quiet," my mother ordered, peering
intently at the window.

"What are you looking at that's so mesmerizing?" I asked, fully expecting a diatribe against blue jays. My mother was continually outraged
by the behavior of blue jays and could not understand their open mendacity and cruelty to other birds. She considered them wanton murderers.

"Look, Kitten," my mother whispered, wonderingly. "Nature's most
exquisite artist."

I circled around to her side of the table and stood behind her chair,
eager to find out what the source of this enchantment was.

"It's marvelous, and absolutely incredible what they are able to ac-
complish! Just look at what she did overnight! From one end of the
window to the other, she not only wove an intricate and exquisite web,
but see what she's caught! Two flies, another spider, and a box-elder
bug. It's dazzling, don't you think?"

What I found marvelous and absolutely incredible was not only my
mother's fascination with these insects, but that she was referring to
a web the spider had woven across the pane of glass facing into the
kitchen. In other words, the spider was creating her masterpiece inside
the kitchen, and she was not, under any circumstances, to be disturbed.
I wondered how my mother hoped to protect such a vulnerable instal-
lation from the swiping hands of frightened kids.

"I'll cordon it off," she announced, jumping up to collect masking tape and a permanent marker from the kitchen drawer. Very carefully, she pulled and then affixed tape to the entire length of one side of the window, then the other, after which she wrote on it in bold letters, DO NOT DISTURB.

"Children are to keep their mitts off! The spider is the da Vinci of insects," she proclaimed, triumphantly.

"How's that, Mums?" I asked.

"There's nothing they can't do! They are sculptors, scientists, and architects. Every silken strand has been spun to her exact specifications. First, she builds, then she hunts, then she eats, and finally . . . she waits," my mother whispered, with dramatic intensity.

"For what?" I asked, picking up my cue.

"For *him*. Her mate. He will be smaller than she is, and he will be helplessly drawn to her scent, so that before he knows it he'll be un-wittingly caught in her web, fighting his way through the maze in his eagerness to claim her. Once he does, and the queen has what she needs"—my mother paused momentarily for effect, then continued—"she will devour him."

"Are you going to sit here all day and all night, waiting for this little moment of insect erotica?"

"Oh, Kitten, don't be average. Can you think of anything *better* I could be doing?"

Standing behind her, my eyes riveted to the female spider hanging motionless in the center of her web, I realized that there was very little, in fact, that could surpass this natural tableau in either beauty or virtuosity.

I pulled my chair closer to the drama, sipping quietly from my cup of coffee. Minutes passed, during which both my mother and I watched intently as the female spider continued to weave her web.

"Never kill a spider, Kitten," my mother warned. "Spiders are our friends."

CHAPTER THIRTY-ONE

We sat in the waiting room, trying to jolly her along. She was calm enough, nestled between her oldest daughter and her youngest son, with her old friend Tim Hagan sitting across the way. Her old friend and my second husband. My father, in rigid denial, had stayed at home. We were a strange and alert little band, pretending to make jokes but only half listening to one another. Our eyes and ears were bent toward the nurse behind the desk, the one calling the numbers, as it were. The mission was a terrible one, and we knew it, but there was nothing to be done about it. Spiders crawling out of wallpaper and strobes blasting through consciousness, glasses broken from an unexplained fall. All of this needed to be attended to, and so here we were, as vigilant as soldiers in a foxhole. No getting out of this, now. I had requested it, my brother Sam had found the neurologist, Tim had flown in from Cleveland, and so it was meant to be. Had to be.

My mother's eyes were like the eyes of birds, watchful and quick. Her expression revealed confusion more than anything else, though she tried gamely to laugh at Sam's silliness. The laughter would escape her, but then it would stop too suddenly, as if shot still. She, too, sat upright like a nun during Mass, her hands clasped in her lap, her face uncertain of its attitude. My husband smiled at her kindly. He would save her, if he could, if he knew how, but we were in the land of the unknowing and had to wait our turn, just like everybody else. While we waited, we dreamed our own private daydreams, and each one of them had a happy ending, or at least a reasonably happy ending. Tim daydreamed that his friend Joan would be rightfully accused of extreme eccentricity; Sam flirted with the option of a mild stroke, but only a mild one, one that would leave her with her mobility and her sense of humor; and I, I wanted the dread that had pooled in the pit of my stomach to disappear, and in its place a feeling of purposefulness to be restored as I was handed a diet and exercise regimen and told to see to it that my mother followed doctor's orders. My mother did not daydream, but was focused intently on her right hand, which she had balled into a tight fist.

"Mrs. Mulgrew?" the nurse called out, looking in our direction. Our little band rose as one.

"Dr. Fortson will see you now. Are you ready?"

My mother looked from me to Sam, from Sam to me. She nodded, and then shrugged.

The nurse, an amiable woman endowed with patience, smiled and came around the nurses' station to deal with us directly.

"The examining room is sort of small, so it's probably best if you only have one or two people go in with you, is that all right?" she asked, quickly appraising the situation.

"I'll stay out here," Tim said, "and you two go in with your mother."

Sensible, thoughtful Tim, who understood how things were.

The examining room was indeed compact, and we were momentarily at a loss as to how to situate ourselves. This occasioned a bout of giggles, as Sam made an exaggerated show of being uncomfortable in the chair, on the exam table, on the surface of the work counter, and finally sat on his haunches in a corner of the room, pretending to pout.

When the door opened, Sam jumped to his feet. Dr. Fortson was a tall, lean, dark-complected man, whose gentle manner immediately put us at our ease.

"Mrs. Mulgrew, I'm Mark Fortson," he said, taking my mother's hand. "And I presume these are your children?"

"I think so," Mother replied, which elicited a small smile from the doctor.

Relief and gratitude washed over me as I watched Dr. Fortson arrange two chairs facing each other. One of these chairs had a small table attached to it, a chair designed for students. My mother was asked to sit in this chair, and Dr. Fortson occupied the other. Sam and I stood behind Dr. Fortson's chair, providing us with an unobstructed view of our mother. Dr. Fortson was at once self-assured and modest, his professionalism innate. He had learned from experience to present himself as calm, unhurried. He had all the time in the world for my mother, and I said to myself, You are wise, Dr. Fortson, because this is a woman who deserves all the time in the world.

"How are you doing, Mrs. Mulgrew?" he asked, leaning forward ever so slightly.

My mother had decided to perform for the doctor, and this concerned me. I had seen her do this only when she was tipsy, happy, or agitated. In this room, sitting across from a man she'd never seen before, she was clearly agitated, but had made up her mind to take the high road. From my mother's point of view, this meant assuming a confidence she didn't have. I was hoping she would not try to be witty.

"What do *you* think?" she answered, wittily.

"I think you're concerned about what happened to you a few weeks ago. You fell out of bed and broke your glasses. Can you tell me about that?"

My mother tensed, twisted her hands in her lap.

"It wasn't good," she said.

"I'm sure it was upsetting. Do you remember how your glasses broke?"

"Something zapped my brain."

My mother looked over at me, and I nodded encouragingly.

"And did you see something else that may have frightened you?" Dr. Fortson inquired. He was, of course, referring to the spiders coming out of the wallpaper.

My mother paused, shrugged lightly.

"Just, you know—I don't know," she uttered.

Dr. Fortson studied my mother for a minute and then said, "Mrs. Mulgrew, can you walk across the room for me?"

This had the effect of brightening my mother's mood, and she immediately jumped up from her chair and walked briskly across the room.

"Can you put one foot directly in front of the other and walk quickly?"

Dr. Fortson was smiling, but we all understood this to be a challenge, and for a moment my mother hesitated. Then, nonchalantly, she put one foot in front of the other and took a step. She wobbled but tried to maintain her equilibrium, and then attempted to sabotage the effort by skipping across the room. She was in high performance mode, and I could feel my shoulders rising.

"Well, you certainly can skip," Dr. Fortson said. "Now, let's do something different. I'd like you to take a short quiz, all right?"

My mother assented, sat down in her chair, and accepted the pencil and paper that Dr. Fortson offered her.

"Mrs. Mulgrew, will you draw the face of a clock and show the time to be one P.M.?"

I tensed, my brother crossed his arms.

After some hesitation, my mother drew something that could, perhaps, have resembled a clock if she were being creative, but this drawing looked more like a ghost, onto whose face she applied two dots.

"Ah," said Dr. Fortson, carefully searching my mother's face.

"Mrs. Mulgrew, may I call you Joan?"

"Yes, of course," my mother said, visibly relaxing. She had misinterpreted Dr. Fortson's response to her drawing and thought he had found it unusually clever.

"Joan, what is the date?"

"The day I am here," she answered, smiling.

"And what is the day of the week?"

"Friday," she replied, correctly.

"Can you tell me what year it is?"

This gave my mother pause, but she forged ahead, as if such a question was unaccountably silly.

"Nineteen . . . Nineteen, oh what? Nineteen you-know-what," she teased.

"And who is the president of the United States?"

Our mother most certainly knew who the president was, he was a Democrat and a good one, and we had often debated his politics versus his morals.

"Who cares?" my mother countered flippantly, something of her old playfulness asserting itself.

"Well, I'm curious to know if you can tell me who the president is."

It was then that my mother looked down and covertly unfolded her right hand, on which she had clearly scribbled certain names and numbers in ink. Dr. Fortson pretended to be astounded.

"Joan, are those crib notes? Are you cheating on your MMSE?"

Sam and I spontaneously burst out laughing, we couldn't help ourselves. Some part of us delighted in the sheer absurdity of this stratagem, in the very cheekiness of it. How like our mother to think that she could outsmart a neurologist, but how distinctly unlike her to want to. The laughter quickly subsided and was replaced by silence as Dr. Fortson sat back in his chair, appraising our mother.

He liked her, I could feel it, and what's more, he respected her. Beneath the masquerade, he saw her for who she was. An exceptional woman, full of life, a woman whose children clearly adored her. He would go on questioning her until he was completely satisfied.

My mother straightforwardly told him that her daughter Tess had died of a brain tumor, but that it had happened years ago and now she painted in her studio, and cooked, and played the piano. She told him she lived in a park, which seemed to amuse him. When he asked her if she liked to read, my mother crossed one leg over the other and responded, "Are you kidding? Have you met my husband?"

There were other questions, seemingly benign, and then the examination came to an end. Dr. Fortson rose and faced the three of us. Briefly, he referred to his clipboard, then waited until he had my mother's full attention. She was in no hurry to give it to him, and tried to make eye contact with Sam, who gently turned her back to Dr. Fortson. A humming began in her throat, and just as suddenly retreated.

"Joan, I think there's a very good chance that you are in the early stages of Alzheimer's disease."

A familiar, terrible blankness fell over my mother's features, the vacancy she had always disappeared into when the news was unbearable.

"How can you be certain after such a short examination?" I asked.

Dr. Fortson regarded my mother with a steady gaze.

"There are other tests, certainly, and I'll see to it that these tests are scheduled. Some are more sophisticated than others, but we have yet to fully understand the exact nature or progress of this disease, and that makes it very hard to diagnose with precision. Judging from today's examination, and from many years of experience, I'm almost sure your mother has atypical Alzheimer's disease."

"How is it atypical?" I asked.

Dr. Fortson looked guardedly at my mother, and I said, "It's all right, she's able to hear this. Aren't you, Mother?"

Yes, my mother nodded. Yes.

"The underlying damage is the same, but the first part of the brain to be affected is not the hippocampus, which is typically the case in patients over sixty-five."

There was no possible rejoinder to this, it was so thick with language I couldn't process. He stood there calmly in his white coat, his arms hanging loosely at his sides, his elegant hands at peace. No doubt, he had spoken these words until he knew them by rote. He had memorized what could not be explained, and I was suddenly overcome with an urge to best him, to bully him, if I could, into a different diagnosis.

"You wouldn't discourage a second opinion, would you?" I demanded, hoping to catch a glint of fear in his eye. There was nothing like fear in his expression; instead his face softened with a pity I found unnerving. Gathering my mother's purse, I abruptly shook Dr. Fortson's hand and walked out the door, aware that his eyes were on us as we slowly moved down the length of the hallway.

❧

DESPITE THE WARM and beautiful autumn day, we huddled together in the parking lot, saying little. My arm had settled around my mother's shoulders, and Sam, I noticed, was lightly holding her hand. Tim stood slightly apart, his head bowed because what can a friend say that isn't first the right of the children?

I had flown in from Los Angeles the day before, after having pleaded for two days off from work. The producers of the television series I was currently shooting did not exactly lead with compassion, nor was it their job to do so, but resentment rose in me as the negotiation intensified, and by the time we had finished, and the two days had been allotted, I felt wrung out and defeated. Having to beg for a day off to take my mother to the neurologist had left me depleted, and I'd arrived in Dubuque exhausted, unprepared for what this day might bring.

The full impact of what had just passed in the examining room had not yet hit me, but I knew it was only a matter of minutes before it did. My mother blinked up at me, the sunlight glancing off her glasses, her white hair like tufts of feathers moving in the breeze, and I said, "Mother, this was just an initial meeting with the doctor. The whole thing needs much more time and attention, and I can promise you, you'll get it. We'll visit the best neurologists in the country and see what they have to say. But now, I think it's time to go home and rest and have a lovely dinner, what do you say?"

Wrapped in her Goodwill trench coat, her face devoid of expression, my mother agreed.

"Sam, I need to go to the market. Will you take Mother home and stay with her until I get back?" I asked my little brother, whose calm demeanor remained unchanged, whose hand still grasped my mother's.

"Of course, I'd love to take my mother home. We might go home and take a nap, or we might stop somewhere and split a beer. Come on, sweetheart, off we go."

Hand in hand, my mother and her youngest son started off in what Sam hoped was a promising direction.

It came to him, suddenly, that he had no idea where he'd parked only two hours before.

CHAPTER THIRTY-TWO

As we drove to the supermarket, I struggled to explain to my husband what had transpired in the examining room. Tim was patient, resigned, a man long accustomed to waiting. I left out any emotional clarification; that part of the account remained elusive, and so what Tim heard was a story that sounded almost comical. When I described the abrupt manner in which the doctor had presented the diagnosis, my husband asked, "Can you think of a better way to do it?"

Driving along a stretch of highway I'd traveled a thousand times before, I felt as if I might suffocate. The schools and churches and benchmarks of my childhood hurtled past me: the tree-lined street where the boy who had given me my first kiss lived; St. Joseph's grammar school, where in first grade I had wet my pants and Sister Leonard, white with fury, had rapped my knuckles with a ruler; the Ground Round where my mother regularly ordered the appetizer platter, a mound of mysterious and, from my mother's point of view delicious, fried foods; and on past the movie theater where I had so often sat with my mother, spontaneously bursting into applause when the lights dimmed and the previews came on and whispering with a kind of delirious anticipation, "Don't you just *love* the previews?" and past the Kennedy Mall and the only Chinese restaurant in town and the tire shop that had sprung up where Long John Silver's once stood, and up John F. Kennedy Road until we turned in to the parking lot of the A & P.

Inside, I suggested that we split up, it would be faster that way. Tim agreed, and walked off to find the butcher's counter. I headed for the produce section, which I somehow remembered was at the far left end of the supermarket, partially hidden from view. There was an urgency to this task, and I walked hurriedly over to the long rows of vegetables, each variety neatly piled in its own crate. I stood for a moment, looking around me. What was I after? Ah, yes, potatoes! I'd make meat loaf and mashed potatoes. Comfort food. My mother would like that.

Looking at the mounds of potatoes, I trembled; the air-conditioning was excessive, I couldn't see where they kept the small plastic bags, and I was about to shout this complaint to a girl in the next aisle wearing a red apron—why on earth do you make it so hard to find the goddam bags? I was about to say to her—when suddenly I reached into the bin containing Idaho potatoes and taking a potato in my hand and feeling its roughness, the earthiness of the skin, I pressed it to my face and started to weep, overcome with grief and unable to control the tears that poured down my cheeks, and equally unable to stand up straight, keening over the potatoes and sensing the first stirring of real terror as well as an intense loneliness, I experienced an almost unbearable yearning for my mother as she was yesterday, as she was ten years ago, and even allowing for the griefs in her life that would need to be re-lived, I would have gone back to them without hesitation, if it meant that today would be taken from her.

CHAPTER THIRTY-THREE

Like Pavlov's dog, I returned to work on *Star Trek: Voyager*. In it, I had found salvation, strength, and purpose. It acted beautifully as an excuse to step away from the more severe challenges of life and cast me daily into a vast and rigid machine over which I had no control. In fact, the crew called it the Machine, fixing wry smiles to early morning, exhausted faces. I took daily comfort in the sheer immutability of Paramount Stages Eight and Nine. Once inside the door of that soundstage, an "otherness" prevailed that was very like the undertaking itself. Otherworldly, contained, meticulously organized. I had only to chuck myself into that Starfleet uniform, and I was magically transported to a world of military make-believe, relieved of mundane concerns. Every morning I plunged into this world as if from a great height. The demands, from my perspective, were all-encompassing, exacting, and rigorous, the rewards almost entirely private.

If, six years into the discipline, I was no longer quite as agreeable as I'd once been, it is because Pavlov's dog had begun to chafe at the leash that had for so long ordered her movements. It became harder and harder to take that early morning dive without a nervous glance backward, into my life. Somewhere in Iowa, light-years from Paramount's Stage Eight, my seventy-year-old mother struggled to understand what exactly she should be doing with the large jar of turpentine she had found in her art studio and, finding no easy solution, had poured the liquid into a saucepan and carried it to the kitchen, where it looked as if it belonged on the stove top, and so that is where she put it. The small fire, extinguished by her alarmed and disgruntled husband, carried reverberations, and soon I received a phone call from

Sam telling me of the incident. The incident had been relayed to him by Joe who, on my father's advice, had downplayed its seriousness. Feeling overwhelmed by the constraints of my job, I asked Sam to bring our mother to Los Angeles as soon as possible. My argument, I assured him, was sound. Our mother was vulnerable in the big, empty house, presided over by a man in open denial of her struggle, and therefore she needed to be removed from any possibility of harm. Furthermore, I continued, she would be seen by the best neurological team at UCLA Medical. This was the second opinion on which so much hinged. No one could contest this, I promised him, and even if they wanted to, they didn't have a leg to stand on. Our mother had signed the official document making me her health-care guardian.

This decision had been arrived at two months earlier, following the diagnosis by Dr. Fortson. After a dinner of meat loaf and mashed potatoes, I had suggested to my mother that she might want to take a bath, and that I would accompany her upstairs.

"Want to split a beer?" I asked her.

My mother watched as I opened a can of Budweiser and poured it evenly into two glasses. Leaving Tim to do the dishes, my mother and I climbed the front stairs to the bathroom, where the colorful prints of Fables de La Fontaine hung in their separate frames on the depleted pear-colored walls, where the mismatched rust and yellow towels were draped carelessly over the rod, where the clean, soft bath mat waited on the tiled floor, and the medicine cabinet holding my mother's bath accessories stood ready to transform the tired room into a sanctuary. Turning on the faucet, I poured a capful of Johnson's baby shampoo under the hot running water, scattered a handful of bath salts into the tub, and folded a washcloth over the rim. Once my mother had immersed herself in the water, I placed her glass of cold beer on the washcloth and, with my own beer in hand, curled up on the floor, my arm resting on the rim of the tub. This was the way it had always been. No one disturbed the sanctity of the bath.

"Isn't that divine, Mums?" I asked, sipping my beer.

"Mmmm," she answered, plucking yet another washcloth from the towel rod behind her, and immediately draping it over her breasts.

I observed her for a moment, her left hand pressed against the washcloth covering her breasts, her right hand holding a glass of beer, her gaze distant. My mother's limbs were slender and soft-skinned, her plump breasts still youthful, only the softness of her abdomen betrayed the wear and tear of childbirth. She had always been unconcerned about this, as if a slight paunch was the price one paid for bearing children. About her breasts, however, she had always been inordinately modest.

Soon, I would have to get on a plane and return to Los Angeles. Communication with my mother, necessarily limited by distance, would be further compromised. There would be no way of knowing with certainty that she was protected. My father's love, though unquestionable, obscured his reason. Among the ranks of her own children, there existed the very real possibility of dissent.

"Mother, I need to ask you something," I said, leaning on the rim of the bathtub with both arms.

My mother looked at me, questioningly. Her eyes were frightened, unsure. She did not fully comprehend what had happened at the doctor's office, nor did she want to. She wanted only to take her bath, the bath she had always regarded as her reward at the end of a long day.

"Mother, I know you're exhausted, but I think we need to talk about something. We're a long way from any answers I'm satisfied with, all of that will come, but in the meantime it's important that you have a legal document protecting you. You need *someone who you trust* to protect you, no matter what. A health-care guardian. Do you understand?"

Drained, my mother nodded, then lowered her head. How she wished she had never called me, never confessed to the spiders coming out of the wallpaper. This was too confusing, too hard, and now her daughter was making yet another demand.

"Who would you like that person to be, Mother? You have to choose," I said.

For a long moment, I watched her struggle with the importance of what was being asked. Forcing herself to process this information, she gathered her knees to her chest and rested her cheek there, like a young girl. Her left hand let go of the washcloth and she dipped her fingers in the water, strumming them lightly on the surface. My mother slowly lifted her hand from the bathwater and, pointing a finger at me, mouthed, "You."

After I had helped my mother into her nightgown and tucked her into bed, I called Sam on the upstairs phone, out of earshot of my father, who sat brooding in the TV Room, nursing a drink, an empty crossword puzzle spread out before him on the coffee table. I told Sam I felt strongly that I should be our mother's health-care guardian as long as he agreed and, in so doing, that he would assure me of both his allegiance and, if necessary, his help.

Sam wholeheartedly approved of my decision, although he, too, was troubled about what our father would perceive as a betrayal. As it turned out, this concern was warranted. My father wanted no part of it and was particularly insulted by my presumption in assuming health-care guardianship. I could see that he considered this strictly his right and was furious that once again his oldest daughter had stormed in and usurped his position, this time undermining his dominance in a way almost unforgivable.

The following day, I arranged to meet with a lawyer and, in the privacy of her office, watched as my mother signed the papers giving me full authority over her health care. Had I been less frightened, maybe I would not have acted so quickly, and so apparently without concern for my siblings, but I was filled with a sense of foreboding that eclipsed all other considerations. It was intolerable to imagine living thousands of miles away in a bubble of ignorance, never knowing with certainty the state of my mother's condition. I did not trust my father, and therefore I feared for my mother.

Before confronting my father, I had anticipated a harsh punishment, but I did not expect to be blamed. His denial of my mother's affliction was not only resolute but critical to his sense of authority, and because his pain was immeasurable and his disorientation extreme, he turned on me with a vehemence that struck like a blow. My father needed me to share his anguish, the fury he felt at having been betrayed, his outrage when, one afternoon shortly following the incident of the fire, Sam arrived at the house, said hello to our father, and half an hour later reappeared with our mother on his arm. She wore her trench coat and carried a small suitcase.

"Where the hell do you think you're going?" my father demanded.

"I'm taking Mom to Los Angeles, Dad. Katy's her health-care guardian and that's what she wants," Sam replied, looking into our father's eyes. Then he led our mother through the kitchen and down the short brick path, where he had parked his car. Sam settled our mother in the passenger seat before turning and glancing back at the house. If he expected to see our father at the window, he did not find him there. Sliding behind the wheel, Sam forced a smile and, taking our mother's hand, said, "Guess what, sweetheart? We're going on an adventure—we're going to see Katy."

CHAPTER THIRTY-FOUR

If a cat shitting indiscriminately all over the house is any kind of a bellwether, then I was forewarned. Ebony nuggets were found in the folds of my gold brocade curtains, in the toe of my slipper, on the silky border of my Turkish rug. The cat himself was disinclined to favor us with his company, and streaked past us at all hours, creating chaos. And to think, only three weeks earlier, he had been the most desirable creature in the world.

"The smartest cat in the kingdom," my mother had promised, her hands clasped in excitement, as she gazed at the animal in its metal cage.

"Will it be fun?" I'd asked, leaning down to get a better look at the tawny feline as he prowled back and forth on the newspapered floor of his pet shop home.

"Fun to study," my mother had assured me, with eyes full of wonder.

I bought the Siamese cat for five hundred dollars and we released him in the living room of my pretty Brentwood house, expecting to see him as soon as he had acclimated himself. He never did grow accustomed to his new environment and, despite our naming him Sebastian and calling his name day and night and putting out tempting dishes of Chicken of the Sea and sitting for hours on the living room couch waiting for him to appear, he refused to show himself. He waited until we had gone to bed, and then practiced a stealth, as well as a repressed hostility, seldom observed in a domesticated animal.

After three weeks, I looked helplessly at my mother and told her I was sorry about Sebastian. She was sitting on the patio, a book lying open in her lap. After a moment, my mother shrugged and said, "Why?"

"Because you haven't been able to study him," I reminded her.

She shrugged again, indifferently, and went back to looking at her book.

"What are you reading, Mother?" I asked.

My mother snapped the book shut and, clasping it to her, said, "Very, very good." By this, I was meant to understand that her fervor for reading remained undimmed, and that I was not to question her further.

The next day, Sebastian reached new heights in debauchery and left neat piles of feces in nearly every room of the house. Lucy, my housekeeper, delivered this news with barely concealed rage.

"Señora, that stupid cat need to go! What you think? He loco!"

Lucy, who had helped me raise my children and whose custodial skills over eighteen years had been incomparable, was defeated by the cat. I decided to get rid of Sebastian as soon as he could be found and successfully wrangled. That night, I approached my mother with the news.

"Mother, I think it's time to find a new home for Sebastian, don't you?"

My mother nodded in agreement, and then said, "Me, too."

Sitting across from her in the living room, observing the same book lying opened to the same page, I felt my heart sink. My mother was not disappointed, she was lonely.

"Do you want a new home?" I asked, attempting levity.

"Yes, *my* home," she replied, quietly but firmly.

Three weeks previously, Sam had delivered my mother to me. She was happy to be in my comfortable house on the west side of Los Angeles, happy to swim at her leisure in the heated pool and to eat Lucy's delicious meals, happy to accompany me to the market, the bookstore, the seaside. When it was time to get in the car and drive to our appointment at UCLA Neurology, my mother appeared composed.

The neurologists at UCLA had been meticulous, compassionate, and decidedly more upbeat than Dr. Fortson. When the battery of tests had been completed and a kind nurse's aide had taken my mother for a snack, the lead neurologist took me aside.

"Unfortunately, the neurologist in Dubuque was pretty much spot-on. I'm not sure I'd diagnose this case as atypical, but I'd say there's very little question that your mother has Alzheimer's disease," the doctor said, looking at me with a studied, almost charming, directness. He was about the same age as Dr. Fortson, but better dressed beneath his white coat, and impeccably groomed. Despite the onerous nature of his task, this doctor conveyed a polished optimism that made me yearn for the likes of Dr. Fortson.

Homesickness is a sickness of the heart, not of the mind. It is deeply subjective and belongs, inarguably, to the sufferer alone. My mother had traveled a long way to accommodate my needs, she had endured the second round of tests at UCLA, she had accepted my long absences while at work, she had been spurned by a cat she had wanted to adore, and now she was ready to go home. I had never before fully understood the depth of her attachment to Derby Grange, probably because I hadn't had to. Ours was an allegiance of escape, not of resignation, and yet here she was, longing to return to a place she had spent a great deal of her married life running away from.

As she sat in a deep-cushioned wicker armchair, the late afternoon California sun dancing on the surface of the pool, a plate of Lucy's cheese empanadas on the tray beside her, and a glass of cold, frothy Corona in her hand, my mother's sadness was palpable. It transcended filial bonds, the life she'd made for herself, with the husband she had chosen, and my mother knew only that she had stayed away too long, and that now she wanted to go home.

CHAPTER THIRTY-FIVE

We spent the day slogging through the bog field of our mother's affliction. Though we were good children all, there was nonetheless a wariness in the air, behind which each sibling retreated as the atmosphere thickened with unspoken resentment. Some of this hostility was aimed at me, I understood that, and I accepted it. The circumstances under which I had lobbied so passionately for the position of health-care guardian were hardly fair. It is conceivable that I had compromised our mother, but I didn't think so. I knew only that the faces in my Brentwood living room, on that winter's day in 2001, were clouded with confusion and distrust. My siblings resented the inconvenience of having to travel to Los Angeles for a meeting that might have been held in Iowa, had it not been for my refusal to deal with my father's unmanageable recalcitrance. I felt strongly that his inability to accept the nature of our mother's affliction put her in harm's way, and that it was imperative to make my siblings understand the gravity of the situation.

It was difficult and unsettling to see them like this. Then again, a family conclave of this nature had never before been requested. The reality of what lay ahead of us was not only daunting, but terrifying, and because of this our vision was blinkered. Fear is a starkly felt emotion, it is not nuanced, and as I looked around the room, I saw how it had manifested itself in each of my siblings.

I thought how unfair it was to strip a family of its one great gift. We knew how to laugh, we had always known how to laugh, and now this, too, was threatened. Who would we be without our laughter? How would we cope? How would Tom manage without his antics, a clownishness so absurd that my mother was helpless to resist? If she didn't immediately respond to his silliness, he'd pick her up, open the oven door, and shove her in. Jenny, on the other hand, brought original material to the table. In a single, brief sketch, she could capture two women in a trailer park discussing paychecks and cheese cubes with a perfect ear, and with timing so impeccable that my mother, delighted, would clap her hands and say, "I think Jenny's the funny one, don't you? Do it again!" How would Jenny navigate the silence? And Joe, wielding a lightning-fast wit, how would he react when his brilliant punch lines failed to dazzle, when my mother would no longer cock her head and say, "He's not only beautiful, he's a polymath"? Or Sam who, while appearing to play the foil, offered the laughter of release when he'd cap off an hour's badinage with a simple, perfect irreverence, which invariably elicited a collective groan of surrender, after which Mother would pat the seat next to her and say, "Come here, my hero."

I recalled a time, seven years earlier, when they had all come to L.A. to celebrate my fortieth birthday, a hedonistic and gaudy event that went on for four days. On the evening of the fourth day, when the party officially ended with me announcing that I needed to go to bed and study my lines in preparation for my reemergence into outer space the following day, there were only a few revelers left. In my bedroom upstairs, I unlatched the French doors that opened onto a deck overlooking the pool and listened as the sounds below drifted up to me. At first, I could hear only murmurs and then, quite distinctly, Tom's voice rang out, "Big Mama, you better watch your mouth or I'm gonna have to do something about it!"

My mother's voice responded. "Like what, Big Daddy? I ain't afraid of you! I got Brother Man here to defend me, don't I, Brother Man?"

"Hell, I don't know about that, Big Mama," Sam shouted. "All's I know is I've had about enough of your bellyaching!"

Screaming, footsteps on the brick patio, shrieks of laughter, and then the sound of my mother being thrown into the pool by Big Daddy and Brother Man, both of whom jumped in after her.

This aquatic revival of *Cat on a Hot Tin Roof,* replete with expletives and hysteria, seemed to go on for hours, during which I lay on my bed, my script unopened beside me, smiling. I would wake up an hour early, I promised myself, and learn my lines then, because while I was prepared to spend the following day in a stupor, I was unwilling to sacrifice this moment.

The atmosphere in my living room on the day of the family conference was heavy. It was without levity, levity wasn't allowed, and in the realization that we had conducted a meeting for over three hours without even the suggestion of laughter, I knew that we had become a different family. The one thing that had set us apart had been taken from us, and though we would joke again, and tease, and strive to recover a flavor of the old exuberance, we would never again laugh as we once had.

When my mother entered the living room in the late afternoon, having awakened from her nap, and found all of her children waiting for her, she stopped, but in the sudden swift movement of bodies coming forward, of arms outstretched and faces lit with love, whatever confusion she may have felt was instantly dispelled, because everything that made sense to my mother was present in that room.

CHAPTER THIRTY-SIX

Lucy came upon me weeping outside and, because such a sight was unnerving, she quickly retreated. Moments later, she reappeared carrying two glasses of white wine, the more generous of which she handed to me.

"You want to talk about it, señora?" she asked, sitting lightly in the chair opposite me.

This was neither customary nor habitual, this coming together for drinks after dinner, but it had gained frequency, now that the boys were older. Lucy never fully reclined in her chair but sat on the edge of the seat, legs crossed, still wrapped in her red apron. Her black hair was pulled back into a ponytail, her dark eyes were fixed on me, and one white-sneakered foot bobbed in the darkness.

"I'm worried, that's all," I said, wiping my nose with a cocktail napkin.

"About Beanie?" Lucy asked, referring to my mother with the nickname that she felt best suited her. In Lucy's mind, there could be only one señora, and that was me.

"About everything, but yes, mostly Mother. I don't know what to do, I feel hamstrung out here, and God knows what's going on back there. They've got a girl coming in every day, but Sam tells me she lives in the boonies, and sometimes she's late, other times she's early, sometimes she doesn't show up at all. She doesn't have a car, so she relies on her husband for a ride and, to hear Sam tell it, he's not the most dependable guy in the world," I explained, taking a long sip of my wine. "I swear to Christ, Lucy, if I weren't contractually bound to this series, I'd move out there and take care of her myself."

Lucy grew thoughtful, her white-sneakered foot pausing in mid-bounce.

"I go, señora," she said.

I looked at her and laughed.

"You're crazy," I responded. "How would you do that?"

"I think you the crazy one, señora. The boys is grown, only you now. You need me and Javier to take care of you? You can't make the bed yourself?"

Stunned, I leaned forward and searched her face. Could she possibly be serious?

"Listen, señora," Lucy demanded. "I an American citizen, my kids everywhere—here, Mexico, Nebraska, one guy even in Iowa. Javier can stay here for now, I go ahead alone. This a really good solution. What you think?"

"I think you're extraordinary," I replied, but Lucy dismissed this with a wave of her hand. The tears, censored by the intensity of the conversation, began to flow again.

"Oh stop, señora, you make yourself sick. Everything is okay. I go to Iowa to take care of Beanie. How hard can it be? Mexico is hard, Campeche is hard, leaving five kids and crossing the border is hard, but this is not hard," she stated, conclusively. She stared at me almost defiantly, then took an unladylike swig of her wine. This gesture, so unlike her, was her way of letting me know that whatever resistance I might offer would be considered insignificant.

"I won't argue with you because first, you're right, and second, you're stronger than I am," I said.

"No, señora, we the same," Lucy declared, her voice lifting with the wine, the hour, the enormity of what had just been settled. "We born in different places, different countries, but we the same kind of person. You save my life, señora, you know that—and now it's my turn to help you. I want to take care of Beanie. You know I love Beanie, señora, I swear to God. I ready to go."

What does mercy feel like? Shakespeare knew: *the quality of mercy is not strained, it droppeth as the gentle rain from heaven.* Whatever sins I had committed, whatever smallness I had practiced, whatever selfishness I had indulged, all were instantly absolved. The gods, present in the fierceness of Lucy's features, in the uplifted, proud chin, in the ramrod-straight back, in the warmth of her skin and the depth of her sable eyes, had chosen to show me mercy, and it had, indeed, fallen as the gentle rain from heaven.

CHAPTER THIRTY-SEVEN

Covert communication was complicated, but my mother perse-vered. She plucked at my sleeve to get my attention and pointed a slender finger first at me, then at herself. She widened her eyes and raised her coffee cup as if we were playing a game of charades.

"More coffee?" I whispered, intensifying the mystery of the game.

My mother shook her head and then, using the same finger, pointed upward.

"To talk," she said, putting a finger to her lips.

I understood. My mother wanted me to accompany her upstairs to her bedroom. She wanted to have a heart-to-heart, and she did not want us to be disturbed. Privacy was of the utmost importance. In the ten minutes we had been sitting at the kitchen table, her eyes had not left my face.

"I think Mother's tired, aren't you, Mother?" I asked, rhetorically.

My mother yawned.

"I'm going to take her up for a nap," I said, "and maybe I'll lie down with her myself for a few minutes."

"Good idea, señora," Lucy said, from her station at the sink. "But first, Pie, you need to take your pills."

In Lucy's vernacular, Pie was all that needed to be salvaged from this overused term of endearment. One was either a sweetie, or a pie, but never both.

Lucy turned to the cabinet above my father's makeshift bar and opened the door. In the three months since she'd arrived, the house had been transformed. An order it had never known showed itself on gleaming surfaces and spotless floors, in pots and pans meticulously organized, in scented laundry folded into sensible piles, in the vase of tiger lilies that sat on the kitchen table, and in this cabinet, where the bottom shelf had been stripped of flatware and now housed two rows of pill bottles, neatly arranged. I moved to Lucy's side and watched as she shook the pills from various bottles onto a small white plate. Vitamin B12, vitamin E, a tiny coral capsule from a bottle labeled Aricept, ginkgo biloba, vitamin B6.

Lucy leaned into me and whispered, conspiratorially, "Beanie don't like the pills. I give her applesauce, maybe pudding, I try to fool her, but she smart. And hard to swallow, señora, sometimes she don't do it, she throw them out."

My mother's aversion to the pills was immediately in evidence, as she pushed the plate away from her and rose to her feet.

"Mother, just take one—for me. Will you do that, please?"

Against my better judgment, I selected the Aricept and handed it to my mother with a glass of water. She looked at me beseechingly. Taking the pills was perceived as penance.

Grudgingly, she took the coral pill from my hand and put it on her tongue. More disturbing than her resistance was watching the futility of the effort. Time and again she regurgitated the pill until, unable to stand it, I said, "All right, that's enough, darling. My God, this is torture."

My mother's expression was grim. She loathed this exercise.

As I was leading her up the front stairs, I noticed that my mother grasped the handrail before she pulled herself to the next step. These were stairs she had run up a thousand times, her hand lightly grazing the banister, her step soundless.

In her bedroom, she indicated that I should close and lock the door. This surprised me, as the likelihood of anyone interrupting us was slim. I did not argue and bolted the door with the brass lock I had insisted my father install thirty-five years earlier, when the bedroom had belonged to me and the threat of being disturbed caused persistent anxiety.

My mother climbed onto her bed, the same bed I had slept in for most of my childhood, an heirloom bequeathed to me by Aunt Jane. Like a disgraced military general, the bed had slowly been stripped of ornamentation until it now resembled nothing more than a pleasant place to lie down. Gone was the elegant green velvet canopy, tented on four tall tasseled posts, sheltering the berth below. Gone the mahogany side frames, the pink corduroy bolsters, the corded neck pillows, the silk duvet.

The house was very still, now, as my mother and I arranged ourselves on the bed. Curiously, my mother did not sit cross-legged, as was her habit, but chose instead to sit on the edge of the bed, legs dangling over the side, her arms braced on either side of her. I had little choice but to sit next to her, near the end of the bed, propped up against one post. My mother's head was down; she had removed her glasses and was twisting them in her hands. Moments passed. Suddenly, she raised her head and looked directly into my eyes.

"I can't do this," she said, tapping the side of her head with her glasses.

I waited.

"Kitten, don't ask me to do this," my mother continued, slowly, turning to face me.

"Do what exactly, Mums?" I asked, and instantly regretted the impulse to interrupt, an impulse I could not easily check when I was afraid.

Using her glasses, my mother pointed to the wall behind me. Her eyes were fixed on a spot directly behind my head. I knew that if I turned to look, I would see nothing there, nothing but the faded floral paper that had covered these walls for too many years. But this, my mother was telling me, this wallpaper is no longer benign, this room is no longer safe.

"Kitten, this is all I have," my mother said, haltingly, and once again she tapped her temple with her glasses, but this time more sharply. I wanted to say, *Please don't do that, darling*, but I stopped myself.

"I have a big problem up here, and I know it won't get better," she went on. "My brain is all I have. Don't ask me not to—to . . ." She hesitated.

"Don't ask you not to do what, Mother?"

She stared at me for a long moment. "Think," she whispered. Then, reaching over, she pulled a book from the bedside table and rested it on her lap.

"Read," my mother said, quietly.

"Are you able to read now?" I asked.

My mother looked at me pityingly, lifted her hands, raised her head as if straining to find something just beyond the reach of her memory. She could no longer see it clearly, not as it was, but she knew it had been there: a large burlap bag, full of library books, deposited on top of the old chest in the TV Room. Next to it, her tired leather purse, clasp undone. Busy little hands rifling through it, searching for the odd quarter. The burlap bag was of no interest to small children, just as the purse was of little interest to my mother. In the course of two weeks, the lumpy bag would have grown thin, its contents come to roost in every part of the house; on my mother's bedside table, next to the sewing machine in The Addition, on the coffee table in the TV Room, beside and on top of the toilet, atop the round kitchen table. My mother's books were part of the infrastructure of the house, like the long windows in the dining room, or the molding on the living room ceiling, and it was unusual to see her without one tucked under her arm. Often, she would lightly kiss the front cover of her book, before placing it under the telephone on the kitchen counter. "Good book?" I'd ask, from my spot at the kitchen table, to which she would reply, "Sheer heaven."

"Everything will stop, but I will know and, Kitten, listen to me." She was fighting for the right words, and she was finding them, but the effort demanded a monumental exertion of will. I nodded, reached for her hand.

She immediately withdrew her hand and, leaning into me, whispered, "I don't want to die that way. I need you to help."

I had been sitting, but now I slid off the bed onto the floor. Crawling a little way toward my mother, I found her lap, and rested my head in it. She stroked my hair lightly, distractedly, almost as she had when I was a girl.

Then, tapping her fingers gently on the top of my head, she whispered, "Pills."

It was almost inaudible, she spoke so softly. I wondered, later, if a part of her had wished not to be heard.

Raising my head, I looked at my mother as she sat on the edge of the bed. She was rigid with exhaustion; this effort had exacted a toll, and now she was utterly drained.

"Let's take a little nap, Mums," I said, easing her down onto the bed. I lay beside her and pulled a yellow cotton blanket over us. Gently, I removed her glasses from her grip and put them on the bedside table.

We lay facing each other, the late afternoon sun no longer brightening the room. My mother's small form was still beneath the blanket, but her eyes were alert. She waited, and while she waited I drew her hand to my lips and kissed it. It was imperative that she rest, that the scratching of her mind stop, if only for a few hours.

"I'll help you, darling," I said at last. "I promise."

CHAPTER THIRTY-EIGHT

I don't know what I thought I was doing, sitting in the small quiet room with its overstuffed chairs and its ambience of coziness. Playing a game, I supposed, though it lacked all of the playfulness of a game. It was something I observed myself doing.

"Can you tell me if there is a particular cocktail of pills that will ensure success, in these circumstances?"

The doctor looked at me, fascinated. Because she was my friend, and innately dramatic, she wanted in on the game, but I wasn't having it.

"It's a simple yes or no answer, isn't it?" I continued, attempting to lean back in my chair. Like all of the furniture in the room, it was expensive, chic, and uncomfortable, not unlike the doctor herself.

"Not entirely," she answered. "Every case is different, but what you are talking about is not as easy as you might think."

"Go on," I said.

"Well, first there is the problem of timing. Each pill would need to be taken individually. Then there is the problem of assimilation and, of course, throughout there is the overriding problem of regurgitation," the doctor explained, regarding me carefully.

I nodded, glancing out the window.

"You know, Kate, it doesn't typically last too long," she said.

"What doesn't last too long?" I asked, suddenly impatient with her manner.

"This stage," the doctor replied. "Very soon, she will forget that she even asked you."

"How soon?" I demanded.

The doctor looked down at her Chanel slippers, then back at me.

"Soon."

CHAPTER THIRTY-NINE

She wore a bracelet now, and walked past the little red Taurus hatchback as if the giving up of that possession had not broken her. It had. Seven years earlier, when I had surprised her with this gift, she had cried out with joy and, approaching the car as if it were a newborn, tenderly kissed the hood. Then, after allowing her hands to travel over the body of the car and peering excitedly into the backseat, she had stopped to exclaim over the size of the trunk, already imagining it stacked high with paintings. Beaming, she had stood and declared, "I will name her Ruby, and she will be mine, mine, mine!"

But seven years had passed, and when I told her that the time had come to stop driving, that it was no longer safe, she stood and stared at me in disbelief. Then, shockingly, her eyes filled with tears and she began to cry, a state to which she seemed oblivious. She wept, and as she wept she fought to retain the one privilege that still promised independence—the right to get in her car and drive away. I talked to her of danger, of children at crosswalks, of tiredness, of forgetfulness. After ten minutes of this lecture she stopped listening, and I watched as her anguish dissolved into indifference. A brief internal scuffle ensued, during which her features underwent a series of swift, inexplicable changes, before a curtain of blankness dropped, obliterating any trace of the distress she had been feeling so acutely only moments before.

Two months later, we decided to take a walk down the gravel road and, as we started out, passing the little red car now sleeping in the shadow of the glen, my mother said, "I have a game."

"Uh-oh. What kind of game, Mother?" I asked, stopping to marvel at the host of tiger lilies that annually bloomed at the foot of the stone gates. I was sure my mother was going to suggest that we visit the bee-hives hidden in the woods.

"Let's go to that house," she suggested, pointing at one of the newly constructed houses on the road. My heart sank. This sudden development of oversize modern houses on a road that had long been a dusty ribbon winding through fields of corn, past farms boasting hundreds of acres of land, continued to appall me. Having grown up in the country-side, with the nearest neighbor a quarter of a mile away and town itself strictly a weekend aspiration, I could not bring myself to accept this strange archipelago of cookie cutter structures, all of which seemed to have erupted overnight, like enormous mushrooms.

Whatever mischief stirred this sudden impulse of my mother's, I knew it wasn't entirely innocent. My mother harbored a resentment of these recently sprouted edifices, all of which offended both her sense of history and her sense of taste, while at the same time arousing in her a mordant curiosity. She wanted to see what lay hidden behind the clean brick walls, so new to the sun and the rain, the front lawns brandishing toy cars and pink plastic swing sets, the two-car garages sheltering brand-new automobiles and bright green lawn tractors. Surpassing her interest in all of these novelties was my mother's overweening curiosity about human beings, particularly human beings she might otherwise never encounter.

"What are you suggesting, that we just walk up and ring the bell?" I asked, stopping in the middle of the road to face my mother.

"Yes, say we're on a walk, and that I'm—you know." She tapped the side of her head.

So, this was how it was going to be: I was to approach the house, ring the bell, and announce to whomever answered that my mother was not quite right in the head but that she wanted very much to see the woman's lovely house and, if it was not too objectionable, would love a guided tour.

I shook my head at the bizarreness of it but had to admire my mother's pluck. As we approached the front door of the house, my mother and I linked arms. We stepped onto the cheerful, unblemished welcome mat and, tightening my smile, I lifted my hand and pressed the doorbell. Almost immediately, the door was opened by a stout, middle-aged woman wearing a man's flannel work shirt and blue jeans. Her unruly blond hair was pulled back into a ponytail and her feet were bare. I instantly surmised that today was housecleaning day, and that my mother and I had not chosen wisely.

"Hi there!" the woman said, smiling warmly.

"How do you do? I wanted to introduce myself. I'm Kate Mulgrew, and this is my mother, Joan," I said. "We live down the road, and we were just out for a walk when my mother told me she has always wanted to see your house. She's fascinated by how people decorate, especially a house this size."

I looked directly into the woman's eyes and smiled conspiratorially, indicating that this was entirely my mother's idea. Whatever wariness she may have felt when she opened the door suddenly dissolved and, as she swung the door wide to allow us in, our neighbor said, "My name's Angie. Come on in. The place is a mess, today's cleaning day, but sure, have a look around if you want."

As we crossed the threshold, my mother and I looked beyond the small foyer and were immediately struck by the immaculate condition of the living room. White pile carpet stretched from one end of the room to the other, and my mother, as if drawn by a magnet, preceded us into the space and whispered, "Blinding."

I laughed and said, "She's blinded by the carpet, and so am I! My God, it's so *clean and bright* in here!" I had seldom seen a room in quite this state of spotlessness.

"Oh, don't look too close," Angie warned, pushing back her hair with one hand. An industrial vacuum cleaner waited on the step leading into the living room, and I wondered if every day wasn't cleaning day in Angie's house.

"Don't you have young children?" I asked, shaking my head in wonder.

"Oh, they don't come in *here*." Angie laughed. "They wouldn't dare!"

"You've got hidden rooms for rambunctious children," I suggested, smiling devilishly. "I can only imagine how spectacular *those* rooms are."

Angie could not resist. Basking in the glow of our awe, our neighbor offered to give us a tour of the house. My mother clapped her hands, and I happily assented.

"You're sure it's not inconvenient?" I asked.

"As long as you don't mind the mess!" Angie warned, in the manner of one raised to conceal pride behind a show of modesty.

My mother's wish had been granted. Past the living room we went, into the oak-paneled, wide-bottomed den, whose walls exhibited framed photographs of Angie's children, beribboned, slick-haired, and miserable; past the large and gleaming utility room; and into the kitchen where, incredibly, a plate of fresh-baked chocolate chip cookies rested on the counter. The space was impeccable. I cocked my head. *Could Angie possibly have been expecting us?* Impulsively, I said, "Looks like you're expecting company."

Angie chuckled. "Oh, no, that's just a snack for the kids when they get home from school. I bake most days."

Incredulous, I turned to my mother, who hummed for a moment and then said, "If you like cookies."

This remark in no way deflated our hostess, whose cookies I was confident had been featured at many a school bake sale, and she continued to lead the way down the hall into the garage.

My mother caught my sleeve and whispered emphatically, *"Bedrooms."*

Angie stopped and asked, "What's that she's asking?"

"She's terrible—she's dying to see the bedrooms," I replied, affecting shyness.

At this, Angie blanched.

"Oh, no, no, no, I can't do that, I'd never forgive myself. Some of the beds aren't even made and Doug—that's my husband—he's got his stuff lying around all over the place." Angie's cheeks reddened, and I understood that the bedrooms signified an intense, if narrow, intimacy that was strictly off-limits to strangers. Quickly, she led the way down a darkened hall that opened into the garage, where two machines gleamed in the shadows: one a black SUV, and the other a dark blue Chevrolet Malibu. The husband must be driving yet a third car, I mused, watching out of the corner of my eye as my mother, humming, approached the garage door and asked, "Does it open?"

Obediently, Angie pushed a button, and the automatic door began to rise.

A blast of sunshine greeted us when we emerged, and my mother threw open her arms and cried, "Life!"

I thanked Angie for her hospitality and her great kindness in indulging our whim. She stood there, arms crossed, and I realized that she had taken a risk in allowing us into her home. There was a good chance that she had recognized who I was, in itself a cause for wariness, but she had in no way demonstrated this. Instead, she had chosen to understand that my mother was not herself, would never be herself again, and that she could put her cleaning aside for a few minutes and make an old woman's dream come true.

When I turned, I saw that my mother had started down the road toward Derby Grange. Her face was tilted toward the sun, in her hand she held a black feather. When I caught up with her, I pulled her arm through mine and asked, "Well? Wasn't that fun?"

My mother considered this for a moment, then tucked the feather in her sleeve, shrugged lightly, and answered, "Medium."

A cloud of dust appeared at the bend in the road, and when it had settled I recognized Sam's car speeding toward us. He overshot us by a few yards, screeched to a halt, then skidded backward. Rolling down his window, he looked at our mother and said, "Hello, sweetheart! Are you collecting feathers? Are you visiting bees? What are you up to?"

"No good," I answered, drily. "You won't believe what she just made me do."

"Well, I want to hear all about it over a beer. Split one with me?" he asked, grinning at our mother.

Our mother stood beside me, her eyes fixed on her son. She blinked, then brought her hands to her chest.

"I think that means we've got a date. I'll race you!" Sam shouted, putting his foot on the gas and disappearing through the stone gates.

I started after him and had taken a few steps before I realized my mother was no longer with me. Turning back, I saw that she was standing where I had left her. She was looking past the stone gates, into the front yard where Sam now stood, waving his arms and shouting at us to hurry up.

My mother spoke so softly I needed to lean in. Not taking her eyes off the figure of her son waiting for her in the front yard, she said, "The one I love."

"Jeez, thanks a lot, Mums," I responded, "I thought *I* was the one you loved."

Pulling the feather from her sleeve, my mother pointed it toward the front yard and said, this time more emphatically, "That *man* is the one I love."

"Well, I should hope so, he's your son," I said.

"Who?" my mother asked, looking up at me apprehensively.

"Sambo, your *son*—you know, Mother, that crazy guy over there shouting at us to hurry up," I said, waving back at my younger brother.

My mother, standing very still, not taking her eyes off Sam's shape in the distance, put her hand on my arm.

"No, no," she whispered, as if shocked by what I'd said. "That is the *man* that I love."

I stared at her for a long moment, then nodded very slowly as I realized that she had meant every word she had uttered and that it was I who had misjudged her intention. Suddenly, and completely without warning, her brain had transformed her son into her lover.

My mother and I slowly made our way across the yard to where my younger brother waited for us, oblivious to the fact that his identity had changed and that walking toward him was a woman who was about to turn his world upside down.

CHAPTER FORTY

Occasionally, our mother's natural personality flashed through the interstices of the affliction, filling us with unreasonable happiness. Unlike the terrifying moments when Tessie's malignancy shifted in her brain, allowing her to run into the dining room after she had lain immobilized for weeks, we experienced our mother's spells of lucidity as wonderful and, despite our better judgment, were made almost giddy with hope. The first hint that this might be happening would be the clear articulation of an opinion, usually involving something insignificant.

"Mother, would you like more milk in your coffee?"

Suddenly, like a bolt from the darkness, would come the answer: "Milk is for babies."

This acted on us like a drug, and my mother would then be assaulted with questions, each of us vying for a moment's recognition. Once, when she appeared to be enjoying a sustained reprieve, I leaned into her and asked, "Darling, how would you like to take a trip to New York?"

My mother jumped up, something I had not seen her do in weeks, and cried, "Yippie ki yo! Yay, team!"

Within the hour, I was on the phone to my travel agent, and the following weekend we were on our way to New York City. My shooting schedule demanded that I remain in Los Angeles during the week, so it had been decided that Sam would accompany our mother on the trip, and that I would meet them Friday night at the Mayflower Hotel. Throughout the preparations, Sam later assured me, she had maintained her enthusiasm. On the flight from Chicago to New York, where

I had arranged for them to be seated in first class, the flight attendant had asked for their drink order, in response to which our mother had winked at Sam and made the universal sign for whiskey by wiggling her right hand. She had already had a long day, and Sam was acutely aware that the affliction could at any time reassert itself, so he'd suggested that she have a Coke instead.

"People who drink Coke are losers," my mother had replied.

In the lobby of the Mayflower Hotel, I waited for my mother and my brother to arrive. As they came through the revolving door, first Mother, then Sam, I knew at once that my mother's perception, her grasp of time and space, had devolved significantly in the past week. She emerged through the glass door, wrapped in her Goodwill trench coat, a look of complete bewilderment on her face. I went to her immediately and, putting my arms around her, exclaimed, "You're here at last!"

Sam came up behind me, kissed my cheek, and whispered, "I think she's pretty tired."

My mother had lapsed into silence but continued to stare at me as a confused child might, a child who wanted to trust this adult woman fawning over her, but who was too disoriented to remember why this trust eluded her.

"I know you're tired, darling," I said, taking my mother's arm, "so let's go upstairs."

As we began to move toward the elevator, my mother quickened her step and, as she half walked, half skipped across the lobby, began to hum. The humming had an urgency to it, an edge, and I understood that my mother needed to go to the bathroom.

"You go up, take the bags, here are the keys, we've got to get to the loo," I explained to Sam, already ushering my mother to the lobby restroom.

She did not make it. Inside the stall, after wrestling with the zipper of her pants, I saw that her adult diaper was soaked through and urine was beginning to leak down her leg. Coaxing her to sit on the toilet, I knelt beside her and said, "Don't worry, darling, we'll go right upstairs and you'll have a lovely bath, all right?"

This bewildered child, who was my mother, sat on the john with her stained pants around her ankles and looked at me with an unmistakable expression of shame.

A year and a half earlier, during my hiatus from *Star Trek: Voyager*, I had taken my mother on a luxury cruise up the Aegean Sea, and we had been delighted when, on our first evening aboard the elegant ship, a porter had delivered to our cabin an embossed envelope containing an invitation to dine at the captain's table. I was seated next to the captain, while my mother held court at the opposite end of the table. Shortly before dinner was served, the captain lifted his glass and, saluting us, launched into a monologue the length and substance of which were astonishingly trying and, although I maintained my composure and kept my eyes fixed on the bridge of the captain's nose (an old and very effective acting trick), my mother had decided that she had not traveled halfway around the world to suffer yet another excruciating bore and, putting her hand to her mouth, yawned loudly.

Hearing this, I turned sharply in her direction and mouthed, *"Mother!"* but she was undeterred. Looking straight at me, she said loudly, "But he's so *boring*." Then she rose and, without excusing herself, walked quickly down the length of the dining room, threading her way through tables occupied by well-heeled patrons, many of whom wondered why this trim, white-haired woman was so anxious to leave her place of privilege. Following her, I watched with growing horror as a stream of urine escaped from the hem of her black silk trousers, running down the sides of her patent leather pumps, leaving a vivid trail on the polished dining room floor. In the cabin, minutes later, my mother acted as if nothing untoward had happened, as if wetting one's pants in public was no big deal and I, as usual, was exaggerating the reality of what had happened simply because it suited my sense of the dramatic.

At the Mayflower, as I guided my mother to the suite upstairs, I realized that there was a strong possibility this trip had been a mistake, that my decision had been impetuous. In a week's time, she had regressed, and I worried that the prospect of having to navigate so much as a city block might overwhelm her.

I ran a bath for my mother and, as lavender-scented steam filled the room, watched as relief smoothed her features. Leaving the bathroom door open a crack, I returned to the sitting room, where Sam stood at the window, looking out over Central Park West.

"Maybe this wasn't such a great idea, Sambo," I said, pulling a bottle of pinot grigio from a bucket of ice.

"She needs a good night's sleep, the poor love," he responded, turning to look at me. "On the flight, she kept asking me the same question over and over."

"What question?" I asked.

"She wants to know what to do about this thing," my brother replied, "this thing with her mind. She's incredibly anxious, and she *knows*. She kept asking me what she should do about her—condition. It was awful."

"How did you handle it?"

"I told her we all loved her, that we were all fighting for her," Sam answered, softly.

"How did she respond to that?"

Sam looked at me, then shifted his gaze to the park.

"She didn't," my brother said.

I plucked a beer from the large bowl of ice on the coffee table and brought it to my brother. Sipping our drinks, we gazed at the city spread out before us and fell into silence as we shared a view that had never ceased to captivate us. Below us, Central Park was disgorging a stream of people, eager to avoid the crush of rush hour, some in pairs but many solitary, unfurling umbrellas, carrying briefcases, bending under the weight of backpacks, all purposefully striding to their respective des-

tinations, delighted that yet another chaotic day had come to an end
and that soon, very soon, cocktails would be ordered and keys inserted
hurriedly into latches, ties ripped from chafed necks, raincoats thrown
carelessly over barstools. Thousands of people would simultaneously
be seeking the same reward for having once again survived the challenges that attend the privilege of living in a great city.

We heard a sound, a slight rustling, and turned to find our mother
standing in the sitting room, dressed in her pajama top, khaki trousers, mismatched socks and, completing this ensemble, the ubiquitous
Goodwill trench coat.

"I am prepared!" she announced, making a beeline for the coffee
table, where she found herself momentarily confounded by the array
of snacks laid out before her.

"You're dressed for just about any occasion, sweetheart," Sam said.

"Drinks," our mother responded, pointing to the bowl of beers,
now sweating in their bath of ice water.

Sam smiled and immediately opened a Bud Light, which he poured
into a short glass and offered to our mother.

I was surprised at her recovery but decided not to overthink it. We
were together, in a city we all loved, and we would make the most of
it. Apparently, Sam agreed with me, because he popped open a second beer and, putting a hand on our mother's shoulder, asked, "What
would you like to do, Mother? Are you hungry? Would you like to
take a walk? We're in *New York*, sweetheart, and we can do anything
you like!"

Our mother, without hesitation, replied, "More drinks!"

At that moment, my husband came through the open door, disheveled from his journey, hair wet with rain, carrying a garment bag.

"Joan!" Tim exclaimed, taking large strides across the room, where
he embraced my mother, who looked at him curiously, almost criti-
cally, before deciding that he, too, must be a member of this clan, and
would therefore be interested in her pursuit of liquid refreshment.

"Drinks," my mother suggested, flirtatiously.

Tim considered this request for a moment, first observing our mother's outfit, then looking questioningly at Sam and me. I was almost certain that my caring, principled husband would advise against drinks but, to my surprise, he said, "Okay, Joan, if that's what you want, then that's what we'll have. But first, I need to take something *off* and you need to put something *on*."

The bar at the Mayflower Hotel was dark, corners of the room illuminated by festive strings of lights, fake ivy strung over the arch which separated the bar from the dining area. At our mother's urging, we had come downstairs and found ourselves hesitating in the doorway, trying to decide our next move. The atmosphere was convivial. A gaggle of patrons had converged onto the stools in the center of the bar and were engaged in lively, competitive chatter.

My mother, whom I presumed was having trouble growing accustomed to the dim light, made her way gingerly down the length of the bar until she had arrived in the middle of the line of strangers, whereupon she smiled at the man to her right, whose telepathic powers were immediately in evidence when he turned to my mother and said, "I think you'd like to join us, wouldn't you, my friend?"

Within seconds, room was made for my mother and myself, and we slid onto the high stools that faced the mirrored bar, overhung with red lights that flickered like small flames.

As grateful as I was for the stranger's kindness, I was nevertheless slightly abashed at having put out an entire bar's length of regulars. The man who had so thoughtfully accommodated us smiled at me, nodded, and then turned to my mother.

"What will you have, my friend?" he asked, cocking his head to one side, as if this was part of a familiar and very pleasant ritual, one that included any and all comers.

"Irish whiskey," my mother answered, with a confidence that surprised me. Standing behind us, Sam chuckled, Tim groaned, and I said, "Make that four, please, bartender. *Lots* of rocks."

When the drinks were placed in front of us, my mother did something I had never seen her do before, and it gave me pause. She studied the drink for a moment, then plunged her fingers into it and shoveled out the ice, which she flicked into the bar drain. Then, lifting her glass, she clinked with the man sitting next to her and said, "To my pub mates!"

This toast had a combustible effect and suddenly, in seamless accord, every patron sitting at the bar lifted his glass and shouted, "To pub mates!"

Glancing furtively at Sam and Tim, I couldn't help but feel the first prickle of complicity as I, too, raised my glass in salutation. Sensing this, Sam leaned into me and whispered, "Let her have her fun. Why not? If this is what she wants, let her have it."

"But what if she gets sick?" I asked, recalling my mother's violent reaction to the medication Dr. Fortson had initially prescribed, Aricept, which he hoped might delay the onset of more symptoms. He had warned me against giving my mother any alcohol, as one poison was likely to react adversely to the other. That conflict had not arisen, because my mother had vomited so convulsively after having taken the Aricept that I stashed the bottle away and the next afternoon offered her a glass of beer instead.

Sam shrugged, then said softly, "We'll know when it's time, but it's not time yet. Another half hour or so."

Comfortably ensconced at the bar, immersed in conversation with strangers she perceived as friends, my mother was avid for more whiskey. She consumed the toffee-colored liquid as if it were water, and no sooner had she downed one than she demanded another. I was convinced that any moment she would throw up all over her new pub mates, but this didn't happen. Instead, the rapport she had developed with the gentlemen on either side of her contained a surprising element of solicitousness. It struck me that these men, whom she had never laid eyes on before, understood my mother's dilemma, and empathized. No words were spoken, but every whiskey placed in front of her was accompanied by a sidelong glance from her pub mate, a look that assured me that my mother was in very good hands. The atmosphere was dense with smoke, laughter, and ribaldry. Although I was seated next to my mother, I was not a part of the central clique, one which fanned out on either side of her. Sam occasionally chimed in, but our mother kept her eyes riveted to the man on her right or the man on her left, as if their presence promised something far more appealing than anything we had to offer.

After two hours had elapsed, and my mother had consumed eight whiskeys with breathtaking dispatch, I nodded to Sam and said, "That's it, Sambo. One more and we'll all end up in jail."

But when we attempted to remove our mother from her barstool, she resisted with a strength and audacity that caught both Sam and me off guard. Our mother fiercely defended her right to stay at the bar, in the company of her pub mates, because wasn't she a mature woman who could do as she liked? Who were we to tear her away from the first pleasure she'd known in months? And yet, tear her away we did, and almost immediately our mother's ebullience collapsed. We watched, incredulous, as the vitality drained out of her. On the elevator, we observed our mother with a new kind of alarm. What had we done? We were complicit, we knew that, but in what? Our mother was not drunk, not in the conventional sense. She had not stumbled as she left the bar, nor had she slurred her words. This drama playing out in our mother's head was one we could not define, but we understood that it hinged on a sliver of hope that had revealed itself through an old, familiar lens. At the bar, she was just another pub mate, one on whom all judgment was suspended. At the bar, for a short time, she knew herself.

Once inside the suite, my mother pleaded to be allowed to go down for one final drink.

"A nightcap with my pub mates!" she implored, her back against the suite door.

We cajoled, we wheedled and, finally, we persuaded our mother to take off her coat and to get into her pajamas. I turned off the light in her bedroom and slipped across the hall to my suite, where my husband, unaccustomed to more than the occasional Irish coffee, was fast asleep under the covers. I slid in beside him and, still restless, picked up my book and tried to read by the dim light of the bedside lamp.

Suddenly, I heard a sound that made me prick up my ears. In hotels, it is the most ordinary of sounds, that of doors opening and clicking shut, and yet this particular sound pulled me from my bed and drew me to the suite door, where I peered through the peek hole into the hallway. Nothing. Unsettled, I pulled on my coat and opened the door, using the open bolt as a doorstop. I put the key in the lock of my mother's suite and entered quietly, not wanting to disturb Sam, who was sleeping on a rollaway in the sitting room. I made out his form under the white duvet and tiptoed into my mother's bedroom. The bed was empty, and her trench coat was missing from the armchair.

Without thinking, I left the suite and made my way down the corridor. At two o'clock in the morning, no one was on the elevator, so I stepped in and pressed the lobby button. When the elevator door opened, I wrapped my coat tightly around my nightgown and hurried to the entrance of the bar. Opening the door, I immediately saw my mother, sitting exactly where she had sat for most of the night, perched between her pub mates, an Irish whiskey on the bar in front of her. She wore her Goodwill trench coat over her blue pajamas, her walking shoes untied beneath her scalloped pajama bottoms. No one at the bar seemed the least surprised by her reappearance. I watched as a wave of laughter rose from the group when my mother said, "I told them that I couldn't say good-bye to my pub mates without a nightcap!"

Sitting unobserved at a table in the corner, I knew that I would wait it out, that it would not be long before the bartender announced last call and the patrons would slowly gather their coats, their briefcases and handbags, throw money on the counter and, bidding the bartender good night, would one by one pull my mother into an embrace and tell her what a wonderful night it had been, how happy they were to have met her, and how they would look forward to many more nights at the Mayflower bar because, after all, they were pub mates now, and pub mates were nothing if not loyal.

Buttoning his coat against the damp night, the man to her right was the last to leave my mother's side and, just before passing me on his way out, he nodded slightly and said, "She's a hell of a woman."

My mother was not surprised when I came up behind her and said, "I think it's time for bed now, darling, don't you?"

Not a word was uttered, she was completely compliant. For the third time that night, we stepped on the elevator and rode silently to our floor. I helped her out of her coat, took off her shoes, and pulled back the covers on the bed. Satisfied that she was comfortable, I leaned in to kiss her forehead and, seeing that her eyes were closed, concluded that whether she was asleep or not was none of my business.

CHAPTER FORTY-ONE

Lucy's sacrifice had been considerable, and yet she never complained. It was not in her nature to indulge feelings of loneliness or despondency. She had been raised in the Mexican state of Campeche, a land of limestone hills and rain forests, a land of poverty, where children were born on dirt floors in shacks that housed twenty people. There was no running water, no plumbing, no electricity, and young girls went to work in the local factory as soon as they were able to stand on their feet for twelve hours straight. The only luxury Lucy had ever known was the devotion of her first love, a boy named Javier, whom she had met in her pueblo when they were both sixteen years old.

The vicissitudes of poverty are harsh, however, and Lucy and Javier were forced to separate when Lucy's family encouraged her to marry an older man, who took her away and immediately impregnated her, which resulted in the birth of a daughter nine months later. This marriage proved to be less than auspicious, and Lucy soon ran away. She subsequently married twice more, each union producing two children, so that at the end of what she considered her salad days, Lucy had been bound to three men by whom she had had a total of five children. Her last husband, roused to fury by Lucy's apparent indolence when she collapsed to the floor in hard labor and refused to make him his dinner, took a bottle of tequila, broke it, and sliced her calves as she lay moaning on the ground.

Lucy escaped, but was forced to leave her children behind when she drew the short straw and fate determined that it was she, of her eleven siblings, who would cross the border in the dead of night, huddled in the back of a truck driven by a coyote who, after seizing her last peso, had deposited her alone and penniless in a strange and foreign land. Because Lucy had learned very young to stand on her feet for sustained periods of time, the journey to Los Angeles was successful, and it was on the outskirts of that sprawling city, in a suburb called Bell, that Lucy was reunited with her mother's sister, Tia Josefina, who gladly offered her niece shelter, but warned her that this came with a proviso, one which Lucy was fully prepared to accept. It happened that Josefina cleaned for me twice a month, and after my second son was born and I had inquired as to whether she knew anyone who might be available to live in my house and help me with my children, Josefina came as close to smiling as her thin, sallow mouth would allow.

The only regret that Lucy harbored, after having brought each of her children as well as a number of her siblings to Los Angeles, was that she had lost touch with her childhood sweetheart, Javier Flores, for whom she still secretly carried a flame. Imagine Lucy's great surprise when one day the phone rang, and it was her sister Paty calling from Bell with the news that Javier had shown up on her doorstep and that there would be a fiesta at her casita that weekend welcoming him to America and that everyone was hoping Lucy would ask Señora Kate to give her the night off. Señora Kate was only too happy to oblige and stood in the doorway watching as Lucy, attired in a black lace dress, a cluster of bougainvillea braided into her long, inky hair, sling-back heels adorning her small feet, and a red shawl wrapped loosely around her shoulders, walked off into a night that would return her to her first and only true love.

That had been ten years ago. Now, months had passed since Lucy had first entered the back door at Derby Grange, months during which she was required to familiarize herself with the habits of not just my mother, but my father, too, and this proved to be by far the greater test. From the moment my father had decided that he would turn his face away from the truth of my mother's affliction, he had developed a detachment that was extremely difficult to penetrate. When he met

Lucy for the first time, my father had acknowledged the small Mexican woman with nothing more than a curt nod, and this is how things stood for many weeks. Lucy had never learned the value of self-pity, however, and had been enculturated to keep her distance from alpha males, so that it was natural for her to assume her duties without undue sensitivity toward my father. She went about the business of tending to my mother, cooking and cleaning and ironing my father's boxer shorts, and all of this she did with grace and efficiency. At night she climbed the back stairs to the small room just off the stairwell, lit a candle for her children and her mother, made the sign of the cross, and crawled into bed.

Although not characteristically given to divulgences of a personal nature, Lucy one day told me that she thought Javier could be quite useful around the property, cutting wood and mowing the broad lawn, cleaning the gutters in the spring and, in winter, salting and shoveling the driveway.

"Javier really keep the place good, señora," she told me, and then added, smiling, "and you know he don't talk too much."

By this time, my father had grown accustomed to laundry impeccably done, a soft-boiled egg and strong coffee served to him in the morning, a cup of soup and a dish of tapioca presented on a tray at night. His mood had softened as he observed Lucy's expert ministrations, the bright sounds that now attended my mother's rising, the soft cajoling in the late afternoon, when it was time for my mother's bath, the undisturbed calm after my mother had been put to bed.

When I approached my father and asked if he would consider allowing Javier to move in and help around the house, and after assuring him that no task was too much for Javier and that his presence would hardly be felt, my father looked at me and said, "Okay, okay, knock it off. If she wants the guy to come that badly, what the hell. Give it a go."

A month later, Javier arrived, and it was just as Lucy had predicted.

Neither seen nor heard, the man moved mysteriously around the property, clearing timber from the glen, mowing the lawn, stacking wood, cleaning out the hedges, reinforcing the fence, washing my father's car, bringing in the groceries, taking out the garbage. On my visits home, I would occasionally observe my father standing at the door of the TV Room, shaking his head as he appraised the firewood stacked neatly on the well-swept side porch.

In time, my father would address both Lucy and Javier by their Christian names and, while he never inquired into their pasts or made any attempt at conversation, he could sometimes be heard saying, "Lucy, how are you?" or "Nice to see you, Javier," which, for my father, was tantamount to a confession of love. Increasingly, the door leading from the TV Room into the kitchen was intentionally propped open, and while a small group sat eating and drinking at the kitchen table, my father could eavesdrop while pretending complete indifference, ensconced on the couch in the TV Room, his crossword puzzle laid out before him.

The dinner ritual gave Lucy great satisfaction, and on my visits home, hours went into the preparation and execution of the perfect meal. Sam would be invited well in advance, and my mother, standing at the back door, would wait for him. When his truck pulled into the driveway, and Sam leapt from the driver's seat shouting, "Hello, sweetheart!" my mother would inhale sharply and clasp her hands to her chest. Coming through the door, Sam would draw my mother into an embrace and say, "You look so pretty tonight, sweetheart." Peering into the kitchen, he would add, "And you other broads aren't so bad, either, especially the one making chicken and rice."

When we were all seated, beers would be popped open, wine would be poured, and Lucy would place in the center of the table a platter of guacamole and tortilla chips and a plate of cheese and crackers. If my mother regarded these hors d'oeuvres with indifference, Lucy would insert a plate into the microwave and within seconds present to my mother a dish of saltines topped with melted cheddar and drizzled with Worcestershire sauce, the sight of which invariably elicited a smile of satisfaction.

In the middle of high-spirited teasing, the wine and beer flowing freely, the back door would suddenly swing open and bang shut, and Joe would be standing there, stamping his feet on the welcome mat, presenting himself with a diffidence that concealed his awkwardness at having interrupted the festive gathering. Immediately, I would rise and go to him, saying, "Bobo, I'm so glad you're here! Join us! Come on, *please*." Joe, after accepting my kiss, would move to the refrigerator and extract a Bud Light, which he popped open as he crossed into the kitchen. When he reached my mother, he would lean over and plant a kiss on her cheek.

"How are you doing today, Mom?" he'd ask.

My mother would hum for a moment, playing with a saltine.

"Sit down, Bo," I'd urge, pulling out a chair for him.

"Maybe later. I'm going to check in on Dad," Joe would answer, already moving away.

When the meal was ready, and the table had been cleared so that places could be properly set with wineglasses, silverware, and my mother's homemade cotton napkins, I noticed a figure hovering in the shadows, just inside the dining room.

"Javier, what are you doing lurking in the dining room? Come in here and sit down!" I ordered, moving toward him. Instinctively, he demurred, but Lucy faced him from across the room and said authoritatively, "Javier, you better do what Señora says or you gonna be in big trouble."

This was the first time Javier had ever joined us at the dinner table. Ordinarily, he'd finish his work around six o'clock, wash up in the bathroom in the back of the house, fix a plate with whatever Lucy had prepared, and disappear upstairs for the rest of the night. Tonight, as we added a chair to the table and quickly assembled a place setting, we took voluble pleasure in Javier's presence, and it was only Lucy who said nothing as she circled the table, positioning platters of arroz con pollo, tomato and avocado salad, thin slices of cantaloupe garnished with mint.

Before she sat, Lucy and I shared a look, and within seconds two plates had been arranged on a tray, complete with cold beers and a small dish of guacamole. As I entered the TV Room, I was met with predictable resistance, which expressed itself in a short volley of dissent.

"Not hungry," my father flatly stated, raising his hands.

"Can't eat it," Joe said, crossing his arms across his chest.

"Okay, I get it, but try to remember your manners. You'll hurt Lucy's feelings, so I'm just going to leave it here," I whispered, making room on the coffee table for the tray.

When I returned to the table, Lucy and Sam were attempting to seduce my mother with small tidbits of food. My mother declined the slice of avocado offered by Lucy but greedily ate the rice from Sam's spoon, after which Sam said, "Isn't that delicious, sweetheart? Wait till you try this!" In this manner, my mother managed to consume what amounted to a balanced meal, an accomplishment that pleased all of us.

Sated, she sat next to Sam, appearing fully content. Her eyes were bright with interest whenever he spoke, and when he laughed, she laughed with him. Javier, too, regarded my brother with an open, guileless expression, one that suggested respect as well as affection. In the short time Javier had been living at Derby Grange, it had been Sam who had shown him around and helped him to understand how things were done. This was no mean feat, as Javier did not speak a word of English and Sam's Spanish was, by his own admission, "entertaining." Nevertheless, a bond had developed between them, and as I listened to their banter, I observed Lucy out of the corner of my eye. She was in her element, sitting at that table, the ubiquitous red apron wrapped around her sturdy body, the impeccably prepared feast reduced to scraps, her eyes shining with satisfaction.

Leaning into my brother, I whispered, "Lucy and Javier are living in sin, you know. And they call themselves Catholics."

Sam looked first at Javier, then Lucy, before he pronounced judgment. "That is a holy bed you two are defiling, you know that, don't you?"

Lucy started to giggle, but Sam cut her off.

"I don't think God would find this very amusing, do you, Luce? I think it would really piss Him off."

With astounding speed and economy, Lucy translated Sam's words for Javier who, looking genuinely abashed, lowered his head and covered his eyes with his hands. Lucy laughed until she wiped tears from the corners of her eyes, imploring, "Stop now, Sam, you really bad. *You* the one going to piss God!"

"No, no, don't change the subject, Luce," my brother interrupted, wiping his mouth with his napkin and throwing it into the air so that it landed in the middle of what had once been a pretty knoll of guacamole.

"I think this shocking behavior has been going on for quite long enough," I declared, sitting back in my chair and folding my arms.

"Javier, don't you think it's time you made an honest woman out of her?" Sam asked, shaking his head in puzzlement.

"Translate, please, Lucy," I demanded.

"Oh, señora, I no say that to Javi! You *crazy*?"

"Never saner," I responded.

"Don't make me do it myself, Luce, 'cause it won't be pretty," Sam warned.

Suddenly Lucy rose from the table and, as she began busily clearing plates and dishes, sliding and scraping with a terrible clatter, she whispered something to Javier that sounded to my ears like a fierce repudiation of love but was, in fact, a fairly direct translation of what Sam and I had said. She then gathered a pile of dirty dishes in her arms and moved abruptly away from the table. An awkward, attenuated silence followed, until, finally, Javier lifted his head and said, "Sí."

"Sí?" I asked, mouth agape.

"Was that a sí, Javier?" Sam pressed, grinning.

"De verdad," Javier answered, softly.

Lucy, her pink-gloved hands plunged in dirty sink water, whirled around and stared at Javier.

Sam, putting his arm around our mother's shoulder, pulled her into him and said, "Well, what do you know, sweetheart? There's going to be a wedding!"

My mother suddenly looked away, as if struck, but when she turned back and lifted her eyes to her son's face, the perplexity that usually masked her features had been wiped away, revealing a girl transfigured by ardor.

CHAPTER FORTY-TWO

The limo rolled slowly through the stone gates, navigating the high banks of snow on either side of the driveway. I watched from the Good Living Room window as the driver opened the passenger door, out of which immediately tumbled my older son, Ian. As he attempted to find his legs, my friend Mary Kay appeared from the other side of the car and extended her hand to him, laughing.

"Oh, God," I mumbled, "they've been drinking."

Jenny looked up from the table we were in the process of setting and cried, "Oh, let me see!"

We studied the tableau for a moment before Jenny speculated that Mary Kay, held captive inside the car, had bravely maintained sobriety while Ian gleefully ravaged the contents of the limousine bar.

"She should have joined him, it would have eased the pain," I said, stepping over the chairs arranged around the table and making my way to the front door.

"At last!" I cried, pulling Mary Kay into an embrace and shouldering her overnight bag. I was delighted that my old friend had made the journey from Los Angeles to share Thanksgiving with my family and had been game enough to find Ian in the chaos of O'Hare, locate the limousine I had ordered, and endure the three-and-a-half-hour drive from Chicago to Dubuque. Weather, in snowstorms so prodigious that the mere thought of flying in one rendered one speechless with panic, often dictated the cancellation of the commuter flight from Chicago to Dubuque. Under these circumstances, a hired limousine seemed less an extravagance than a reasonable compromise.

Ian, wearing a quilted jacket and sporting a beanie, stumbled up the path and, stopped by my hand, submitted to a kiss. The stubble of his beard scratched my cheek and I thought, When did that happen?

"Did you enjoy that little drive from O'Hare with Mary Kay?" I asked, with a wry smile.

"I did," Ian replied. "I find Mary Kay very good company."

As we entered the house, Mary Kay laughed lightly and said, "I don't think he required *any* company, he seemed perfectly happy with his *own*."

Voices rose in greeting as the last two stragglers, for whom we had been waiting since morning, walked into the TV Room and were swamped by members of my clan, all of whom had assembled to celebrate the holiday. Alec, my younger son, who had traveled with me from Los Angeles to Dubuque, sprang to his feet and shouted, "Where the *fuck* have you been, bro?" Everyone had come with the implicit understanding that this would be a Thanksgiving to remember, and to cherish. Our father would be seated in his customary place at the head of the table, and our mother would be seated in hers, facing him from the opposite end. Tradition dictated that I would sit at my father's right, and Sam at my mother's. All of my siblings would be gathered around this table, causing a number of the spouses to vie for a seat, bony and big bottoms alike pressed cheek to cheek on the same worn cushion. Most of the kids were relegated to the Good Living Room or the kitchen, depending on age and disposition. Lucy and I would shuttle between the rooms, arms laden with dishes, subduing arguments and herding recalcitrant teenagers into their appointed chairs.

With my sisters and sisters-in-law assisting us in the kitchen, the buffet was organized quickly. Eased in between generous platters of turkey and ham, mashed potatoes and green beans, there would be additional items less easy to identify. Sam's wife, Wendy, would have prepared a mysterious pasta dish and baked loaves of bread, all shapes and sizes, artfully presented in a wire basket of her creation. Something odd but chutney-like might assert itself next to the butter dish, and the gravy bowl was a perpetual disappointment, appearing in its tiny white cradle under the shadow of the huge turkey platter. Dessert was understood to be outside of our habit, so anything that looked even remotely sweet would be immediately greeted with skepticism. Store-bought pies could be found the next day, sunken and sodden in their aluminum tins, excavated as if by a raccoon.

The wine, my brother Tom's domain, was good and plentiful. Bottles of pinot noir and sauvignon blanc shared the counter with china plates, silverware wrapped in cloth napkins, and glasses. On the table stood two antique silver candelabras, each sprouting six candles, secured in their tiny basins by bits of paper towel. Mismatched pitchers of ice water, a heatedly debated nod to convention, were grudgingly placed next to the bottles of wine. Sprigs of rosemary and evergreen were put in small vases and placed under the candelabras.

When everything was in order, it was announced that dinner was served, and a line quickly formed in the dining room. First, the small children were served by their mothers, followed by the teenagers who, over the years, had learned prudence in helping themselves to portions sufficient to quell their hunger, but never to sate it. The adults came last, and it was an unspoken rule that I would fix a plate for our father, and that Sam would do the same for our mother. When I placed the modest repast in front of my father, he invariably raised his hands in alarm and the time-honored exchange would follow:

"Too much!"

"Dad, it's nothing. Please, just eat it."

"Unlikely."

"Well, then, *pretend* you're eating it."

Mother, on a typical Thanksgiving, would receive her plate with delight, making the appropriate sounds of pleasure. A light, quick smacking of her lips, a coo of surprise, and a fork plunged immediately into the pat of butter smoothed onto the side of the plate, which she would pop into her mouth with the deftness of a baby bird.

This Thanksgiving, my mother regarded her plate with indifference, studying the items on it with bemused detachment. Sam, sitting beside her, leaned over and cut her turkey into small bites, then forked a piece and brought it to our mother's lips. Her attention could be won, now, only by certain people, people sensitive to my mother's deliquescence. Lucy's kindness and efficiency could motivate my mother to react, but only Sam seemed to possess the ability to move her. As the forkful of meat reached our mother's lips, she would gaze into Sam's eyes as if willing him to show her the way, and this is what he did. With infinite patience and indicating with his own mouth what he wanted her to do, Sam would say, "This is delicious, sweetheart. You need to open up." Mesmerized, my mother would part her lips, Sam would slip the bit of turkey into her mouth, she would begin to chew, and everyone at the table would sigh with relief.

As the meal unfolded, laughter erupted from time to time, and the teasing, which had for so long defined our communication, revealed itself in short, colorful bursts. In spite of this, we were all waiting. Acutely sensitive to our mother's every utterance and gesture, each of us hung suspended in limbo. Would today be the day when our mother would look at us and say, as she so often had in years past, "How much do you think this meal would cost in New York?"

My mother sat in her chair, her hands folded in her lap, and waited. Her eyes, once keen and mischievous, wandered over us, settling on nothing, until they found Sam, where they assumed a sudden interest. She fixed her gaze on her youngest son, as if enthralled. Her expression also conveyed fear, and suggested that lurking behind the relief of finding a face she understood was the far greater threat that it could just as suddenly be snatched away. To observe this in real time was to observe a theft so ingenious that no one could be sure of what had happened, only that in a moment's time our mother's face had lost its vitality and had once again become expressionless.

While my mother's eyes rested on her son's face, she was with us, and could even be compelled to smile. If Sam smiled, my mother smiled, and attending this smile was a hint of the mother of old, which so captivated us that Jenny sat down next to our mother and, taking her hand, pointed at Joe, who was sitting across the table.

"Mother, do you know who that is?" Jenny asked.

Immediately, the atmosphere became charged. This question would never have been allowed had my father been present, but he had left the table earlier, excusing himself after consuming exactly one forkful of mashed potatoes and a glass of red wine.

Joe was instantly on his guard and, faced with his baby sister's pointed finger, asked, "Christ, Jenny, what the hell kind of game is this?"

"Shhh," Jenny scolded. "Mother, do you know that man's name?"

Our mother looked straight at Joe and shook her head, no.

"That's the Alzheimer's talking," Joe said gruffly, scraping back his chair and heading into the kitchen for another beer.

For a moment, everyone was quiet.

Then Jenny pointed her finger at Tom, seated at the other end of the table.

"How about that man? Do you know his name?"

Tom grinned and leaned on the table, cupping his face in his hands.

"Your favorite," he whispered.

Our mother seemed about to smile, as she peered quizzically at her oldest son.

"You see?" Tom asked.

"Mother, what is his name?" Jenny asked, again pointing at Tom.

Our mother allowed herself to look at Tom for a moment before she shook her head and whispered, "No."

Tom continued to smile and, pausing to consider, said, "It doesn't change the fact that I'm your favorite."

Laura had slipped away earlier, having intuited that this was a diversion she wanted no part of.

Now holding both of our mother's hands, Jenny asked, "Who am I, darling? Do you know *my* name? I'm your baby."

This clue elicited murmurs of disapproval, as it was considered cheating.

Our mother's countenance brightened as she stared at Jenny with what could only be interpreted as affection. Then she lifted her hand and, pointing her finger in imitation of her youngest daughter, said, playfully, "No, no, no."

"I think I deserve another chance, she just needs another minute," Jenny pleaded.

Joe, having returned, leaned against the doorframe and said, "No way. Same rules apply for everyone. You lose. Next."

The afternoon had deepened into evening, but in my memory the room had retained a muted light, so that I can recall every detail of my mother's face as she was directed to look at me down the long table. A stillness prevailed, while her eyes settled on my face.

"Who is that woman, Mother?" Jenny asked. "What is her name?"

My mother studied me for a long moment, during which it seemed not only possible but probable that she would recall my name, a bright pebble drawn from a deep well. My siblings, leaning in, stared at our mother with unusual intensity. Finally, my mother whispered, "I don't know. I don't know."

Sam took my mother's hand and said, "That's all right, sweetheart. You know that's Katy."

"And who is that man holding your hand?" Jenny demanded, impatiently.

My mother put her hand on Sam's sleeve, and plucked lightly at the fabric of his shirt. Then she lifted her eyes to his face, and whispered, "The one I love."

This elicited a few startled, nervous chuckles, but soon an awkward silence fell over us. We were no more than a band of children, weary and fractious, and yet my little sister, having walked the plank, thought it only fair that Sam should be made to walk it, as well.

"But what is his *name*?"

My mother gazed into Sam's eyes, transfixed, and then spoke. "His name is Jesus."

Silence. Raised eyebrows. Sam lowered his eyes, a shy, tight smile on his lips. He had generously, even gallantly played along for weeks. Not once had he denied our mother her fantasy, which had dodged the plaques and tangles in her brain and rooted itself in a romance with her son. Another synaptic whim, and my little brother had been elevated to Jesus Christ. This development stopped everyone. My brother's elevation from lover to the Son of God, as bizarre as it was, carried with it a pinched envy, as each of us silently considered the cause for this advancement. There was no question that my mother's affliction caused these deviations, but the fact that each seismic shift revolved around Sam was no accident. In the years following Tessie's death, Sam had been unusually present to our mother. He had sat with her for hours, talking quietly, eating meals with her, walking with her. When it came time to pursue a higher education, he did not go away but chose to remain in Dubuque and attend a local college. He stayed home, providing the relationship between mother and son with the kind of nourishment it needed to establish deep, invisible roots.

We all knew that Sam and our mother had an unusual, even exceptional relationship, but to see it made so starkly visible was disturbing. Glancing around the table, I read in the expressions of my siblings a strange vulnerability, as if each of them were silently acknowledging a different kind of loss. I think it occurred to all of us that in the twisted thicket of my mother's brain the only recognition that had survived was one of love, and that the person assigned this recognition was Sam.

From the vantage point of having had a long history of my own with our mother, I empathized with my brother, and wondered how he would navigate this next, impassable course. Beloved son had been acceptable, if occasionally unsettling to his older brothers, who continually vied for space in our mother's affection. The role of lover had demanded an altogether different sympathy, one Sam was forced to assume in order to appease our mother.

But nothing could have prepared my soft-spoken, gentle-mannered little brother for this final, astounding transfiguration. In a dining room gone uncomfortably still, my mother looked at Sam but no longer saw her youngest son. She saw only the love of her life, and the name she gave him was Jesus.

CHAPTER FORTY-THREE

On the morning of Lucy's wedding, my father sat on the couch in the TV Room and feigned indifference. After so many years, it could be argued that this was no longer pretense, but reality. His cup of coffee, his crossword puzzles, and his cigarettes were all he needed to detach himself from the palpable excitement felt throughout the house. Lucy was getting married, and the wedding was to be held at the old Dancer McDonald House in town. The house was brick and glass and, from the moment I first glimpsed it, driving down Prairie Street with Sam, I knew it was what I wanted for Lucy and Javier. It's possible that Lucy may have preferred something simpler, but I somehow doubted it. Hidden behind that strong reserve, a veneer Lucy had carefully cultivated, a young girl waited, and she was growing impatient. With each passing year, the young girl was finding her dream harder and harder to cling to, what with children desperate for a better life and visas languishing on the desks of greedy immigration lawyers and the constant, unremitting care of other people's loved ones. The old Dancer McDonald House would fulfill part of the young girl's dream, the part that would raise her above the throng, lifting her high over the heads of those who could never know what she had known, and in the moment of separating herself from a crowd of blue-eyed women holding glasses of champagne, she would step onto the dais and reveal to them her shining uniqueness, and in that moment the young girl would be vindicated.

Before that dream could be realized, however, there was a list of chores to attend to, and Lucy could not be persuaded to put them aside. Foremost among these obligations was my mother, and how she must appear when she walked through the front door of the old Dancer Mc-Donald House. I pleaded with Lucy to let me handle my mother and assured her that it would be my pleasure to do so, but Lucy's conviction superseded common sense and, in the end, my mother emerged from her bedroom looking as she had looked on that evening less than two years before, when she had sat at the captain's table aboard the Seabourn cruise, at the beginning of our adventure on the Aegean Sea.

Impeccably groomed, her short white hair washed and curled, makeup applied to brighten her cheeks and lips, black silk trousers and white silk blouse flawlessly dry-cleaned, a strand of pearls fastened around her neck, my mother was led down the front stairs and into the TV Room, where she was duly presented to my father, whose discomfort was evident when he looked up from his book and was made to acknowledge my mother's presence.

"Doesn't Mother look terrific, Dad?" I asked, standing in the middle of the room, my arm tucked into my mother's.

"You bet," my father responded and, as he bent his head to resume reading an impressively dense biography of Ulysses S. Grant, it was clear that nothing more would be forthcoming. Because my mother no longer recognized him, my father had retreated behind the lines of a defense that he felt would protect him from further assault. He acted as if he didn't care, which was his way of judging my mother's affliction as somehow contrived, the result of too many cooks in the kitchen, stirring a pot that should have been left to simmer away, uninterrupted. My father could not credit what had happened to his wife; it was beyond his capacity to do so. Were he to admit to the vicissitudes of aging, thereby lending credibility to the ravages of time and mind, he would be conceding to an opponent he had battled for many years, and it was not in my father's character to do so. Acceptance of my mother's affliction would have connoted failure, which is why he returned to his book after only a perfunctory glance at my mother, whose appearance must have shaken him. Outwardly, she had changed little, and this twisted something in my father so sharply that it was all he could do to remain silent.

"Dad, you're coming to the wedding, aren't you?" I asked, still standing next to my mother, who had begun humming.

"Not my scene," my father replied, without looking up.

"But it's *Lucy's* scene, and I know she'd love to see you there."

"She knows I wish her well," my father said, curtly.

"Actions speak louder than words," I said.

"End of conversation," he warned, glancing at me over his book with narrowed eyes.

I guided my mother into the kitchen, where I poured her a cup of coffee and prepared a soft-boiled egg. It was becoming increasingly difficult to gauge her needs, so Lucy adhered to a strict schedule of feeding, followed by an equally strict schedule of using the toilet, both of which required attention before we set off for the long drive into town. Draping an oversize tea towel around her neck, I began to spoon-feed my mother tiny bites of the egg, generously flavored with butter and salt. Her gaze drifted aimlessly around the room, assuming focus only when I touched her mouth with the spoon. Hers was the distracted attention of an infant who, while taking in the pudding, is at the same time diverted by light, or sound, or tiredness.

Today, my mother's distractibility was heightened, and it was all I could do to persuade her to eat a few bites of the soft egg before she clenched her teeth, making it clear that mealtime was over.

"What is it, darling? What's bothering you? This is a good day. We're going to a wedding!" I promised her, pulling the tea towel from her neck. The humming increased in volume, and my mother began drumming her fingers lightly on the table. She looked expectantly at the back door, the humming constant, a tuneless melody lodged in a crevice of her memory. I thought it might soothe her if I led her to the back door, so that she could look out the window. My mother stood stock-still, peering out with an intensity I had not observed in weeks.

"Who are you expecting, Mums? Sam isn't coming out today. He's waiting for you at the wedding," I assured her, taking her hand and guiding her into the bathroom. Unlike our struggle over the soft-boiled egg, only minutes before, my mother's eyes were now riveted on me. The strength of her gaze, and the quality of anticipation that attended it, indicated to me that my mother very much wanted an answer to the puzzle that was causing her considerable agitation. It was the understanding of the puzzle that eluded her. She would no sooner arrive at the edge of what it was she wanted to know than it would be sucked away from her, circling frantically on the fringes of her consciousness before vanishing. I read all of this in my mother's expression but was helpless to perceive the actual source of her perplexity. Sighing, I knelt on the bathroom rug and, putting a hand on my mother's knee as she sat on the toilet said, "It will be all right, darling. Wait and see. This is a *big* day and we don't want to be late, so let's get going."

In the kitchen, I quickly made a fresh pot of coffee and laid out a dish of rice pudding for my father, then placed a can of Ensure next to the bottle of Popov that waited like an aging mistress on top of the old dishwasher. There was a rustling sound and, when I turned, Lucy stood in the doorway of the kitchen, attired in a peach dress, wearing the string of pearls and matching earrings I had given her for her fortieth birthday. Lucy had explained to me that while out scouting for secondhand finds with my mother, she had happened upon this gown in a consignment shop on Main Street. Although it was originally intended as formal wear, Lucy had purchased it for ten dollars, and had transformed it into an elegant dress, shortening the hem to just below her knee, replacing the long zipper in the back with stitching that shaped the bodice, so that when she had finished, the garment looked as if it had been custom-made for her.

"Oh, Luce, qué bonita!" I exclaimed, in my pidgin Spanish, staring at her. On the table sat two boxes that had been delivered by the florist first thing that morning. In one rested the bridal bouquet, an arrangement of white lilies and roses, and in the other a white carnation for Javier, lying next to a spray of wild roses. I chose the two prettiest roses and carefully threaded them into Lucy's black hair, which she had arranged into a chignon.

"Now, you're perfect," I declared, standing back to appraise her.

I gathered the flowers in one hand and, taking my mother's arm with the other, headed for the car. As I opened the back door, I heard Lucy's voice coming from the TV Room.

"Adiós, señor. I sorry you not coming."

"Not up to it, Lucy. But you have my heartiest congratulations," my father said.

Inside the car, I placed the bridal bouquet on my mother's lap. She studied the roses through the cellophane window of the box and then her eyes jumped to my face, bright with excitement.

"The bridal bouquet," I whispered, glancing at Lucy where she sat in the backseat, smoothing the folds of her wedding dress, lightly touching the flowers in her hair.

As we approached the old Dancer McDonald House, I noted that the street was lined with cars and realized, with a rush of satisfaction, that most of the guests had already arrived. Sam and I had invited not only everyone in Dubuque who had met Lucy, but anyone who knew and loved my mother as well. The broad lawn was crowded with people sipping from flutes of champagne, a preceremony feature I had insisted on.

Pulling up to the curb in front of the house, I saw Sam waiting for us outside the door that opened into the glass conservatory. He strode quickly down the brick path and, beaming at our mother, opened her door and extended his hand.

"Hello, sweetheart! You look beautiful," he said, kissing our mother on the cheek. Entranced, she stared at him until Sam, laughing, opened the back door and helped Lucy out.

"Wow, Lucy. Javier might forget his English when he sees how gorgeous you are."

"What English, Sam? I tell him, when the priest asks you a question, you look at me and I nod and you say *yes*, you got that? Javi no talk today, Sam. Only say yes, yes, yes," Lucy explained, as if she were preparing to marry a small and rather backward child.

Tucking our mother's hand into his arm, Sam started up the path toward the conservatory. Handing the car keys to the valet, I turned to Lucy and said, "The time has come, señorita. Shall we?"

As we moved toward the house, several guests spotted us and, calling Lucy's name, lifted their flutes in salutation. Small clusters of people in colorful summer clothing decorated the broad lawn, while the conservatory held the rest of the congregation, most of whom had gathered around the large silver bowls, each containing several bottles of champagne, tightly packed in shaved ice.

"I think we should go inside and see that everything's ready," I whispered to Lucy. As we approached the conservatory, the enormity of what was about to unfold played over Lucy's features. Unsmiling, she held herself with a dignity bordering on severity, and looked around to locate Javier. The husband-to-be was, of course, inside the ballroom, where he was found busily straightening chairs and smoothing tablecloths. Lucy admonished him for wrinkling his newly acquired olive-green guayabera as she moved to his side and began, reflexively, rearranging wineglasses and plates.

Out of the corner of my eye, I watched as Sam escorted our mother around the conservatory, introducing her to people whose names she had once known. Our mother clung to his arm. Whenever a woman approached them to say hello, my mother would tighten her grip on Sam's arm and fasten her eyes on his face, willing him to look at her. If he did not immediately return her gaze, my mother would start to hum and pluck at his sleeve, compelling him to return his attention to her.

Champagne in hand, I crossed the room and interrupted them.

"It's about that time, don't you think?" I asked, glancing at the depleted bottles of champagne.

"Past time, I'd say. Let's get this show on the road. What do you say, sweetheart?" Sam replied, kissing my mother gently on the forehead.

My mother looked nervously from Sam to me, and back again.

"You come with me, darling," I said, gently detaching my mother's hand from Sam's arm. At first, she refused to come with me, and stood rooted to her place next to Sam.

"We need to get ready for the wedding now, sweetheart," Sam whispered to our mother, "so you need to go with Katy."

With this encouragement, my mother released her hold on her son and, looking at him with unabashed tenderness, allowed herself to be led away.

The ballroom, with its high ceiling and graceful lines, held ten tables, each of which was surrounded by ten chairs. In this way, no one's sight line would be compromised. The bride and groom would take their place at the front of the ballroom, where a small raised space had been marked by a simple arch draped with white silk and strung with a garland of wildflowers.

"Here we are, darling, sit down," I said, ushering my mother to her chair. She looked at me as if I had deliberately tricked her into sitting at this table and refused to take the seat I offered. Glancing frenziedly around the room, she grew increasingly agitated until Sam appeared, carrying two glasses of beer.

"For you, sweetheart," he said, giving one glass to our mother, "but let's not get crazy."

Visibly relieved to see her son, my mother clasped the glass of beer in both hands and settled into the chair between mine and Sam's. Guests strolled in, searching for the appropriate table, filling the room with a sense of anticipation.

Sam, leaning back, slung his arm around the back of our mother's chair, which she seemed to interpret as some kind of cue, because she instantly nestled into the crook of his arm and tapped his nose lightly with her finger. Sam, playing the game, tapped my mother's nose in return.

"You're a little mischief maker," he said to our mother, who suddenly and unmistakably beamed, a gesture so unexpected that both Sam and I spontaneously laughed in appreciation.

Out of nowhere, a pair of arms snaked around Sam's neck and, resting her head on his shoulder, Wendy said, "Sammy, I've been looking all over for you."

Sam's wife was short, dark, and curvaceous, with luxuriant black hair that she wore in any number of bohemian styles, each designed to suit both her mood and the occasion. For Lucy's wedding, she wore a tight-fitting calf-length red lace dress with long fingerless black gloves and had coiled her hair into a loose bun on the top of her head, allowing long tendrils to fall on either side of her face. Her eyes had been lined with kohl, and she had painted her full lips with a blood-red matte, so that her appearance was at once exotic and sensual.

Sam, indicating the chair to his left, said, "It's going to start any minute." Wendy pulled the chair out and, adjusting herself on its seat, turned to wave a gloved hand at someone across the room. When Sam lifted his free arm and placed it on the back of Wendy's chair, my mother stiffened.

She looked at me and, sensing her agitation, I leaned in and asked if something was bothering her. Only moments earlier, she had been smiling, a wonderful and increasingly rare expression of genuine pleasure. Now, her face had tightened, the smile had vanished, and her eyes indicated that she was not pleased with the sudden addition of this overly familiar woman with long black hair and red lips. My mother's growing anxiety manifested itself in the uncontrollable drumming of her fingers on the table, and in the increased humming that had begun in the back of her throat and now lodged itself in the front of her mouth, unable to retreat or escape.

In the time it took for me to process what this meant, the atmosphere had shifted. A silence had fallen over the room that within seconds had expanded into an expectation so persuasive that the assembled guests rose to their feet as if by pulled by invisible strings. Sam, Wendy, and I stood, but when I reached down to help my mother to her feet, I saw that she was crouched in her chair, both hands clasped over her stomach, her head bobbing up and down. Intuitively, I leaned down and put my mouth to her ear.

"Mother, are you all right? Do you need to go to the bathroom?" I whispered.

My mother did not have time to respond before the first bars of Mendelssohn's Wedding March could be heard heralding the entrance of the bride and, standing on tiptoe and peering frantically over the heads of the people in front of me, I could just make out Javier under the festooned arch. He wore no jacket and stood rigidly in his olive-green guayabera and dark pleated trousers. His face, glistening with perspiration, was turned to the door from which his bride would soon emerge, and then, suddenly, there she was, radiant in her secondhand peach rayon dress, the wild roses in her black hair announcing her separateness, her stern face, keeper of a thousand tales of conquest and triumph.

I had seen what I had come to see and bent down to speak to my mother.

"Let's go to the bathroom, Mums. Come on," I urged, taking her by the arm and helping her to stand. My mother was uncertain on her feet, and her face, as she turned to look at Sam, registered confusion and alarm.

"What is it, darling? Do you want to talk to Sam?" I asked, already extending my arm to touch Sam's shoulder.

"No, no, no," my mother responded, adamantly, and then, clutching my hand, demanded, "Who is *that* woman?"

My mother was darting baleful glances at Wendy who, in her innocence, turned to flash my mother a big smile.

"You know who that is, Mother, it's Wendy. Sam's wife," I said, quietly and clearly.

The humming could be heard again, almost as a warning bell, and my mother suddenly stiffened. Just as I started to guide her away from the table, I heard her whimper and, glancing down, saw that the cushion on her chair was damp. I glanced at her backside and with a prickle of dread saw that my mother was wetting her pants, the dark stain spreading down the legs of her silk trousers. Even as I tried to pull her to safety, she resisted leaving the table where her son stood, shoulder to shoulder with his wife. My mother's face, livid with alarm and despair, began to fracture, and I knew I had only a few minutes to get her to the bathroom before we would be noticed. Wrapping my arm tight around her waist, I led her out of the ballroom, up a short, winding staircase, and into the cramped bathroom, where a single shaded bulb illuminated the surroundings.

Maneuvering my mother into the stall, I latched the door behind us and, pulling down her pants, guided her onto the toilet. She sat there, gazing at me in bewilderment, deeply shaken. None of what had transpired in the past fifteen minutes made any sense, none of it had order or clarity, and yet I recognized in my mother's blanched face the sense of a betrayal. As she sat on the toilet, her hands clasped tightly in her lap, her soiled silk trousers bunched around her ankles, her anguish was palpable. She seemed to be vaguely aware of her incontinence, and of the shame she should be feeling because of it, but that was not the dominant humiliation. As she searched my face for answers that did not exist, something in my mother collapsed, and I instinctively reached for her hands.

"You'll be all right, my darling, don't worry," I said, gently.

There was a pause while my mother struggled to find words, any words, that might convey her feelings. Words hung in her brain like bats in a cave.

"The one I love," my mother whispered, haltingly.

I stroked her cheek.

"You mean Sam?"

She looked at me, deeply perplexed.

"Oh, I see," I said and, sitting back on my haunches, studied her. The time had come to cross over, and to do it lightly, never letting go of her hand.

"You mean Jesus, don't you? Jesus is the one you love, and he's waiting for you downstairs."

My mother tilted her head to one side and regarded me with an expression of such pity that I almost felt ashamed. I had fallen from grace because I had somehow been complicit in the betrayal that she had been made to suffer. I knew, too, huddled in the confines of that stall, that others were equally culpable.

Wendy, wrapping her arms around my brother's neck, had been culpable.

Sam, placing his arm on the back of Wendy's chair, had been culpable.

Jesus, the one she loved, had done the unforgivable.

He had broken her heart.

CHAPTER FORTY-FOUR

Before it skidded into murk, her mind paused at a moment of girlishness. An old friend of my mother's, whose name was Barney Ziv, came to visit her at Derby Grange, and with him was his wife, Irene. My mother had known the Zivs for many years, and loved them both, but it was Barney whom she had met first. This meeting took place in the early 1950s in Chicago, where Barney was a young broker for Merrill Lynch, and my mother was acting as Jack Kennedy's personal secretary during his senatorial race against Henry Cabot Lodge Jr. It was a heady time for my mother, a time of high spirits and high stakes, during which she shared an apartment with Jean Kennedy, worked for JFK, and most Sunday mornings sat in Mass just a few pews away from Tom Mulgrew, a young advertising executive. The atmosphere had been one of almost dizzying excitement, working for one of the most promising, talented, and attractive young politicians of his time, someone whom my mother had known since she had taken the Cape Codder to Hyannis when she was twelve years old and was met at the pier by her friend Jean, who was accompanied by her handsome, sun-bronzed brothers Jack and Bobby. The Kennedy alliance notwithstanding, Chicago in the fifties was full of young people seeking their fortune, a landlocked, boozy, ambitious town on the verge of greatness.

In those days, and to those people, she was known as Jicky. The Kennedys had bestowed this nickname on my mother one evening during a lively debate at the dinner table in Hyannis. They teased my mother into wholeness, which is how she learned to read affection, and how she navigated her way through life. After a thorough indoctrination in the art of irreverence, the Kennedys had sent my mother off with an eye for mischief and a wit honed for deployment.

There were many weekends when Jack left his headquarters in Chicago and returned to the Cape, always extending an invitation to my mother to join him because that, too, was part of the Kennedy mystique—if you were outside the circle, chances were you'd stay outside, but if you were in, you were in forever. My mother often said yes, because nothing was more fun than Hyannis with the Kennedys, who spent their days in the sea, swimming and sailing, and their nights over spirited dinners invariably followed by a movie shown in the projection room, after which someone might suggest a midnight dip in the moonlit ocean. These were times my mother had cherished, but suddenly the bird was on the wing and she found herself, unaccountably, without a serious beau. My mother regarded this as less a dilemma than a challenge because, after all, she had been schooled by the best in the arts of coquetry and found herself, at the ripe age of twenty-four, eager to swim in the uncharted waters of mature romance.

Picture her, sitting on a barstool in the Cape Cod Room at the Drake Hotel: five feet, four inches tall, petite, gamine, with a head of thick auburn hair falling in loose waves to her shoulders, slender legs crossed at the knee, wearing a navy pencil skirt and a white blouse tucked and belted around a twenty-two-inch waist. Her small, slightly upturned nose was dusted with freckles, her eyes were sharp and sky blue, her mouth was attractive if not sensual, with a thin upper lip and a fuller lower lip. In slapdash fashion, she would have spat into a thin box of mascara, passed the brush lightly over her lashes, drawn her mouth from a tube of Russian red lipstick, and run a brush through her hair. The physical effect would have been immediate and striking, and over the course of an evening all types of men would have been drawn to that barstool, and many drinks bought and placed in front of my mother who, with her customary frankness and piercing wit, had made her preferences known without much fanfare. Shrugging, she had said, "I just don't like the cut of your jib, and there's nothing I can do about it."

One Saturday night, my mother had explained to me, the barstool next to hers was suddenly appropriated by a long-legged man wearing gabardine trousers, a madras jacket, horn-rimmed glasses, and a Stetson fedora. He did not at first ask my mother if he could buy her a drink but instead leaned against the counter and, studying her with amusement, said, "Woe betide the man whose jib doesn't cut it with you, baby." This opening remark satisfied my mother, who extended her hand and stated that her name was Joan, but that her friends called her Jicky.

IN THE TV Room at Derby Grange, my father is strangely absent. Barney Ziv is sitting in an armless chair in front of the fireplace and my mother is standing before him, laughing. Because we have not seen her laugh like this in a long time, Lucy and I exchange a look conveying both amusement and concern. It is wonderful to see my mother laugh again, it is delightful, but it is strategically miscalculated. Barney is now an eighty-year-old man and, while he has retained his sense of humor, his hair is gray and thinning, his eyes are tired behind expensive tortoiseshell glasses, and he looks at my mother as if this is a game that he is not fully prepared to play. His wife sits across the room on a floral armchair, nestled into the corner. Unlike her husband, she is smiling a little sadly because she understands the nature of this game, and she is silently willing him to participate.

Without preamble, my mother leans into Barney and, plucking his glasses from his nose, perches coyly on his knee. She twirls the glasses in her hand, she tilts her head coquettishly to one side, she takes Barney's pink silk tie between her fingers and flutters it against his cheek. My mother is surprisingly nimble and crosses her legs as she sits on Barney's knee, so that her feet no longer touch the floor. As she swings one leg in the air, she leans back ever so slightly to gaze at Barney, openly offering her face. Barney laughs uncomfortably and shifts in his chair, but he is not so cruel as to release my mother, who has been his friend for many years and who he knows is suffering from an affliction over which she has no control. He had prepared himself for the worst, but he had not expected this, and is shocked to find that the creature sitting on his knee is in fact the girl he had met more than fifty years before, at the Cape Cod Room in the Drake Hotel. As my mother plays with Barney's hair, I look anxiously at Irene. She returns my gaze with eyes full of warmth and sadness, and nods slightly to let me know that if this trick of memory is giving Jicky pleasure, it is just fine with her, and that I should not interrupt this happiness.

When it is time for them to leave, my mother is plunged into despondency and clings to Barney with desperation. Again and again, he is compelled to kiss her on the forehead, on the cheek, lightly on the lips. My mother is in agony but cannot understand why; she knows only that if she lets go of Barney's hand she will return to a place that fills her with terror. Irene attempts to hold my mother, but her eyes are fixed on Barney, who gently guides my mother down the brick path, where his car is waiting. There is a split second of unbearable anguish, during which it is clear that my mother fully expects to get in the car with Barney and drive away with him. Barney extricates himself from my mother's grasp and puts her hand in mine, so that she is tethered when the moment comes, but my mother is frantic now and disdains Irene's embrace; she cannot believe that Barney is leaving without her, and yet the moment comes and suddenly, inexplicably, Barney is settled behind the wheel and he is blowing kisses to my mother but she is frozen with despair, and tears she is not aware of stream down her cheeks as Barney drives off, honking his horn all the way down the gravel road until, in a cloud of dust, the car disappears from view.

CHAPTER FORTY-FIVE

In The Addition, my mother converted the bedroom in which Tessie had died into an art studio. In this room, with its windows looking out onto the orchard, she had bookshelves installed, which she filled with biographies of great painters. On one of the shelves, she placed her boom box and next to it, a collection of tapes arranged in two shoe boxes: Puccini, Verdi, Bellini, Berlioz, Bizet. Callas, Sutherland, Price, Tebaldi. An easel dominated the center of the room, behind which stood an old wardrobe trunk, and on this trunk rested the articles of my mother's pleasure: black and white feathers, mason jars filled with brushes, tubes of oil paints in disarray, boxes of pastels lying in their respective cots, the corpses of butterflies and moths, some impaled on white cork, some curled lifelessly, their wings already folded into dust. Large tables stood against the opposite wall, spread with paper and hardback sketch pads, charcoal nibs, acrylics, oils, and inks of every kind. These tables often displayed death masks and shadow boxes, which were sometimes propped against a book my mother was reading. In the corner sat an armchair, low to the ground, once upholstered in green corduroy, a fabric long since transformed by wine stains, streaks of oil paint, and cigarette burns left by visiting artists and grandchildren. Next to the chair, a small table supported a rose-shaded reading lamp.

Her studio smelled of varnish, acrylics, and coffee. The walls were covered with sketches, paintings already framed and hung, sections of maps that intrigued her. Quotes were written in her looping, elegant script, and might attend a painting or, more often, stand alone. Under a monarch butterfly pinned inside a small white box: *Glory be to God for dapped things.* Beneath the portrait of a middle-aged woman wearing a head scarf:

GIVE LITTLE ANGUISH
LIVES WILL FRET.
GIVE AVALANCHES—
AND THEY'LL SLANT,

My mother loved the faces and forms of women, and those are what she preferred to paint. Two women carrying parasols, two women in intimate conversation, two women strolling on the beach. She called them "Doubles" and, predictably, women responded to them. Many of these women fancied themselves artists, and soon there developed a small colony of female painters who spent many afternoons eating lunch at my mother's kitchen table or taking a picnic into the countryside and afterward painting *en plein air.* Most of the time, however, my mother sought solitude within the confines of her studio where, left to her own devices, she might lie still for hours, her face encased in wet clay. When the death mask was drying, she'd show it to me and, after a moment's consideration, say, "I don't know. It's missing something, don't you think?"

The death masks and the shadow boxes were diversions, fanciful departures from her driving passion, which was women. There was the odd rendering of a bishop staring out from beneath his imposing miter, or a Sicilian peasant in rough pastel, or a trapeze artist in midair. But in every corner of the studio, covering every inch of wall space, hung paintings of women. The Doubles proliferated like daffodils, and I would spend long minutes examining them. They spoke to and about my mother's romantic nature, and of her deepest longings. These small paintings revealed the intensity of female friendship, the beauty and grace of the female body, unburdened, lissome, ignorant of grief. My mother sent most of these Doubles to her best friend, Jean Kennedy

Smith who, many years after my mother's death returned all of them to me with this note: *Your mother gave these to me over the years but now I think it's time that you should have them.*

In her art, she was searching, always searching. Among the hundreds of faces of women that she painted, she was looking for the one face she could never find, and this is why her talent deepened so quickly. There was an urgency behind each portrait, and a deftness, demanding a response.

At her last solo art show in Dubuque, my mother dressed in her uniform of black silk trousers and cream blouse, every painting was sold. The gallery on Main Street was crowded with all of the people who had known my mother well, many from the time she had first arrived in that foreign place, many more drawn to my mother over the years because hers was a different conversation, one they were hungry for. My mother stood in the middle of the gallery, her face suffused with pleasure, her glass half filled with beer, fingering her Mikimoto pearls and sighing as one red dot after another appeared until, finally, she looked at me, and winked.

ALTHOUGH SHE COULD not have known it at the time, my mother gave her last painting to me. Uncertainly, she handed the shadow box to me, and watched me closely as I studied it. I observed the figure of a woman, concealed behind glass, sitting on a staircase and peering through the spindles of a balustrade. The woman is older, her hair is short, dark, and unkempt, she wears a soiled apron, her features are indistinct, almost blurred. Upon closer inspection, it is clear that the woman is clinging to the spindles, with both hands, her face almost pressed against them. Then my eye is drawn to the lower right corner of the shadow box, where it appears the artist may have made a mistake. With a sharp intake of breath, it dawns on me that this is not a mistake at all, but very much the artist's intention.

A large black moth, captured in the woods and placed in a jar to die, had been removed from its death chamber and impaled on the painting of the woman behind the spindles, pierced through with a hatpin that had once borne a crown of pearl.

In the last painting my mother would give to me she had left a message, within which she had hidden her epitaph.

CHAPTER FORTY-SIX

In the fifth year of her affliction, in the middle of winter, Sam and I took our mother for a walk. Down the familiar gravel road, through the stone gates, stopping at the entrance to the meadow where the bees, for so many years, had been kept. She walked very differently, now. The quick, light step and the girlish gait had eroded, the once agile limbs had grown rigid. Her stride was halting, uncertain, not unlike the disequilibrium toddlers exhibit when they first find their feet. Our arms linked through hers, we talked of many things we thought our mother would enjoy, of crows on the wing against a gray November sky, of rodents burrowing beneath the snow, and of the snow itself, settling in congealed clumps on the still-green ground. Our mother would glance at me, or Sam, if our voices were particularly animated, but mostly she kept her eyes straight ahead. The humming which for so long had served as a guide to her mood, had been silenced. She looked about her as if she were vaguely alarmed to find herself where she was.

When we stopped to gaze into the meadow where the bee houses still stood, barren in a barren field, our mother straightened. Sam was talking about the bees and the old beekeeper in his wide, funny hat and the big, wonderful jars of honey he would bring to the house. The piece of land on which the bees were cultivated belonged to our father and those jars of golden honey were given to us by the beekeeper in lieu of rent. We always felt we got the better part of the deal because the pure, rich honey was delivered in generous glass jars, more than enough of them to last us until well into the following year.

"The bees aren't there anymore, darling," Sam explained. "It's wintertime."

My mother tilted her head skyward. *Wintertime* had meaning, *bees* had meaning, but the two together overwhelmed her.

Pointing to the large brick house a hundred yards down the road, I said, "And that's where we went and forced the nice lady to give us a tour of her house, the one with the white carpet that nobody was allowed to walk on and cookies on the kitchen counter that she baked *every day*, do you remember, Mums?"

Her eyes skidded across the road, then back to me. My mother's face no longer questioned, no longer pretended, but assumed instead a studied detachment, as if this was just another in a long line of unanswerable questions best handled with a short, indifferent shrug.

We turned back toward our house, walking slowly under the arbor of trees that shaded the driveway. Occasionally, our mother would stop and stare at something on the ground and, bending down, we would retrieve a leaf or a feather and place it in her hand. Not so very long ago, she would have responded reflexively, tucking the feather expertly in her sleeve, poking the leaf gently into her pocket. Now, she looked at the leaf for a moment before letting it fall from her fingers. The feather intrigued her, she turned it this way and that to try to discern its meaning. Finding none, she let it go, and did not watch as it drifted to the ground.

As we approached the front porch, our mother extricated herself from our grasp, and walked ahead of us, alone. Sam and I exchanged a glance that said, She never could bear walking three abreast. We smiled and started laughing, but then we heard what sounded like a whimper and, turning, we saw our mother hesitate, but before we could reach her side she had lurched forward, stumbled, and fallen. She lay facedown in the snow, her arms outstretched in front of her, her body rigid. When we leaned down to help her up, we were startled to hear her cry, "No! No!" We knew intuitively that this was an order, that we were not to touch her. Our mother continued to lie there, her face hidden in the dirt-edged, crusty snow, slapping the cold ground with her bare hands, and my brother and I were powerless to do anything because the loss of her legs beneath her had so profoundly mortified her that she refused to be comforted.

Watching our mother as she lay prostrate on the frozen ground, my brother and I did not speak. Nothing moved in the yard, the birds were still, and we could do nothing but wait as another ending announced itself.

CHAPTER FORTY-SEVEN

My mother's essential self had always been elusive, so that the docile, simple creature she eroded into provided a kind of reassurance. All of the things we were wary of in her previous self had melted away, allowing us to speak to her in ways that would have been unthinkable six years before. The fawning, the baby talk, the bright, false smiles, all of the behaviors that once would have repulsed her, she now accepted from each and every one of us with hollow sweetness. She was like a beloved child who had been struck by lightning.

Lucy nursed my mother with a devotion I lacked, one that was crucial to my mother's comfort and well-being. She bathed her and fed her and washed her hair. In the morning, she sat my mother on the edge of her bed and worked sweatpants up her stiff legs, pulled a turtleneck over her head and slid unresponsive arms through sleeves, glided socks onto her cold feet, and tied her shoes with double knots. In the evening, she laid her back on the bed and changed her diaper, an impossible challenge given my mother's inflexibility, and yet Lucy accomplished this task with efficiency and grace, never once pausing in her ministrations, her voice measured, tender, confident.

It's not that I was incapable of performing these tasks; I had no aversion to changing my mother's diaper or sitting with her while she struggled to defecate. These things did not offend me. What got in the way of true devotion was my inability to let go of the past. Often, she would look at me with an expression of terrible sadness, one that I interpreted as regret. Regret that she had been reduced to this, regret that I had to witness it, and while on one level I realized that my mother was far beyond the discernment of such an emotion, on another I could pretend that in the far recesses of what was left of her mind, I still had meaning.

It was then that my memory would provide redemption, calling up moments I thought I had lost. My mother's eyes, incapable of registering the simplest thought, helped me to reach into the past.

I recalled a warm autumn day when Tom, standing in the kitchen, warned my mother that he would give her just one more chance to answer the million-dollar question.

"Now, Mother, for the last time, what is the square root of sixty-four?" my brother asked, sternly.

Our mother, looking up sheepishly, asked, "One?"

"That's it, you lose!" Tom exclaimed and, crossing the room in three strides, picked our mother up, threw her over his shoulder, opened the door of the oven with his foot, and shoved her in, her little legs sticking out, yellow sneakers bobbing up and down.

Convulsive laughter emanated from inside the oven, bringing those of us on the outside to our knees, tears streaming down our cheeks.

"I'm going to wet my pants!" my mother cried, still stuck inside.

With one hand, Tom pulled her from the oven, whereupon she fell to her knees, helpless with laughter, and scrabbled across the kitchen floor, wetting her pants and sobbing with hilarity.

On another evening, my mother sat at the kitchen table working on a miniature clay sculpture of Jesus, when my father opened the back door and asked her what the hell she was doing.

"A miniature of Jesus," my mother responded, drily.

"Hmm," my father said, fixing himself a drink. He sauntered over to the table and, sitting beside my mother and indicating the small sculpture, asked, "May I?"

Reluctantly, my mother passed the figurine to my father who, after taking a good quaff of his scotch, examined the clay form and set to work. Two minutes later, he presented his masterpiece to my mother.

Onto the miniature of Jesus he had deftly attached an erect, if very tiny, penis.

"Now, that's a miniature you can be proud of!" my father proclaimed, whereupon my mother collapsed and, sliding to the floor, clung to my father's pant leg, shrieking with laughter.

"Jick, you are beginning to piss little Jesus off," my father admonished, sitting back and appraising his handiwork, while my mother lay at his feet, completely undone.

⋆⋆⋆⋆⋆

QUITE UNEXPECTEDLY, I was awarded an honorary doctorate by Seton Hill University, a small liberal arts school in Greensburg, Pennsylvania. I was in my early thirties with two small children, a difficult marriage, and a wildly fluctuating career, so this honor, aside from being deeply gratifying, provided me with the perfect opportunity to escape for a few days into a world of lofty ideals and high-mindedness. It was, after all, a Catholic university for women, where my name had been pulled from a hatful of candidates because a majority of the student body had admired my performance as St. Elizabeth Ann Seton in the ABC Circle film *A Time for Miracles*. That, combined with my Catholic upbringing and a propensity for playing morally incorruptible characters, won me the vaunted degree of doctor of letters.

When I called my mother to tell her the news, she was momentarily speechless.

"But you didn't graduate from college, Kitty Kat, did you?"

"No, Mother darling, I did not."

"Did you even *go* to college? Didn't you instantly become an actress?"

"No, Mother, I went to conservatory first, which is where I learned how to act. Admittedly, I dropped out when I was offered my first part."

"Your life is very odd, Kitten. Everything is backward, isn't it? You just sort of stride around, doing things, and getting things that seem sort of magical. You could have been a doctor, or a violinist, or an abbess. What am I saying? You *are* a doctor! An honorary doctor of letters! How terrific! But very odd."

"Will you come?" I asked, flipping through my address book for my travel agent's number.

"Are you stark raving mad? This will be absolute heaven!"

"I'll send you the ticket."

"I mean it, Kitten," my mother said.

"Which part?"

"You would have been a terrific abbess."

WHEN WE ARRIVED in Greensburg, we were greeted by the president of Seton Hill, a kind woman with abundant blond hair and an attitude of tired benevolence which I took to be the result less of running a women's university than of having mothered seven children. She drove us to our lodgings, which turned out to be a quaint, tastefully appointed inn on the outskirts of town. My mother and I were very happy. We ordered tea in our room and were pleased when a tray arrived bearing tiny crustless sandwiches, assorted pastries, a pot of tea, and a small carafe of sherry. The sherry was immediately poured, the sandwiches devoured, and the pastries abandoned. We then lay down on our respective beds and started to laugh. As frustrating as it is that I cannot now recall the substance of the lunacy that led to this laughter, I vividly remember the laughter itself, a slow-starting, restrained chortle that expanded into full-blown hysterics, so that in no time both my mother and I were writhing atop our small beds, weeping, begging each other to stop until, unable to contain herself, my mother simply fell out of her bed and hit the floor, a casualty attended by a series of soft percussive farts.

AS I HELPED my mother off the toilet, holding her with one hand while reaching for her diaper with the other, I wondered how it was that we did not notice when the laughter left her, so subtle was its dissolution, and so absolute.

CHAPTER FORTY-EIGHT

My mother loved her bath. It was the simple happiness of hours snatched from the pandemonium of a house filled with children. The bathroom door would be closed, the lock turned, and my mother would say, "Kitten, run the water for me, will you?" As she relaxed in the scalding water, a look of pure bliss would suffuse her features. Sitting up in the tub, her preferred posture and one that signified the height of relaxation, she would place one washcloth over her lap, another over her breasts, look at me as I leaned against the side of the tub, and say, "Did anything interesting happen to you today? Start at the beginning, and remember, Kitty Kat, it's all in the details."

Now, years later, a bathtub was installed in the room that was once my mother's studio. It had been cleared and reappointed and, just as was the case after my sister's death, denuded of any sense of meaning, so that it would be impossible to guess that this room had at one time held all of the secrets of my mother's most realized happiness. Mysteries and old comforts were stored in her bedroom upstairs, a place no longer accessible to my mother. Her limbs had stiffened, she could no longer direct them to move up the stairs, or down. A small bed had been placed against the wall in the Good Living Room, a table and reading lamp next to it. This is where my mother now slept, under a soft comforter, next to the tall windows looking out over the broad, sylvan lawn.

After an early dinner, Lucy would prepare my mother for her bath and, if I was home, I would assist her. The temperature of the water had to meet certain specifications, neither too hot nor too cold, a condition that my mother, had she been aware, would have disdained. The bath

bubbles were poured liberally from a bottle of Johnson's baby shampoo, the lavender salts scooped out of a glass jar and scattered over the
surface, hands run smoothly back and forth through the water to balance the temperature. When my mother's clothing had been removed,
an exercise achieved by seating her on a chair and gently draping a
towel over her naked body, Lucy would reach for my mother's hands
and say, "Okay, Beanie, time for what you love. You ready for your
bath? Come on, pie, let's go."

I moved forward to take my mother's arm. I wanted to help her into
the tub, but she refused to move. She stood there, a bath towel held
by Lucy covering her body, frozen in place. Suddenly, she looked at
me with undisguised panic. She had no understanding of the large,
water-filled basin, steam rising from its surface like smoke, nor could
she grasp her nakedness other than to sense its wrongness. I held my
mother's hand and said, "It's all right, darling, the water is good. You'll
like it, I promise. Let's try."

At the side of the tub, where for most of her life my mother had instinctively raised her leg to step into the bath, she stopped. I looked at
Lucy, Lucy looked at me, and in this brief exchange we shared the fear
that is palpable when there is very little room left.

Kneeling, I put my hand around my mother's ankle and tried to
coax her to lift her leg. The strength of her resistance was unexpected;
it was as if she were rooted to the ground. Lucy steadied my mother
while I took her leg firmly in my hands and forced it to bend, causing
my mother to cry out in alarm. When her foot touched the water, her
expression changed from panic to aversion, and I knew then that we
had to hurry. Working together, Lucy and I lowered my mother into
the water. I quickly lathered a washcloth with soap and started to run
the cloth over her body, all the while murmuring softly, "It's good,
darling. It's your bath, you love your bath."

Her expression, as I moved the cloth in gentle, concentric circles
over her back, revealed a frightened, wary resignation. Why was she

not able to sense the memory of the bath, and the pleasure it had always given her? Taking my mother's slender fingers one by one into my hand, I carefully soaped them, rinsed them, studied them. I knew these hands as well as I knew my own; knew the earthy, scullery smell of them, the surprisingly delicate touch of her fingers, the unvarnished nails that she pared herself with kitchen scissors, the elegance they assumed in repose. These were hands I had sought since earliest consciousness and, as I watched the washcloth slide from her breasts into the tepid water without the remotest twinge of embarrassment crossing my mother's features, I realized with a dull, heavy certainty that she would never again in her life know pleasure.

CHAPTER FORTY-NINE

Following Tessie's death, I feared the family would be constitutionally unable to withstand another breach. The premature and wholly unnatural way in which my sister died had created a fissure, felt by those of us who survived her. It only ever revealed itself in the way our laughter ebbed when she was mentioned, or in the sudden cessation of our teasing. Her absence was felt as keenly as a nightmare which, upon waking, proves to be the reality. Over time, the understanding that we would never see her again was pocketed, and taken out only when we were very careful, or very drunk. The wound, stitched tightly and well scarred, could nevertheless open at the least provocation, so close did it sit to the surface of feeling.

My father had tried to honor his own grief, but because it was unfathomable he was never sufficiently prepared for the fall. When Tessie died, he had buckled under the weight of her casket and fallen to the ground, sobbing, "I never thought I'd see you go out like this, kid." At Uncle Bob's funeral, my father had entered the church and, recognizing the figure in the casket to be his beloved younger brother, stood frozen in disbelief. Certainly, he had known he was attending his brother's funeral, and yet, when confronted with the reality of his death, was so profoundly shaken that he could not move.

My parents, who had lived their lives with incontrovertible courage, had never accepted the stages of grief, and therefore were unable to ritualize their sorrow. Intolerable sadness was tolerated by closing the book on a life, one never to be reopened. If I attempted to talk about Tessie with my mother, I would be met by a blank look, the ghost of a smile, and the end of the conversation. My father was more forthcoming, but he knew his limits. He might indulge a few fond memories, leading to what one hoped might be an exploration of feelings, but when the opportunity for real communication appeared, he withdrew behind a sentimentalized but nonetheless impermeable façade. I understood that they were guarding their privacy, which they prized above all else, but theirs was such a fierce and solitary defense that those of us left in its wake floundered.

With our father dead and our mother lost, we surviving siblings became unmoored. Unusual behaviors revealed themselves at inauspicious times. Simmering beneath the surface of our loneliness was a kind of inarticulable fury, reducing each of us to a meanness we despised. We longed to reach out to one another, but at every turn this instinct was thwarted, tangled in a web of suspicion and resentment. As much as we had loved one another in the fullness of life, we hated what we had become when that wholeness was eclipsed by loss. Mendacity, jealousy, and rage percolated on the back burner while egoism masqueraded as generosity. In our confusion, we second-guessed one another, and because we had never learned to confront each other with frank vulnerability, we fell back into the roles assigned to us at birth.

Observing my siblings at this time, I was struck by the willfulness of grief, and by its extraordinary subjectivity. Laura loved my mother in a way entirely unfamiliar to me, while my father's death seemed only to have deepened Joe's devotion, his bereavement in stark contrast to my own. Tom, the oldest, assumed a patriarchal authority, the newness of which was burdensome. His was the way of lightheartedness, of the confidence of love, and to be suddenly thrust into a position contrary to his nature weighed heavily on him. In New York, Jenny struggled with two toddlers and an ineffable longing for her mother who, when awake, blinked at the ceiling above her and thought of nothing. Occasionally, in the late afternoon, Sam would steal into our mother's room and sit beside her, holding her hand. He avoided Joe, aware of the vast chasm between their singular griefs, and Joe, had he been able, would have avoided everyone. I came and went, leaning on the door-jamb and watching as Lucy gently washed my mother's rigid face, her blue-veined, slender hands. Lucy's expression was set, aggrieved, her indomitable spirit in shadow.

It was a house divided, but exactly how it came to be so remained a conundrum. We had always been competitive, pugnacious, mischievous, and thought it our right to be so, given the limitations of parental attention. Whatever ill will we bore one another, it was always within the accepted confines of sibling rivalry, but in the absence of parents to inspire that rivalry we lost confidence in ourselves, and in our love for one another. We fought for life to continue as it had always been, we fought for our right to be in the house that we loved, we fought for stature, for respect, for equality. We fought to be known in a new way, as siblings without parents. It was a swift and terrible tide to swim against.

After a visit home, I would return to New York and spend days ruminating on what I had just experienced, wondering how and why tensions had risen to such a fever pitch. It was as if we had all been in a catastrophic accident, leaving some severely damaged, others stunned, everyone debilitated. The house had come to represent the love of our parents, and in that spectral world we struggled to reclaim them, each of us longing to proclaim our specialness to two people who were no longer there.

A balance might have been achieved, had we viewed our mother as sentient. Instead, the emptiness that filled the house after our father died was edged with the anguish of having a mother who, though she existed, could do nothing to assuage our fears. The increasing vacancy of her mind juxtaposed with her strikingly familiar physicality lent a kind of surreal terror to the atmosphere where, in hushed, brittle tones, we hissed at one another about who deserved what. Occasionally, when the tension became intolerable, there would be shouting, the pounding of a fist on a table, the slamming of a door. There could be no justification for these violent displays of volatility, save one. We were inconsolable.

And how deeply we loved, I thought, watching Joe as he stood before the bonfire, hands stuffed in pockets, staring into the flames, or noticing with what quiet unobtrusiveness Sam stole into our mother's room, gently closing the door behind him. Tom, his sandy hair streaked with gray, no longer entertained us as he once did, but sat at the kitchen table, lost in thought. He maintained an equilibrium that eluded the rest of us, but even this virtue could abrade, when the mood was foreboding and the slightest touch incendiary. Jenny, coiled with resentment at not having had either parent as long as the rest, sought relief in vehemence, but could sometimes be seen kneeling next to our mother's bed, tears streaming down her cheeks, tears she would immediately wipe away if Laura walked into the room, having stopped by for a short visit.

I pretended to go about my business and, having the luxury of a New York apartment to return to, considered myself well out of the mess. In the past year, I had transferred my mother's health-care guardianship to Sam, who, on-site, could act more quickly and with far greater efficiency than I could from the Upper West Side, but even this capitulation hurt. Nothing could alleviate the constant anxiety that plagued me, the certainty that I had somehow neglected something in my mother's care, that if anything happened in my absence I would be responsible. I, more deluded than any of my siblings, imagined myself still important to my mother's happiness.

The most chilling aspect of my mother's affliction was the way in which it had settled over us, with infinite precision, coercing us into accepting this new mother, while inexorably leading us away from the one we had adored. This normalization of an affliction that had stripped our mother of personhood stole over the house like an undetectable poison, so that in time her presence came to serve as a reflection of our own deficiencies, creating strife and conflict among us.

In this twilight, we hovered over our mother, and waited.

CHAPTER FIFTY

S he no swallow so good now, señora," Lucy said, sipping her coffee. A bright morning in May, the birds in full-throated song outside the open window, the sun glinting through the leaves of trees. Spring at Derby Grange, shimmering with anticipation.

"What do you mean, exactly?" I asked, leaning forward on the kitchen table, chin in hands.

"She try, señora, but it too hard to get down, so now sometime I use a dropper, fill it with some Ensure, some custard, soup, and wait till I see Beanie swallow. It take a long time, señora, and sometime I scary she might choke. What I do then? We so far from town."

I sat back heavily and sighed. Lucy, whose spine was never less than ramrod straight, conveyed a weariness that lived, now, in her bones, evident in the way she rose from a chair, in the deliberateness of her step, in the foreboding that crouched inside her.

"How much longer can you manage like this, Luce? Tell me honestly."

My mother's inert form was extremely difficult to move, complicating even the simplest of chores. Her petite frame concealed the rigidity of her muscles, which had slowly calcified. There was no direction coming from her mind to advise her body of its abilities, no memory to recall its suppleness. She lay in her bed, inflexible and unyielding, forcing Lucy and Javier to apply both strength and strategy to the changing of a diaper, the turning over for a sponge bath, the lifting of her body to allow for a lightning-fast replacement of linens.

"I all right now, señora, but next week? Who knows? Why you think she don't eat, señora? Beanie always love food."

"She doesn't eat because her brain isn't sending her the message to eat," I answered, fiddling with a spoon, rubbing its shallow bowl with my thumb, something I had often seen my mother do.

Lucy understood this and nodded gravely. The insidiousness of my mother's affliction continued to astonish and appall her.

"What going on up there, you think, señora? Anything?"

"I think a lot of soldiers have jumped to their death up there," I replied, laying the spoon gently on a blue-and-white cotton napkin.

In the Good Living Room, I sat on the edge of my mother's bed. More and more, she slept. Her white hair had been brushed back from her face, revealing small, symmetrical features, enviable skin, perfect ears. Her mouth, thin-lipped and tightly shut, precluded beauty, but what that mouth had articulated would put beauty to shame, I thought. I smoothed her hair very gently so as not to wake her, but suddenly her eyes opened and fixed themselves on mine. There was no longer the soft adjustment from sleep to wakefulness, what remained was the effect of a light, abruptly switched on. My mother knew to look into my eyes, she still understood that eyes, like open windows, were to be sought, and now she gazed at me, unblinking.

Still, and despite my better judgment, the warning bell in my heart sounded, and I would look deeply into her eyes and imagine that I saw there what no one else could see. In the far recesses of what was left of her cognition, I thought I could glimpse—behind the vacancy, almost lost in the deliquescence—a terror. My mother's pale blue eyes, anchored by pinpoint pupils, fastened onto my own with what I was sure was the last, supreme effort at communication. She did not know me, she did not know herself, but in some primitive corner of her ravaged brain she knew that she had fallen into an abyss, and if she could only find her way back to the moment before she had lost her footing and slipped off the cliff into darkness, if she could only find that moment, she would remember to grasp my hand.

"Where are you, my darling?" I whispered, leaning down to kiss my mother's forehead.

Her eyes fixed on mine, I knew very well how she had come to be where she was. This is what happens, I thought, when you are sent un-mothered and unmoored into life. This is what becomes of a good mind throttled by blow after blow of unexpected and unexamined griefs, of a heart so hungry for solace that it mistakes persuasion for love, of a yearning so unfathomable that not children or friendships or artistic catharsis can fill it. I thought of her early migraines, and her dismissal of them, of the cool cloth laid on the livid brow, the blood pooling at the base of her brain. I thought of Maggie's death and my mother's trauma, the shock of leaning over the small crib in the early light of dawn, the tiny figure, blue and lifeless, and how and where that shock had settled. I thought of Tessie's death and the daily horror of being forced to bear witness to the suffering of her own child, beloved and utterly lost. I thought of the betrayal she had endured when Father O'Byrne had not attended Tessie's funeral, his presence having been requested at a golf tournament somewhere in Colorado. I thought of the unbearable smallness of this excuse, his cowardice in the light of what had passed between him and my mother, and the devastation of that indiscretion.

It is only an organ, the brain, just as the heart is only an organ, and hearts will stop when they have been broken. We give full marks to the broken heart but are less tolerant of the broken mind. Concerned and purposeful, we put our faith in science, convinced that a solution lies in the magic bullet of medicine, that the chemistry of the brain is somehow more fixable than the chemistry of love.

Injustice is random, of this I was well aware. Was I not the child of a mother who, when I wept about the unfairness of a marriage gone wrong and the havoc it was wreaking on the children, had looked at me sadly and said, "Life isn't fair, Kitty Kat girl, so get on with it."

I gave Lucy the night off and prepared a nice dinner for my brothers, who stopped by later in the afternoon. We sat and talked about the state of our mother's affliction, the emptiness of the house, the future without a name. Joe left first, saying that he would look in on our mother in the morning, when she would be more alert.

Our mother, hearing none of this, lay in her narrow bed, turning to stone.

CHAPTER FIFTY-ONE

Tom listened impatiently and then said, "All right, let's take a look at some nursing homes, some assisted living facilities, just to get an idea."

"And then?" I asked.

"We'll figure it out," he answered, shortly. Tom was not a man given to terseness, it didn't suit him. Suffering unnerved him, and he found the apparent suffering of his mother demoralizing. He had watched as Lucy applied the small spoon to our mother's lips, he had seen the complete lack of responsiveness and, finally, when the dropper was inserted into her mouth and our mother had struggled unsuccessfully to swallow, her eyes widening in alarm, he had turned and walked out of the room.

"Where to?" I asked, settling into the passenger seat. "I don't know this town anymore."

"You never knew it," Tom replied. "Let's face it, you were just passing through."

"And stranded, half the time. Always begging for a ride because you commandeered the car. So unfair. That car was meant to be split three ways, if you'll recall," I said, adjusting my seat belt.

"Not easy to split things two ways, let alone three," Tom said.

"Not to mention six," I stated, glancing at my brother sideways. Tom sighed and shook his head.

"Derby Grange is turning into a shit show, isn't it?" he asked.

"That's an understatement, but we both know it's about something else, something much bigger than a house and forty acres of land," I suggested.

We drove in silence for a while, and then my brother said, "Dad's death was bad but this thing with Mom is worse. Everyone's losing it."

"So, tell me again why we are visiting these nursing homes," I demanded, turning to face him in the car.

"Jesus, Bate, because we don't want her to choke to death in the middle of the night with Lucy and Javier panicked out of their minds and an ambulance an hour away, that's why," Tom responded, defensively.

"What about a twenty-four-hour nurse on-site, at the house?" I knew this would be dismissed but was curious to hear what my brother would have to say.

"There is no nurse in Dubuque County better able to handle our mother than Lucy. And besides, it would drive Lucy nuts," Tom said, emphatically.

"Not to mention Bo. That would be the last straw," I added.

We looked at each other and said nothing. The tension at Derby Grange was palpable. The house now stood only to serve our mother's needs, and to shelter Lucy and Javier. Everyone longed to restore meaning to the place, but not everyone could live in the house. In his will, our father had divided Derby Grange equally six ways and, while in principle this was equitable, in practice it was extremely complicated. The house and property could accommodate only one of us, and this reality forced us into making a choice as to who should live in the place we all loved so well. This decision, sufficiently excruciating to cause conflict among us, was exacerbated by our mother's emotional absence.

"Ah, here we are at the highly reputable Brightview Home. You ready to check this out?" I asked, as my brother pulled into the parking lot and turned off the ignition.

Inside, we were greeted by a stout, pleasant woman in her middle age, whose vigorous gray hair and authoritative demeanor suggested that she had at one time been a nun. Tom and I were immediately subdued and accepted the pamphlets she offered as if they were exam forms being handed to us by an eighth-grade teacher.

Up one corridor and down another, we followed this figure of near-imperious stature, weaving through breakfast rooms and sunporches, through game rooms and libraries, passing through desolate spaces where we encountered white-haired nonagenarians lost in thought, or conversation, or sleep, walking slowly through the dining hall, where a number of people sat finishing their nondescript lunches served on plastic trays, appetite no longer a drive but a test of endurance, the cloying smell of ammonia and mushroom soup permeating the atmosphere, until we arrived at the door of an en suite room the woman thought might best suit our mother's needs.

In that moment, I was happy to have had the training of an actor and entered the room with the same inscrutable pleasantness I had exhibited when searching for an apartment in Manhattan. The woman, whose bearing had lost some of its importance as soon as we had entered the residential wing, stood to the side and watched our faces with the beady-eyed alertness of a crow.

While Tom strolled into the bathroom, making small sounds of approval regarding the appliances attached to the shower, I studied the bedroom, turning slowly in place to illustrate to the woman that the economy of the space was unexpected, and that I was not to be hurried.

The discipline required to conceal my reaction was considerable. This was a place utterly devoid of life, a place where old people came to count their days before dying, and in that counting was the drip, drip, drip of indifference, stripping them of any sense of self they may once have clung to. The clean, tidy bed where so many had lain, with its floral polyester bedspread and its two flattened pillows in faded pink cases, the requisite vase of plastic flowers on the round table beneath the window, through which one glimpsed other drab buildings, squatting in the distance, the beige recliner stained with the remnants of someone else's coffee, the empty closet able to accommodate no more than those articles absolutely necessary for subsistence, the open door leading into the corridor.

"I noticed that everyone keeps their bedroom door open. Is that choice, or protocol?" I asked, peering into the bathroom, where I met my brother's frankly horrified expression, and quickly backed out.

"Oh, we like our residents to feel free to visit each other. We encourage friendships here," the woman explained, proudly. Every instinct in my body told me that at no time in its entire history had friendship blossomed in this arid, lifeless place.

"Well, it's quite impressive," I said, buttoning my coat, "but, naturally, we're going to have to give it serious consideration. There are six of us kids weighing in on this decision, and you know how that goes."

The woman's expression told me that she knew only too well how that went and that, in her experience, it generally went south. Her self-regard was such that she would not demean herself by pandering, but when she asked for our personal contact information, my brother said, quite pragmatically, "We're going to look at all of our options before making a decision. I'm sure you can understand that. She is, after all, our mother. We'll call you when we know what we want to do."

As soon as we had passed through the front door into the sunshine, I started to cry and, turning to my brother, said, "You were brilliant."

"Then why are you crying?"

"Because it's unbearable to think of my mother in that place, unbearable to know that that's where unwanted old people are shuffled off to. The whole thing was ghastly."

"You know what's not ghastly?" my brother asked, flipping the car keys in the air and catching them deftly with his other hand.

Brushing the tears from my cheeks, I studied him for a moment before answering.

"A cheeseburger and a beer?"

"Now you're talking my lingo, hermana. Vámanos!"

Biting into an oversize burger at the Ground Round, I observed my brother's eating habits, which mirrored my own. We ate quickly, intensely, and with no apparent relish. The goal was to absorb as much fuel as possible in the least amount of time. Tom was slightly more fastidious than I and had the discipline to return his burger to the plate after each wolfish bite, whereas I allowed for no such leisure and consumed the entire burger without once putting it down.

"That nursing home made you a little peckish, huh?" my brother asked, popping a French fry into his mouth.

"Stress eating," I replied.

"You've been stress eating since you were two," Tom declared.

"My size four pants don't feel it," I said.

"Six."

"Screw you."

We paused as the waitress gathered our plates.

"Bom, what are we going to do?"

We looked at each other, searching for an answer.

"We could move her closer to town, so that in the event of an emergency a hospital would only be minutes away. Much less pressure on Lucy, easier for the family to visit Mom, more convenient when the time comes for, you know—"

"Hospice," I interjected.

"Yeah. And gives us the time and space to sort out Derby Grange. It's practical, all around."

"Practical, but sad. Dad would never have allowed such a thing," I said, curious to see how this opinion would settle.

"Dad was of sound mind, and he died very quickly," my brother responded. "Mom doesn't know where she is, or who she is. She won't know the difference."

"We don't know that," I said, a little too defensively.

My brother regarded me carefully. He didn't want to hurt me, but he was growing tired of the unrelenting importance I attached to every aspect of my mother's care and wanted to resolve the issue efficiently and with as little drama as possible. This dynamic defined our relationship and had served it well. We seldom disagreed and, despite distinct differences in personality, had always loved and trusted each other. In a sense, we had started out together, the first son and the first daughter, and this distinction at once set us apart and balanced us. Tribally, we shared equal power.

"Bate, you know as well as I do that she's not here anymore. Maybe we could find a small house somewhere close to the hospital, something affordable, and just make a quick and easy transition," Tom suggested, his tone confidential.

We sat in silence for a moment.

"You and I would split it, is what you mean. Keep the others out of it," I said.

"Exactly. I'll take care of the down payment and whatever else is needed up-front and you and I can settle later on. Agreed?"

I shouldn't have been surprised. Tom had always been generous, sometimes inordinately so. I often wondered if this was in reaction to our father's penuriousness, a failing my brother had determined early in his life not to perpetuate. Sitting across from him, I couldn't help but feel the sadness of time lost; it was impossible not to marvel at all we had known, the secrets and intimacies of a childhood defined by a place that we had loved but that could no longer protect us or our mother who, we knew with terrible certainty, would never have left of her own volition.

Tom had changed remarkably little in fifty-two years. Trim, agile, light on his feet, he had features favoring the Kiernan side of the family. In this moment and in this light, he looked very much like our mother. I wondered if he was aware of that genetic inheritance, and if it pleased him.

When the waitress came to the table, my brother and I rose in our seats and reached for the check at the same time.

CHAPTER FIFTY-TWO

Everyone detested the house on Devon Drive, and yet that is where we took her to die. Reason abandoned us at this time, and what prevailed was a sense of survival. Even now, I cannot remember the exact justification for this decision, other than that it seemed to resolve a number of conflicts among us. Derby Grange awaited ownership, and until that was determined the home in which my mother had lived for almost fifty years was, in effect, off-limits.

Of course, there were any number of practical reasons applied to this solution, but in retrospect they seemed contrived and insubstantial. We wanted her near a hospital, in the event of an emergency. We did not want to risk an awful accident at home, in whatever form. We wanted all of the family close by.

I can't even recall if I was present when she was physically moved from Derby Grange to the tidy little house on a quiet, tree-lined street in town. So many memories have dissipated in the mind-blunting of that period, when every thought, every feeling, every action was born out of intense anxiety. In the removal of our mother from the place she had lived in and loved for fifty years, we were declaring her death imminent, and perhaps that is why, in my mind's eye, Derby Grange had been shuttered, the windows latched, the doors locked. Most likely, it was a sunny day in June when she was lifted from her bed, as inflexible as wood and yet as light as a feather, wrapped in blankets, her diaper fresh, her hair combed. Lifted up by two men, Sam and Javier, and carried carefully to the backseat of Sam's SUV, where she was laid against cushions, her head propped up on pillows, her eyes staring straight ahead.

As they drove down the sun-dappled driveway, under an archway of trees she would never see again, past the glen where feathers had been found and tucked in a sweater's sleeve, where tiger lilies danced like orange beacons in the dusk, where children and grandchildren had shrieked with pleasure on the swing that Joe had fashioned out of two long planks of wood and anchored to the branches of the tall maple tree that shaded it, past the bonfire that, even in its dereliction, waited for the family to gather, for the flames to mesmerize, for the laughter and the singing she would never again hear, down, down the driveway my father had paved with Mulgrew Blacktop and, looking back, to the house itself, standing amid a copse of trees, its rooms lit with candlelight, tall windows beckoning, the brick and mortar of two hundred years, the births and the deaths of children, the paintings framed and hung on every wall, the ornate mirrors, the sage walls and the salmon ceiling of the dining room, the art studio, where everything was forgiven, the upstairs bedrooms and the floral wallpaper, the bed she had once shared with my father, the narrow back stairs and the hundreds of secrets they had known, the orchard with its crooked fruit, the grape arbor, where daughters married, the forgotten statue of St. Francis, through the stone gates, past the bee houses, down the gravel road, past the Breitbach farmhouse and the ramshackle red barn, past the rolling cornfields, the green valleys, onto the new road that would take her, for the last time, away.

My mother, by all accounts incapable of thought, had nevertheless fixed her gaze on the disappearing view of her house, and had not closed her eyes until the car turned onto the highway. Someone told me this, or perhaps I was there, sitting beside her in the back of the car. I must have been present when she was again lifted out of the car and this time carried a much shorter distance, up a common concrete walkway, through an unfamiliar front door, and into the bright living room where a bed had been made up for her, against the wall. This was a house without shadows, without mystery, without guile. It represented itself well; clean, new, well maintained, the kitchen a veritable homage to the baker who had once lived there. Gleaming surfaces, spotless carpets, air-conditioning—an unheard-of luxury growing up—at a low, constant hum. The thermostat confounded us because we had no way of measuring our mother's comfort, and therefore this amenity became a source of irritation.

As she was unfolded into her new bed, with all the attendant fussing, my mother's eyes remained open. I hurried to sit beside her, to smooth the sheet over her chest, to adjust the pillow under her unyielding head. I wanted to observe the effects of this disruption and, seeing none, wondered why I was not appeased. The entire purpose behind this enterprise had been to bring peace to a family in turmoil, but that calm eluded me. What washed over me instead was shame.

The furniture in the living room was moved to accommodate the six of us. This is where we would hold our final vigil and, unsurprisingly, each of us chose a place we marked as our own. Tom appropriated the couch, which rested against the length of the front wall. Jenny often joined him there, but she was just as likely to perch at the foot of our mother's bed. Across the room, facing the bed, was an armchair, and this is where Joe sat, leaning forward, his arms planted on his knees. Laura claimed the ottoman next to Joe's armchair, in front of the faux fireplace. Sam drew a chair from the kitchen table and placed it at the end of our mother's bed, availing himself of the best possible view of her face. My position was beside the bed, in a small, upright chair next to the bed table, which held, on a single tray, all of the articles that would ease my mother's discomfort: ice chips in a glass, a small carafe of water, a sponge, a washcloth, a box of Kleenex, a comb, a jar of expensive body cream, a tube of ChapStick. When I left my chair to go into the kitchen or use the bathroom, Lucy would slip into it, usually bearing a small plate of comfort foods with which to stimulate my mother's appetite.

My mother's days and nights were passed in limbo. It was rare and wonderful when she opened her eyes, and then we would all gather around her, those eyes as compelling as the sun. Her gaze settled on nothing, the vacancy behind it unfathomable, the obliteration of the brain complete, and yet we sprang into action when her eyelids fluttered open, and an egg would be boiled in no time, flavored with butter and salt and gently brought to her lips, but she would not respond. Nevertheless, Lucy persevered, and the dropper was daily eased between my mother's lips, the nutrient dispensed slowly into her mouth. Ice chips were folded in a thin dampened cloth, a glass of Ensure sat half full, a flexible straw resting inside it.

One evening, toward the end of the first week in the house on Devon Drive, Lucy prepared a small dish of custard, which she brought to my mother's bedside. I took the dish from her, placed a napkin under my mother's chin, and waited. An hour passed and then, as if pulled from a deep sleep, my mother opened her eyes. Immediately, I spooned a tiny portion of the custard and brought it to her mouth. My mother did not look at me, she did not look at anyone, but to our amazement she suddenly parted her lips and then, in a gesture reminiscent of defiance, snapped her teeth together and shut her mouth, tight. Her intention was unmistakable. She would take no more nourishment.

In the small living room, everyone was still. It was as if we'd seen a ghost, the last remnant of a mother who had, however reflexively, asserted her will. In that moment, no one breathed, because whereas we had anticipated any eventuality—choking, resistance, physical struggle—we had not anticipated our mother's small, primitive act of defiance. In much the same way my father had looked steadily into my eyes and said, I don't fear death, but I don't welcome it, either, my mother had made a decision, the finality of which stunned us with its clarity. In that moment, I knew my parents to be of the same stripe, and suddenly understood the bedrock of their bond, and why they had endured.

These were two people who despised illness but were not afraid to face death, and what lay beyond it. They would meet God—or oblivion—philosophically. Had I been able to accommodate my mother's wish to end her life in the early months of her diagnosis, she would have thanked me, kissed me good-bye and, having locked the door behind me, taken the pills without hesitation. So it was with my father, who refused to extend his life unnaturally. Theirs was a spartan courage, and that is what they had recognized in one another, and what they had admired.

Leaning in, I put my lips to my mother's ear and whispered, "I understand, darling." I longed to stay there, longed to rest my head on my mother's breast, but there were other siblings with the same longing, and now there would not be much time.

I rose and, looking at my brothers and sisters, said, "I'm going to call my husband, and then I'm going to make dinner. Let's have some wine."

CHAPTER FIFTY-THREE

The waiting had begun. I asked my husband to come, and one day he walked through the front door on Devon Drive, his thin, worn garment bag slung over his broad shoulder, his kind face drawn with pity. After greeting Sam and Jenny, Tim went directly to my mother's bedside, knelt on the carpet before her and, putting his hand over hers, said, "Thank you for being my great friend, Joan." When he stood, I motioned to him to join me in the front bedroom, which I had requisitioned. As soon as the door had closed, he dropped his garment bag and took me in his arms. I buried my head in his shoulder and wept. My husband's presence offered a reprieve, the first I'd had in many days, and we lay down on the bed, no more than a foot apart, facing each other. In a strained whisper, I divulged everything that had been repressed for days, every gnawing anxiety, every poorly concealed irritation, every unexpected sadness and, as always, he listened attentively, stroking my cheek.

"And my mother was the one who insisted that you and I meet in Ireland. She knew, didn't she?" I asked, muffling my sobs with the pillow.

"I don't know if she had an intuition about us, but I sure as hell know that she loved *you*," my husband replied, pulling me into the crook of his arm.

Like a child, I nestled into him, breathing deeply as I lay against his chest, feeling the warmth of his skin beneath the fabric of his crisp white shirt.

"How do you know?" I entreated, softly, listening with one ear to the beating of his heart.

Tim chuckled. He would indulge me, this time, because he knew I was depleted, and he understood that I needed reassurance and that it had to come from someone I trusted unconditionally.

"Before I met you, if we were at a dinner party with Jean Smith in New York, or visiting Jean at the Residence in Dublin, and someone asked your mother about her family, she'd say that she had a daughter who was a successful and very accomplished stage actress."

"Not a television actress?" I asked, tilting my head back to look into his eyes.

"No, 'an accomplished stage actress' is what she'd say."

"With pride?" I whispered, tracing his eyebrow with my finger.

"Of course. Your mother was nothing if not a snob. And, as we both know," my husband said, turning me on my side and spooning me in anticipation of a nap, "the apple didn't fall too far from the tree."

Tim's presence steadied me, but genuine comfort was beyond my reach. I was in a constant state of hypervigilance, at times barely able to conceal my agitation. All of my nervous energy was applied to the preparation of meals for those of us holding vigil, to the daily grind of considerations no longer significant, the sponge bathing of my mother's rigid body, the ice chips hourly placed between her unyielding lips, the purposeless grooming, the pointless changing of the linens, the ceaseless activity we wove like a chrysalis around our mother's still form.

We inhabited our tensions with awkwardness, as if they were suits of armor. The suspense of living near death in a small room containing the people most entitled to bear witness to this rite of passage was sometimes intolerable. Bottled-up resentments could, without warning, reach dangerous levels of toxicity.

One afternoon, a week after our mother had closed her mouth to food, Joe said something I considered so thoughtless and provocative that I opened the front door and stormed off down the block. What he said remains elusive, as do most of the brittle exchanges that took place during this period, but how he said it, and the force with which it struck, sent me into a blind fury. As I stalked down the suburban street in my ubiquitous red apron, past blond-brick single-level houses boasting miniature manicured lawns, beneath leafy trees I could not recognize, my feet landing hard on hot concrete, I sensed my brother in full pursuit. He called my name, but I ignored him, and continued marching down the block. "Kate!" Joe called out again, and this time caught up with me, stepping in front of me to make me stop.

In the middle of the afternoon on that quiet, well-mannered street, I abandoned all restraint and erupted. I accused my brother of selfishness, of sabotage, of cruelty, and with each salvo I discharged my voice rose in pitch, so that anyone looking out of their living room window might shrink back in alarm at the sight of a wild-eyed woman in a red apron, hurling invectives at a handsome, distraught middle-aged man crouched before her, gripping his head.

"Jesus, Kate, for Christ's sake, lower your voice," my brother pleaded, as my shrillness reverberated down Devon Drive, disturbing its Sunday afternoon equanimity.

"Don't fucking tell me to lower my voice, don't you *fucking* tell me to lower my voice, are you out of your goddam mind? I have *fucking* had it! It is *fucking enough*!" I shouted, and as I shouted I began to wail, tears streaming down my cheeks, weeks of pent-up sadness and impotence erupting all at once, without warning, in a messy, profane display of anguish.

My brother, never before having seen me completely lose control, was caught off guard, and stood there in the middle of the block staring at me, his expression at once sheepish and apprehensive. Wiping my eyes with my apron, I shook my head and muttered, "Oh, what does it matter. Nothing matters. Nothing matters anymore."

Joe reached out and, putting a hand on my shoulder, said, "That's not true, Kate, and you know it. Come on, get a grip."

As we faced off in the middle of Devon Drive, the absurdity of the confrontation struck me. Neither of us, in that moment, could have articulated the precise source of conflict, and that is because there was none. The source of our conflict, of every conflict that had arisen in the past months, was rooted in exhaustion, the inexpressible exhaustion that comes of having lived with the specter of death for eight consecutive years. Our father had died two years earlier, but six years before that our mother had been handed a death sentence, and from that moment forward we had striven to prepare ourselves for this inevitability, and yet we continued to surprise ourselves with unexpected bursts of rage. This is why my brother and I stood, heads already bowed with regret, in the middle of Devon Drive on a fine Sunday afternoon, not a thousand feet from our dying mother, and why we did not move until we had repaired this rupture, which we did by agreeing that this was hard, and would undoubtedly get much harder, and that it was imperative to hold fast and remember that we loved each other.

When I looked into my brother's eyes I saw, as I had seen often since our father's death, a terrible, ineffable sadness, which he was capable of quickly covering with anger or detachment, leading everyone to assume he was pissed off most of the time. He wasn't. He was lost, and so was I, and our reconciliation came as swiftly as the storm that had preceded it, as he shook his head at his older sister in her greasy apron and wild hair, with her big mouth and her dirty talk, and she in turn wagged a scolding finger at her younger brother with his still beautiful face and his ridiculous self-consciousness over a private tiff in a public place about nothing of substance, nothing at all but parents gone missing and the utter hopelessness of that feeling, and still here we were, and, suddenly washed over with relief, giving way to a spontaneous spasm of laughter, and the careful slinging of arms around each other's shoulders, and the slow return to the tidy little house on Devon Drive, on a beautiful summer's day.

"Jesus," my brother said, "you look like shit."

"The neighbors are going to think I'm a complete wack job."

"Don't say I didn't warn you."

CHAPTER FIFTY-FOUR

For ten days she had not eaten and had absorbed only the liquid dispensed through ice chips or the flexible straw forced between her teeth. Her breathing was shallow, but regular. She did not stir.

My siblings and I agreed that it was time to make the necessary phone calls. Our mother appeared to be in a deep sleep, and yet common sense told us that it could only, now, be a matter of days before her autonomic nervous system shut down completely, and our mother would then stop breathing.

The phone calls also signified a public admission that our mother would soon be dead. Most people, I had learned in my life, feared death, but my mother's closest friends were not most people.

Mary Eleanore Shanley Harriss, otherwise known as Effie because of her height and its resemblance to the Eiffel Tower, and Jean Kennedy Smith had met my mother at Eden Hall at the Sacred Heart boarding school when they had been very young girls and, in the way of precocious, mischievous, lonely girls sent away to school for the first time, had instantly become fast and, as the years would prove, enduring friends. They would have been considered, by today's standards, almost laughingly homogeneous. All three were Irish-American, Roman Catholic, well-bred girls born into good eastern families, and all would acquire a familiarity with tragedy before they had reached the age of thirty.

Being chosen as a godparent within the Catholic tradition in the very conservative era of the fifties was considered an honor and, although Tom was arguably more privileged to have Jean Kennedy Smith selected as his guardian, I had always regarded myself as lucky to have been given Effie Harriss as a godmother. When I was a child, she had blown into my life with an energy and a glamour that had dazzled me, looming over me while smoking a Virginia Slim through the telescope of a black cigarette holder, in the other hand precariously balancing a martini, her full-throated, viscous laughter punctuating each inanity I mumbled and leaning down to look me square in the face, exclaiming, "I like the cut of your jib, god girl!"

Effie told me she would be on the next available flight out of Mc-Allen, Texas.

"Listen, god girl, tell Jicky to hold on until I get there, will you? Just whisper it in her ear," Effie said, hanging up the phone. The conversation had been concise and decisive, a shorthand used by someone accustomed to hearing bad news. She had lost her husband before she reached the age of thirty and, in the decade following his death, both of her sons had died tragically in unrelated airplane accidents. Effie's faith had seen her through, she had never buckled, never gone mad, never gone under. "She's one hell of a tough, beautiful dame," my father used to say about her, lifting his glass. He had been a little in love with Effie, and my mother, proud of her brave, high-spirited friend, had not been displeased.

Jean Smith would be the more challenging phone call, and I implored my husband to make it for me. Tim had been Jean's great friend long before he knew I existed, and over the years had become well versed in the habits and idiosyncrasies of the Kennedys. He had regularly been Jean's escort after her husband, Steve, died, and both he and my mother had often traveled together to visit their mutual friend. My husband knew Jean Smith far better than I did, and yet he demurred.

"It's not my place," Tim said, digging in his heels.

"What do you mean? You're my husband," I replied, heatedly.

"Exactly. This is about Joan, not me. It needs to come from you, her daughter," Tim insisted.

Reluctantly, I picked up the phone and dialed. When an assistant answered, and I related the purpose of my call, Jean was informed and immediately came on the line. Typically, she was direct, unsentimental, and curious.

"How bad is she?" Jean asked.

I hesitated.

"Bad enough to warrant this phone call, Jean. She's had nothing to eat or drink for days, she's in a coma, her breathing is increasingly shallow, it can't be long now, and I thought you'd want to know."

"Well, yah, of course I want to know, kid, but I mean, how *close* to the end is she, do you think?" Jean persisted, as if speaking to a hospice nurse or an unusually friendly neurologist.

Tim sat on the bed, listening in, trying his best to interpret my frantic pantomimes, and failing. Covering the phone with one hand, I whispered, "I think I should tell her not to bother. It will be all about *her*, if she comes, and I'm not up to it. What do you think?"

I knew that this was, essentially, my decision, and that Jean would honor my wishes. Theirs had been a long and remarkable friendship. Jean was my mother's oldest friend, it was only right that she should be notified and encouraged to attend the funeral. Jean's were the questions of someone who had known a preponderance of tragedy, whose view of death was an admixture of the clinical and the philosophical. She wanted and deserved to be guided, and yet I couldn't bring myself to tell her to come. I envisioned the effort involved in preparing for her arrival, the attention she would require, the obligation Tim would naturally feel, and I knew that I was not big enough to sacrifice my husband at this time, so near to this death.

"It could be a few days, Jean, maybe even another week. It's a long trip from Bridgehampton to Dubuque, easier to get to Paris, actually, and I'm just not sure it's the wisest thing to do. You'll be exhausted by the time you get here," I said, my voice gaining conviction.

There was a silence on the other end of the phone, during which Jean calculated the pros and cons of making the trip. It wasn't about love, I knew that, or loyalty, but about the vicissitudes of aging, and the fortitude required to withstand yet another loss, and whether it wouldn't be better, in fact *more loving*, to abandon protocol and mourn in private, where she could remember Eden Hall and the first time she had laid eyes on Joan Kiernan, whom she had dubbed Jicky and who had remained Jicky ever after, and life on the Cape, when her brothers were alive and the world was full of promise, and the years of adventure and travel and then marriage and children and still they had clung tight to each other, through all of it, through the deaths and the love affairs and the triumphs and the laughter—yes, Jean must have thought to herself, let me remember how Jicky and I laughed, let me remember that, in peace.

Tim took the phone from me and, in a voice that would brook no opposition, said, "Listen, Jean, our good friend will probably be dead and buried by the time you get here, and what's the point of that? Joan would not approve of you making this trip, it's not worth it. You and I will meet in New York and have dinner, share all the memories. Stay put. I'll call you when it's all over."

"It's terrific Effie's coming all the way from McAllen, don't you think? My God, she's like some kind of Viking, isn't she?"

Jean was not willing to end the conversation on a perfunctory note, so I drew closer to my husband, eager to eavesdrop on the final exchange between my mother's best friend and my husband.

Tim laughed and said, "Yeah, you girls were a cross between Amazons and the Three Musketeers. You and Joan had one of the great friendships, that's the important thing. The rest is irrelevant."

This calmed Jean and, with a bit of her old spirit, she quipped, "Listen, kid, tell Effie that she is there to represent both of us and that I expect her to comport herself with great dignity."

I had not expected to be put through to the abbess when I called Our Lady of the Mississippi Abbey, and I was not disappointed. Mother Columba held dominion over a community of thirty hardworking nuns: those who worked in the candy shop making the caramels that provided most of the revenue for the priory; those who worked in the fields harvesting corn and grain; those too old for manual labor, and those too young to know with certainty that this was where they belonged, postulants arriving at the front door of the motherhouse, straight off the farm, thrown into the singular rigor that defined the Order of Cistercians of the Strict Observance.

When she returned my call, I found myself startled, as I always did, by the soft, sweet cadence of her voice. Beneath those mellifluous tones beat the heart of a lioness, whose formidable intellectual vigor and quest for spiritual enlightenment had shaped her into a person of rare authenticity. Columba was interested in an examined life and did not waste her time on superficial relationships. There was steel in her ambition to know God, and thirty years earlier when, on a winter's morning after Mass in the abbey chapel, a trim, freckled woman had approached her and asked her if she was allowed to drink beer and eat cheeseburgers and, if so, would she be her guest at a hole-in-the-wall two miles down the road, she had immediately recognized in my mother a fellow pilgrim.

"I'll come tomorrow, Kate, and spend some time with Joan. It's time to say good-bye, isn't it?" Mother Columba asked, with disarming simplicity. For a moment, I couldn't speak.

EFFIE AND I sat on the back deck of the house on Devon Drive, waiting for Mother Columba. My siblings were inside, keeping vigil around our mother's bed. Effie, broadened and blurred by age, had nevertheless retained her vital, indomitable spirit, and this made her appear still beautiful, despite her bewilderment. She sat on an unfamiliar metal chair on an unfamiliar deck, attached to a house that had no meaning, and questioned me.

"But listen, god girl, why isn't Jicky at Derby Grange? I don't get it."

I knew I would not be able to articulate a satisfying answer, having been unable to do so for myself, and decided to appeal to her compassion.

"We were all very confused after Dad died, and there's been a lot of conflict about the house and the property and who should have it and how we should share it, and then Mother got worse and it frightened everybody to think she might choke to death out there, and so one day Tom and I decided to buy this house so that Mother would be closer to a hospital, closer to everything and everybody, and it just seemed the most practical and convenient solution to a lot of problems, do you understand?" I asked, watching as Lucy placed a fresh cup of coffee in front of Effie.

Effie had envisioned keeping vigil at Derby Grange, where she and my mother had taken long walks down the gravel road, where they had sat together in the swing that Joe built, their sneakered feet lifted in unison, where dinner parties went on until the wee hours, and where she could then be found sitting next to my father on the front porch, flirting under a blue moon, drinking wine and smoking Virginia Slims.

Inexplicably, I was overcome with embarrassment and said, "I'm sorry, Effie, that we can't be at Derby Grange. I hope you don't mind too much."

"Oh listen, kiddo, it doesn't matter. Jicky is all that matters. I wanted to see my friend one last time on this earth." Effie paused, sipped her coffee, and then tilted her head dramatically to one side.

"But I can't believe you produced those strapping boys—two giants! And you kept your figure, but I suppose you have to, don't you, in your game?" she asked, turning to peer at my son Ian, who was lurking in the long grasses at the side of the house. Ian looked up and grinned wickedly at my godmother, who waved and said, "Hi there, young giant!"

Lucy again walked onto the deck, wiping her hands on her tired apron, and whispered, "Mother Columba here, señora. She with Beanie."

Immediately, I rose and motioned for Effie to stay seated, indicating that I would like a word with Columba before making introductions. Effie, true to form, put a finger to her lips and made her way to the open screen door, where she could observe the drama about to unfold.

Inside the small living room, Mother Columba sat on my mother's bed, wearing her tunic, scapular, and cincture. She had replaced the traditional coif with a dark blue head scarf, which she had wrapped hurriedly around her head, exposing a fringe of thick white-gray hair. Sturdy black shoes showed from under her serge skirt, and the silver cross that hung around her neck touched my mother's breast as Columba leaned forward, taking my mother's hand in her own.

Drawn as if to a magical liturgy, I settled quietly in the room with my siblings, and we watched as Mother Columba attempted to shepherd our mother through the valley of death.

"Now, Joan," Columba began, in a gentle, seductive voice, "I think you're very tired, and it's time to rest. You've stopped eating and drinking, so you're showing us that you're ready to let go of life, and just think, Joan, you're going to see what you and I have talked about for thirty years, you're going to see your God. You're going to understand what you've been longing to understand your entire life. So, now, Joan, don't worry anymore, you're not disappointing anyone, all of your children are here, and they want you to rest, they want you to know that it's time to say good-bye."

A muffled sob came from the kitchen and, glancing back, I saw Lucy pull the apron up over her face and I caught a glimpse of Effie, mesmerized, leaning against the screen door. Sam stood at the base of our mother's bed, his hands folded in front of him, his head bowed. In the middle of the room, the oldest child stood next to the youngest, Jenny a head shorter than Tom, while Laura looked on from her station in front of the fireplace. Joe stood behind his chair, both hands resting on the seat back. Ian, too, I could see out of the corner of my eye, was attracted to the unorthodox nature of these ministrations, and I watched as he inched closer to the scene, his eyes riveted to the figure of Mother Columba.

I searched my mother's face for any sign of recognition, for the merest hint of a smile, for the slightest furrowing of her brow, but there was nothing. This surprised all of us knowing, as we did, that if any voice had the power to penetrate the veil that now hung over my mother, it was Columba's.

Minutes passed, and then Columba straightened and said, "I have to go soon, Joan, so you need to hurry up. Don't resist death, Joan, you have nothing to be afraid of. It's time."

My mother's breathing, visible only by the slight rising of her chest, continued unabated. Mother Columba sighed, smiled wistfully, and said, "In the end, for so many, life is stronger than death, but I thought Joan would be eager to go, after suffering for so long."

Another day passed, then two, until the end of another week saw a weary, despondent Effie on the phone to her family, saying she didn't know when it would end, that it looked like Jicky might live forever. She felt herself becoming a burden, or she felt the burden of time suspended and, after another day had passed and we entered the third week of our mother's stasis, I sat down next to my godmother and told her to go home.

"You've done so much more than anyone could have asked for. You've been terrific, and you were an absolutely world-class friend, you know that. This was the important part, Effie. You came to say good-bye, and you've done that, done it beautifully. I'm so grateful to you, we all are. Go home now. It's enough."

And so my godmother left, followed by my mother's older brother Pat, a professional Catholic who had flown in from New Jersey, agitated his way into the death chamber, and slammed the door on his way out, oblivious to his sister's condition, wanting only to have attended the funeral Mass, and shouting as my husband wrangled him into the car to drive him to the airport, "Well, good-bye, Joanie, and I hope you make it to heaven! Bye now!"

Gone, all gone. In the absence of visitors, the house resumed its torpor. The clock over the mantel in the room where my mother lay ticked off the hours, hours stretched on the rack, and we couldn't believe that someone without sentience, without a mind, could so forcefully assert the will to go on living.

CHAPTER FIFTY-FIVE

There was no baffling vacillation, we did not have to follow the jerky graph of our mother's heart. We were somewhere between midnight and dawn, the silence was profound, our vigilance was coming to an end. Then why did we look so embattled, so fatigued? Because the last days had remained the last days for such a long time, during which there had been no relief. It had been torturous, the final letting-go, not only in its attenuation, but in its unrelenting sameness. The six of us were gathered in the room, her breathing had changed, it felt like minutes passed as we hung there suspended, leaning forward, ready. And then, another breath would claw its way upward, her chest lifted and dropped by an unseen hand. Incredulous, we watched.

The silence was disturbed by one pronouncement, which came from Joe who, as usual, sat in his chair, arms braced on his thighs.

"A watched pot never boils," he said.

I looked at my brother.

"What did you say?" I asked.

"You heard me."

When I turned back to my mother, a blueness had appeared around her nose and the edges of her eyes. I had been warned about this by one of the death experts. Saying nothing to my siblings, I put my hand to my mother's cheek. Cold as clay.

Before you slip away, I thought, *remember me.*

If you can, remember me.

I will remember you.

CHAPTER FIFTY-SIX

My mother was laid to rest in a casket that had been designed by my brother Sam and handcrafted by the Trappist monks who worked for him. At New Melleray Abbey, in a large warehouse adjacent to the monastery, monks toiled in absolute silence to perfect my brother's vision, and as they worked they prayed, creating for my mother a mystical cradle.

While we waited for the coffin to arrive at the house on Devon Drive, Jenny and I prepared our mother for the final indignity that would be demanded of her. A large basin was filled with warm water, into which Lucy added washcloths, lavender oil, and bars of soap. Gently, we turned our mother's body so that we could remove her nightgown, a manipulation that required us to lift her body while, at the same time, slipping the nightgown off. As I pulled the nightgown over my mother's torso, I gasped. Her skin was severely mottled with large bruises that spread over her back like dark contiguous shadows, settling in emaciated rib grooves, over still girlish hips, down the length of long, slender limbs. We washed her with great care and spoke very little. Jenny held our mother's hand in her own, moving the bar of soap through her fingers again and again. When I realized that my sister was trying to remove our mother's wedding ring, I asked her what she thought she was doing.

"I want something to remember her by, Kate, something to cherish," my sister pleaded.

"Do not take that wedding ring off her finger, Jenny," I said, staring at her.

Something about my sister's need to have my mother's wedding ring and the strength of my resistance clarified the discrepancy in how we perceived our mother. I could not bear the idea of putting her into the ground without leaving intact that one immutable, unassailable symbol of a life shared. Jenny could not bear the idea of being abandoned.

Dispatched to the country, Lucy had returned with the only articles of clothing she could find that she considered appropriate for the burial. The house was not as we had left it, she told me, and she had no choice but to open boxes at random, withdrawing the few items that appeared, if not familiar, at least satisfactory. As she handed me the pleated gray wool pants, the unfamiliar white blouse with its plastic buttons, and the shapeless gray cardigan, she looked on the verge of tears.

Lucy had shared my morbid daydream. Deep in the ground, my mother's body would slowly decompose, until in due time nothing would be left but a skeleton. Nothing, that is, except the shroud in which she was buried, and in my mind's eye this should be the ensemble that had carried her through the great adventures of her adult life. The dinner parties and art exhibits, the soirees and opening nights, the illicit and the sublime, the private and the triumphant. Through all of this she had worn her uniform of black silk trousers, silver Chanel knit sweater over the cream silk blouse with its low-hanging bow, the whimsical sash of Indian cotton at her waist. It was nearly impossible to imagine the devastated silhouette, the corpse identifiable by heavy wool slacks and dull sweater buttoned over a polyester blouse, no visible sign of her dash, her femininity, her longing. She would be buried like any other mother, in conventional clothing, and for this I was sure she would never forgive me.

My brothers carried the casket through the wide doors in the back of the house on Devon Drive, and situated it in the sunken living room, a few feet from the bed in which our mother had died. It was a simple but elegant pine casket, lined with soft white fabric. Joe and Sam and Tom lifted our mother's body from the bed and slowly carried it to the open coffin, where they laid her down with a gentleness I had not known they possessed, but which did not surprise me. The casket was flanked by two tall candlesticks, and a kneeler was brought and placed before my mother's body, so that each of us could say good-bye in the privacy of this foreign living room, within the confines of this strange house. At no time had we considered a funeral home; we had known from the get-go that we would wake her the Irish way, and we were pleased with this arrangement.

Without formality but with great discretion, each of us came privately to bid our mother good-bye. I prepared meals in the kitchen, I watched, and I waited. When at last the house was still, my brothers and sisters silhouetted against the moonlight on the deck, the smoke from Jenny's cigarette drifting into the night, Laura stretched out on the floor of the cedar deck, her arms cradling her head, Joe and Tom talking in soft murmurs, Sam lying alone on our mother's bed, my chance presented itself. I approached the casket and knelt before my mother. From my pocket, I withdrew a slightly frayed photograph that had been taken on the grounds of Mohonk Mountain House in upstate New York one summer long ago when my mother and my grandfather had surprised me with a visit and we had decided to drive up to New Paltz. In it, my grandfather is leaning against the trunk of a large maple tree, and my mother and I are sitting cross-legged on the ground. The three generations are grinning, as if having just shared a corny joke.

Because saying good-bye in a small house surrounded by siblings is fraught with suspense, I moved quickly. Leaning over my mother to kiss her cheek, I slipped the photograph into the sleeve of her cardigan and whispered, "I didn't have time to find one of just the two of us." Settling back on the kneeler, I gazed at my mother's ashen face. I was not unsettled by the pale, waxen skin stretched tightly over her cheekbones or the terrible stillness of her form. It seemed to me she had been like this for a very long time, but I was suddenly overcome by a wave of helplessness and began to weep. Someone knelt by my side and placed a stiff arm around me, a long-fingered, trembling hand hesitantly cupped my shoulder. This was my elder son's hand, Ian's hand, and this was the first time in many years that he had been moved to comfort me. We knelt, side by side, in silence. I felt the carefulness of his arm, the curious and strangely brave quality of his sympathy, the way in which he did not dare rest the full weight of his limb across my shoulders. Habit compelled me to turn to him, but instinct directed me otherwise, and the two of us knelt there for some time in the thickness of the night, the tall candles illuminating my mother's face, her body lying where it would now always lie, tears streaming down my cheeks, longing to rest my head against my son's shoulder but knowing that I would not, because some blessings must not be disturbed, and side by side we thought our separate thoughts, and it was enough.

CHAPTER FIFTY-SEVEN

The funeral Mass was held in the chapel at Our Lady of the Mississippi Abbey. Midmorning light illuminated the tall stained-glass windows, softening the faces of the sisters who sat on one side of the chapel, wimpled heads alternately bent over missals or lifted in song. I cannot, now, remember the details of the Mass, except that a priest unknown to me officiated and spoke about my mother as if she were familiar to him, which she was not. A few of my siblings spoke, standing at the podium, reading the words they had so meticulously composed the night before. I was struck by Jenny's composure, her small, gallant form in the quiet of the chapel, the pride with which she held herself, the uncommon valor of her words. Sam rose, and when he turned to face us at the lectern, I saw that all of the sisters were beaming and that, caught in the glow of their affection, my brother could not help but smile. Of the grandchildren, I remember only Rory, whose sweet, grave eyes implored us to appreciate his grandmother's eccentricities, the ones that had delighted and disarmed, the ones that had marked and shaped him long before the affliction had turned them into ghosts.

When the Mass was over, we filed out through the side door, my brothers walking ahead, bearing the coffin on their shoulders. As we passed the fountain that had been erected twenty years earlier in memory of my sister Tess, I paused to read the inscription that circled the base and afterward I stood there for a moment, looking out over the falling hills of the Mississippi Valley. The words of Mother Columba's eulogy looped through my mind.

The former abbess had stepped onto the chancel, crossed herself, and moved slowly toward the lectern, where she had paused. A moment passed, and then she looked up and, gathering us in her gaze, began to speak in her gentle, powerful voice. In the quiet of the chapel, as dust motes danced in the long bars of light that shafted through the windows, Mother Columba told us that she had never known anyone like our mother. She had never known a person to match our mother's intellectual curiosity, the abbess said, or anyone less intellectually satisfied. Joan, Columba said, had had a life of suffering, and this had mystified and perplexed our mother, to the extent that she sought answers in every aspect of her experience. Through marriage, through children, through religion, through art, through all of these practices she sought enlightenment, and yet her suffering prevailed. In the end, the nun said, Joan was defined by her suffering, although she had concealed it well.

Then, in a matter-of-fact tone, Columba enumerated my mother's griefs: the loss of her mother when she was three years old, the loss of a child early in her marriage, the loss of another child fourteen years later which, in Columba's opinion, had left my mother a changed person. She no longer pursued a spiritual dimension, instead she took up painting, a passion she had left behind when she married and had children. This creative gift had provided her with the distraction she needed to continue leading a meaningful life, but very soon it became apparent that she was struggling with yet another affliction, one that would cause her more suffering than she could ever have imagined. In the years of decay that followed, Columba explained, Joan would slowly lose her mind, the right to her own thoughts, the consciousness of her own suffering. Consigned to years of wakeful oblivion, Joan met her death as someone entirely unknown to herself. And now, at last, Mother Columba said, Joan could rest.

I recalled that the nun had stood there for a moment, her head bowed, as if in deep reflection. If it was a prayer that wanted expression, she suppressed it. Instead, she walked to the front of the altar, faced the crucifix, and crossed herself. She avoided my eyes as she stepped down from the chancel and slipped into her pew.

"The Mass has ended," said the strange priest who had never met my mother. "Go in peace."

AFTERWORD

I found the poem introducing Part One, "My Father," when my brother Joe handed me a portfolio bearing the title "A Selection of the World's Great Masterpeices." Looking inside, I realized that my mother had removed all of the original pages containing prints by great painters and had replaced them with pages of typed poems and letters, all written by my father, all of them addressed to her.

My father begins with an air of whimsicality, with the title

A COLLECTION OF POEMS
Written in the Fourth Person

The last poem in the sequence, just before the letters begin, is telling:

THE BOSTON SHE PARTY

Oh, to be in Boston
Now that Jackson's there!
And Sarge and Chuck and Joey Boy
And strangers, tall and fair.
Up to the Cape on weekends,
Then back to the rallies again.
But nothing can stir my cold, cold heart
Except—all sorts of men.
So it's hey-diddle-dee

And a heigh-heigh-ho
With a kiss-kiss-kiss for all.
I'll snag myself a Boston man
And marry in the fall.
Yippee!

Then, as the letters intensify, it is clear that my father is growing increasingly anxious, and fears that he might lose my mother. In the final letter, dated October 1, 1952, he writes:

```
Are you really in love with me? I hope you are—
thoroughly, finally, determinedly, convincingly,
generously, tenderly, fiercely, blindly, wantonly in
love with me. Because that's how I'm in love with
you—and, if it's mutual, we're in business. If you
love me—and if you're sure it's you that's doing
the loving, not your advisors—let's get the hell
married.
```

It was this portfolio that inspired *How to Forget*. From my father's pen, and my mother's ingenuity, evolved the story I have written.

ACKNOWLEDGMENTS

In the middle of writing this book, alone in a beautiful house in Ireland, I needed readers. I found them in my friends Eithne Verling, Jonathun Arun, Tina and Des McCarthy, Trish Ford, and Irene Byrne. The Irish were surprisingly emotional, and very generous. The Americans were equally attentive and inspired confidence: thank you Vicky Jenkins, Kevin Tighe, Becky Fletcher, and Daniel Davis. My dear friend Samantha Eggar reinvigorated the writing process with her honesty and her passion.

For the tough calls, I sought my sister Jenny Beck and my great friend Beth Danon, both of whom provided encouragement. Beth simply told me she wanted more and Jenny, whose counsel I feared might be a double-edged sword, was instead a very objective reader, honest, smart, and considered in her criticism.

My thanks to Anne Roiphe whose guidance was, as always, in valuable.

I doubt the book could have been written without the fact-finding genius of my brother Joe, who responded to my many anxious texts with promptness, equanimity, and humor, and to whom I am deeply grateful.

Special thanks to Linda Hope, who provided me with the perfect place in which to write, and whose generosity has gone a long way toward shepherding this book into the world.

Again, I am very grateful for the guidance, expertise, and friendship of my literary agent, Christopher Schelling.

My team at HarperCollins/William Morrow Imprint has been exceptional: thank you to Ryan Cury, Anwesha Basu, Benjamin Steinberg,

Mumtaz Mustafa, Bonni Leon-Berman, Stephanie Vallejo, Susan Brown, Andrew DiCecco, and especially Nate Lanman who, it soon became evident, can do anything.

My editor, Jen Brehl, has made this undertaking one of great discipline and great pleasure. Throughout, she has exercised a sensitivity and an acuity which, while inspiring confidence, at the same time encouraged excellence.

Mine is the gratitude of a sophomore writer who has stumbled across a great editor, which is to say—inestimable.

My children, Ian, Alec, and Danielle, are to be commended and thanked for their insightful, brave, and loving counsel.

Finally, to my daily reader over nightly cocktails, to my source of constant support and unflagging devotion, my love and gratitude to Bennett Zier.